British Imperialism in the Nineteenth Century

Each volume in the 'Problems in Focus' series is designed to make available to students important new work on key historical problems and periods that they encounter in their courses. Each volume is devoted to a central topic or theme, and the most important aspects of this are dealt with by specially commissioned studies from scholars in the relevant field. The editorial Introduction reviews the problem or period as a whole, and each chapter provides an assessment of the particular aspect, pointing out the areas of development and controversy, and indicating where conclusions can be drawn or where further work is necessary. An annotated bibliography serves as a guide to further reading.

PROBLEMS IN FOCUS SERIES

TITLES IN PRINT

Church and Society in England: Henry VIII to James I
edited by Felicity Heal and Rosemary O'Day
The Reign of James VI and I
edited by Alan G. R. Smith
The Origins of the English Civil War
edited by Conrad Russell
The Interregnum: The Quest for Settlement 1646-1660
edited by G. E. Aylmer
The Restored Monarchy 1660-1688
edited by J. R. Jones
Britain after the Glorious Revolution 1689-1714
edited by Geoffrey Holmes
Popular Movements, c. 1830-1850
edited by J. T. Ward
Europe's Balance of Power 1815-1848
edited by Alan Sked
The Edwardian Age: Conflict and Stability 1900-1914
edited by Alan O'Day
The Mid-Tudor Polity c. 1540-1560
edited by Jennifer Loach and Robert Tittler
Slavery and British Society 1776-1846
edited by James Walvin
Reactions to the English Civil War 1642-1649
edited by John Morrill
Britain in the Age of Walpole
edited by Jeremy Black
The Reign of Elizabeth I
edited by Christopher Haigh
British Imperialism in the Nineteenth Century
edited by C. C. Eldridge
The Revolution in Ireland, 1879-1923
edited by D. G. Boyce
Later Victorian Britain, 1867-1900
edited by T. R. Gourvish and Alan O'Day

FURTHER TITLES ARE IN PREPARATION

British Imperialism in the Nineteenth Century

EDITED BY
C. C. ELDRIDGE

MACMILLAN

First published 1984
Reprinted 1987, 1989

Published by
MACMILLAN EDUCATION LTD
Houndmills, Basingstoke, Hampshire RG21 2XS
and London
Companies and representatives
throughout the world

Printed in the People's Republic of China

British Library Cataloguing in Publication Data
Eldridge, C. C.
British imperialism in the 19th century.—(Problems in focus)
1. Imperialism   2. Great Britain—
Foreign relations—1837–1901
I. Title   II. Series
321'.03'0941   JV1016
ISBN 0–333–26907–1
ISBN 0–333–26909–8 Pbk

Contents

List of Maps

List of Abbreviations

CHBE	*Cambridge History of the British Empire*
CHR	*Canadian Historical Review*
EHR	*English Historical Review*
EconHR	*Economic History Review*
HJ	*Historical Journal*
JAH	*Journal of African History*
JEH	*Journal of Economic History*
JICH	*Journal of Imperial and Commonwealth History*
P&P	*Past and Present*

Acknowledgements

The editor gratefully acknowledges financial assistance received from the Pantyfedwen Fund of Saint David's University College for the preparation of the manuscript for publication. He also wishes to thank Sarah Mahaffy, Vanessa Peerless and Judy Marshall of Macmillan for their constant encouragement, help and advice during the production of the volume.

The editor and publisher wish to thank Hodder & Stoughton Educational for permission to reproduce the map on p. 64, depicting India on the eve of the Indian mutiny. This was originally published in *Victorian Imperialism* by C. C. Eldridge, The map on p. 127, Africa in 1914, is reproduced with the permission of Cambridge University Press, and first appeared in *Africa Since 1800* by R. Oliver and A. Atmore.

Introduction

C. C. ELDRIDGE

The beginnings of British imperial history, as a separate branch of historical enquiry, are usually traced back to the publication of Sir John Seeley's eloquent lectures on *The Expansion of England* in 1883. The study of imperial history, therefore, like some ageing Britannia, is approximately one hundred years old. Her vitality is surprising, not simply because at the age of seventy her rather tired frame was assaulted by 'vandals' from the Fens, but because she also suffered, in the 1960s, a near-death experience. However, her constitution proved to be unexpectedly robust, her spirits revived and, learning to walk once again, even though her body still bore the marks of earlier experiences and her mind was especially prone to bouts of confusion, she underwent a rejuvenating process which restored her bodily vigour. Discussions concerning the significance of Great Britain's imperial past are as lively today as they were a century ago.

Seeley's lectures were in their own day something of a sensation. They were lectures with a purpose and a message. He began:

> It is a favourite maxim of mine that history, while it should be scientific in its method, should pursue a practical object. That is, it should not merely gratify the reader's curiosity about the past, but modify his view of the present and his forecast of the future. . . . Here is no bad question for historical students at the opening of an academic year, the opening perhaps to some of their academic course. You are asked to think over English history as a whole and consider if you cannot find some meaning, some method in it, if you cannot state some conclusion to which it leads.

He urged his students, like many an academic since, to 'Break the drowsy spell of narrative; ask yourself questions; set yourself problems; your mind will at once take up a new attitude; you will become an investigator; you will cease to be solemn and begin to be serious'. The reward would be real enough for once the moral has been discovered

> we close the history of our country, not with minds fatigued and bewildered as though from reading a story that has been too much spun out, but enlightened and more deeply interested than ever, because partly prepared for what is to come next.

Seeley's intent is clear, he wished to mould the ideas of his students by heightening their historical consciousness. His message was equally clear. The lectures, which have been described as a panoramic survey sweeping the heavens with a telescope, were basically a reinterpretation of British seventeenth- and eighteenth-century history along the lines of the expansion of the state. Beginning with his famous statement 'We seem, as it were, to have conquered and peopled half the world in a fit of absence of mind', his intention was to increase his students' awareness of empire and to create a new imperial spirit. The history of the last two centuries was the history of the creation of 'Greater Britain'. This was the clue which 'binds together the past of England and her future'. That Seeley was largely successful in his proselytising mission there can hardly be any doubt. On publication, his lectures became an immediate best-seller, selling 80,000 copies in their first two years in print. In fact, the volume remained continuously in print until 1956, a new paperback edition appearing in 1971. Seeley's entry in the *Dictionary of National Biography* records with some justification that the book 'contributed perhaps more than any other single utterance to the change of feeling respecting the relations between Great Britain and her colonies which marks the end of the nineteenth century'.

Of more relevance to our present purpose, however, is the profound impact of Seeley's central thesis on the thinking of subsequent generations of historians. His own writing was not based on meticulous historical investigation by any means, the whole appeal of his lectures stemmed from the broad coverage of large themes, the sweeping generalisation and the penetrating insight. It was left for later imperial historians to fill in the detail by the application of the more rigorous techniques of modern historical research. That they should work within the framework of ideas so brilliantly established by Seeley was natural enough. Thus the virtues and prejudices of Seeley's own approach were passed on to succeeding generations and imperial history acquired many enduring characteristics, notably the concept of the evolutionary growth of the British empire, the unwavering focus on the view from the centre which precluded any discussion of colonial interests and ignored the possibility of any interchange between local conditions and British policy, the almost exclusive concentration on constitutional and political relations, the narrowing of the focus to the colonies of British settlement and the West Indies with only limited treatment of India in a category of its own. All these preoccupations are clearly evident in the first authoritative account of the growth of the empire based on printed primary sources, H. E. Egerton's *A Short History of British Colonial Policy* (1897), which confirmed the ground-plan for future scholarly investigation as imperial history came of age in the early twentieth century. The same preoccupations dominated the planning of the *Cambridge History of the British Empire* in the 1920s: three volumes on general imperial policy, mainly constitutional and administrative history, one volume each on the Dominions, and two volumes devoted to the administration of India. It was an empire in which tropical dependencies appeared to have no worthwhile history of their own, in which the British toiled while the indigenous inhabitants were permanently asleep, an empire in which economics had no proper place at all. It was the empire viewed through Seeley's telescope.

In fact, Seeley's imprint on imperial history lasted for much of the first half of the twentieth century. In some respects there was a succession of Seeleys. Egerton was followed by Sir Charles Lucas, A. P. Newton and A. B. Keith and in the 1920s C. A. Bodelsen and R. L. Schuyler continued to build on Seeley's framework. The traditional school of imperial historiography was established and the chronological stages of British imperial expansion were clearly defined. In the early nineteenth century the lessons of the American War of

Independence and the writings of Adam Smith were gradually absorbed, the old colonial system was overthrown and the empire ceased to be of value in an age of free trade. A temporary revival in the tempo of growth under the influence of the Colonial Reformers was quickly nipped in the bud by the 'Manchester School', and the age of separatism dawned, reaching its climax in 1868–70. Thereafter a reaction set in and belligerent expansionism became the order of the day in the age of the new imperialism which finally ended with the onset of war in 1914. It was a tidy thesis which could easily be extended beyond 1914 to cover the coming of the Commonwealth. Indeed, at Oxford University a missionary fervour for Commonwealth, lasting from Sir Reginald Coupland to Vincent Harlow, sought to bring Seeley's evolutionary process to its logical and desirable conclusion.

With the publication of the first volume of Harlow's *The Founding of the Second British Empire, 1763–93* (1952), however, the study of imperial history began to change for Harlow turned from the study of current imperial problems in the past to the study of the past itself as seen through the eyes of contemporaries. The perspective also began to change as Harlow discovered that the 'second' British empire differed from that of Seeley since it was predominantly a coloured empire ruled autocratically from Whitehall. In fact, he discovered there were several different kinds of British empire. Moreover, realising that trade not dominion was the ultimate aim, Harlow was among the first historians to take 'informal empire' into account as he studied local crises and expansion in distant lands.

It was in Cambridge, however, that the chill east wind was to blow strongest. There, belief in empire and Commonwealth as unified fields of historical study, despite Seeley's initial promptings, had never developed, the emphasis being placed on a wider process of expansion. Thus Oxford's historical method presenting the imperial record teleologically in terms of an ideal end seemed 'unhistorical', and, partly in reaction to Oxford's 'Liberal Anglican School' and partly under the influence of the events of the day – in the early 1950s the end of the European empires was in sight and the shadows of the United States and Russia had stretched over a large part of the globe – a complete reappraisal of Britain's former role in the world was undertaken as the two collaborators-in-chief, John Gallagher and Ronald Robinson, appeared on the scene with the publication of their now celebrated article 'The Imperialism of Free Trade' (*Economic History Review*, 1953). In some fifteen pages they challenged and virtually demolished the previously accepted framework of British imperial history which had held sway since Seeley had first suggested the outlines in 1883.

In 'The Imperialism of Free Trade', Robinson and Gallagher turned the traditional interpretation of the mid-Victorian years on its head by including within their survey the 'informal empire', areas beyond the confines of formal rule but nonetheless dominated by Great Britain in a variety of ways. They were thus able to postulate a fundamental continuity in British expansion and policy but a discontinuity in British activity and mode of expansion. Subsequently, in *Africa and the Victorians* (1961), when assessing British motives for participating in the scramble for Africa, Robinson and Gallagher examined the 'official mind' (the self-image and aspirations of the bureaucracy and policy-makers) and suggested that far from late-Victorian imperialism being the product of the assertion of an aggressive, self-confident spirit overseas, it was more the product of late-Victorian pessimism and fear. The frontiers of fear were on the move and the British found themselves reluctantly drawn into areas overseas by 'local crises' and the subimperialism of the people on the spot. Strategy was the guiding factor, since the protection of India and its approach routes was at the bottom of it all. Thus traditional explanations of the scramble for Africa were also turned on their head: the Eurocentric approach had been departed from and political motives were given pride of place, economic exploitation being the result of imperialism, not its cause.

In the chapter on 'The Partition of Africa' in the *New Cambridge Modern History* vol. XI (1962), the 'Cambridge pantomime horse' clopped on to the European stage. Attention was now extended to the motives of the European powers. Here the African context was developed more fully, the theory of the 'local crisis' enlarged upon and proto-nationalism (incipient

African nationalist movements) seen as the counterpart of local
subimperialism. This essay has been called the most Afrocen-
tric interpretation of the scramble for Africa ever advanced.

The threads of the argument were finally drawn together by
'the thinker' in the partnership in Ronald Robinson's paper
'Non-European Foundations of European Imperialism: sketch
for a Theory of Collaboration' published in E. R. J. Owen and
R. B. Sutcliffe (eds), *Studies in the Theory of Imperialism* (1972).
Here imperialism emerges as a set of reflex actions between
European and non-European components. The strategic
imperative and economic drive from Europe resulted in
imperialism only when they operated at cross-purposes with
the non-European component of indigenous collaboration and
resistance. Hence far from imperialism being a systemic
process it was the product of virtually random interactions
between European impulses and purely internal developments
in the domestic history of other less developed parts of the
world. The trigger for action was a breakdown in the mechan-
ism of collaboration, the course and the character of the
ensuing relationships being shaped more by the subjects on the
periphery than the so-called 'policy-makers' in the metropolis.
Once again, with a few deft strokes of the pen Robinson had
constructed a compelling 'excentric' theory of imperialism
which not only embraced the process of informal empire, its
breakdown, the onset of colonial rule and the manner in which
it was sustained, but also explained the reason why, once
collaboration turned into non-cooperation, it ended in decolonisation. It was a neat and satisfying interpretation, bringing the
process back to where it had begun.

While it is possible to point to the work of a number of earlier
writers and historians whose ideas influenced the development
of Robinson's and Gallagher's theses, their achievement in
providing an intellectual framework for the fruitful discussion
of difficult concepts cannot be gainsaid. The ensuing debates
and controversies have carried forward the study of imperialism a long way. Although Robinson may modestly deny that
the result was a historiographical revolution, their writings
certainly stimulated a renaissance of studies in British imperial
history which, in broadening the subject's horizons and
recharging its batteries, enabled it to survive numerous attacks

on its academic relevance and respectability in a decade which not only witnessed the establishment of African, Asian and other regional histories as rigorous academic disciplines but also witnessed a period of disillusionment with the New Commonwealth. That British imperial history is such a lively subject today is in no small part due to the provocative writings, the wit and the style of Ronald Robinson and the late Jack Gallagher. Indeed, the publication of Robinson–Gallagher extracts, the views of their critics and new assessments has become an industry in its own right – witness W. R. Louis (ed.) *Imperialism: The Robinson and Gallagher Controversy* (New York, 1976). So great has been the reappraisal of British imperial history in the last thirty years that two substantial revisionist volumes on the British empire have appeared: Bernard Porter's splendid *The Lion's Share. A Short History of British Imperialism, 1850–1970* (1975) and Ronald Hyam's more detailed *Britain's Imperial Century, 1815–1914. A Study of Empire and Expansion* (1976). The present volume continues in the same vein: some contributors reassessing the controversies which have surrounded certain aspects of Robinson's and Gallagher's work, another dissecting one of their principal theories, others engaged on reviewing the recent literature and putting forward their own interpretations. It is all a testimony to the vitality of the subject.

However, before introducing the essays contained in this volume it is necessary to begin with a word of caution since the debate about British imperialism, and the growth of knowledge which has accompanied it, has become so voluminous as to defy easy comprehension. At the heart of much of the confusion lies the word 'imperialism' itself. Like most 'isms' it has proved extraordinarily difficult to pin down. In fact, there is no universally agreed definition and almost every writer necessarily begins with his own definition simply because such deep ideological and political differences lie behind the semantic battle that the definition frequently dictates the type and the extent of the conclusions which can, or cannot, be drawn. As a result controversy deepens and misunderstandings multiply as those engaged in debate talk at cross-purposes.

Imperialism is fraught with ambiguities. Yet, despite numerous suggestions that it should be abolished, as its use almost always tends to confuse rather than to clarify any argument, it has nevertheless retained its place in the international vocabulary. It has become an umbrella word to describe the relationship between a dominant and a subservient society; it has become a political football and has come to mean all things to all men. Whether imperialism is basically a political, economic, intellectual or psychological phenomenon usually depends on the aspects of imperialism which are chosen as the fundamental or defining ones. There are also many questions concerning its scope. Should the term be limited to the forcible establishment of political control by one state over others through such means as colonies and protectorates or should it be extended to include the exertion of influence by strong nations over weaker states through the real or potential exercise of force and the exploitation of economic advantages by industrial countries at the expense of non-industrial countries? Should its use be limited, as Marxists insist, to describe a particular stage in the evolution of capitalism? Should it be used solely in connection with developments overseas or can it be applied to relationships within Europe, the United States or even the United Kingdom – the treatment of the Irish, the Welsh and the Scots by their more powerful neighbour, for example? The term is obviously capable of infinite expansion, especially when its intellectual, sociological and psychological roots are included, until it is in danger of being reduced to a convenient shorthand for an agglomeration of causally unrelated events. As new aspects of imperialism are highlighted and added to the list of factors to be examined, soon nothing short of a *total* history of the period in question will suffice if the historian is to attempt to do justice to the phenomenon.

No such attempt is made in this volume. Eight themes of central importance to British imperialism in the nineteenth century have been selected for study, mainly because they are either subjects of controversy, where some guidance for students was thought to be helpful, or because recent research has thrown new light on the subject and a reassessment was thought to be desirable. While contributors have endeavoured to explain the current state of historical scholarship, they have also been encouraged to present their own synthesis as to the probable explanation of the factors involved. Geographical coverage of the empire has not proved possible, especially as the volume has not been confined to the areas of formal rule. Imperialism has been interpreted, broadly, as the extension of British rule or control (or the disposition to establish such rule or control) whether direct or indirect, political, economic or cultural, over another nation or people together with the ideas justifying this process. The definition is not without problems since contemporary and later usages can vary so much and these will be constantly referred to throughout the volume.

In fact, problems of definition and perspective immediately arise, in the first chapter, in Paul Kennedy's survey of the arguments surrounding Gallagher and Robinson's 'continuity thesis', a debate which has dominated discussions concerning British policy in the early and mid-Victorian period for the last thirty years. As he points out, the stance to be adopted does not simply depend on the acceptance of a much broader definition of imperialism than the territorial and juridical definition used by an older school of historians, it also depends on one's assessment of the type of action which can be held (within the broader definition) to constitute imperialistic activity. The vaguer the definition, the more likelihood there is of disagreement. Most historians have come to accept that imperialism should cover not solely the acquisition of colonies but also a variety of relationships between dominant and subservient states, and in the British case most would now agree that the 'received version' of events which presumed a sharp break in policy and attitudes about 1815 or 1846 or 1872 is no longer acceptable. But there is still no agreement about the 'continuity thesis'. Gallagher and Robinson may have been successful in demonstrating that the years 1815–70 were not dominated by an aversion to empire, they may also have been successful, both in their 1953 article and in *Africa and the Victorians*, in demonstrating that annexation remained a last resort in the late-Victorian period, a period more dominated by fear and uncertainty than confidence and aggression; but they have not been successful in convincing all historians that an 'imperialism of free trade' existed along with satellite economies in the earlier part of the century or that late-Victorian policy-makers remained aloof from the real world and immune to the changes in the political, economic and intellectual climate of their day.

Indeed, there is a striking difference between the intervention-prone governments of the early and mid-Victorian years, prepared to act in the interests of British trade in Latin America, the Balkans and China during a period when Britain was allegedly the 'workshop of the world' (portrayed in the 1953 article), and the 'official mind' (seen in operation in *Africa and the Victorians*) whose decisions were based on strategy and political needs in an age dominated by economic depression. Paul Kennedy concludes that there *was* a 'new' imperialism in the closing decades of the nineteenth century: the world of Salisbury, Chamberlain, Rosebery and Milner was very different from that of Castlereagh, Canning and even Palmerston. Their policies varied accordingly. Gallagher and Robinson's 'seductive idea of an overall continuity' has been 'expanded upon until it becomes the major, but distorting feature of their interpretation'.

Nevertheless, as Kennedy admits, Gallagher and Robinson have done tremendous service in enhancing our understanding of the processes by which Britain expanded and protected her interests abroad. A variety of control strategies were used. Thus the British government could adopt mercantilist techniques of formal rule to develop India at the same time as informal techniques of free trade were used, to the same end, in other parts of the world. Similarly, they see the introduction of responsible government into the colonies of British settlement not as a separatist device but as an alternative means for preserving British national interests: 'By slackening the formal political bond at the appropriate time, it was possible to rely on economic dependence and mutual good-feeling to keep the colonies bound to Britain whilst still using them as agents for further British expansion'.

This is a view echoed in the second chapter of this book when Peter Burroughs asserts that devolution of authority could sometimes be more effective than centralised supervision. At first sight it may seem surprising that an essay on such a familiar (some might say hackneyed) topic as 'Colonial Self-government' should appear in a 'Problems in Focus' volume – especially as the white parts of the empire do not tend to receive much space in accounts of British imperialism today, a failing which this volume shares. Nevertheless the introduction of responsible government into the colonies of British settlement has always had a hallowed place in imperial, and more recently Commonwealth, history not simply because it provided a solution to the dilemma which had confronted the British at the time of the American War of Independence but because it blazed a trail through local self-government to dominion status and the Commonwealth relationship which exists today, a trail subsequently followed by India and other Asian, African and Caribbean communities. Not so long ago it was customary to trace the origins of the Commonwealth back to the Magna Carta of the second British empire: Lord Durham's *Report* in 1839 on the situation in the Canadas following the rebellions of 1837. Few, however, would care to be so dogmatic today.

Even this well-documented topic has had its controversies. The content and significance of Durham's *Report* has come under heavy fire and the reasons for the British *volte face* in 1846 in agreeing to the introduction of internal self-government have also attracted much discussion. In addition, a number of historians have emphasised Britain's positive contribution in encouraging responsible government not only in British North America but in the Australian colonies where the Duke of Newcastle, as Colonial Secretary in 1853, insisted (even before public expectations were aroused) that the new constitutions being drafted in New South Wales, Victoria, South Australia and Van Diemen's Land should conform to the system of self-government recently established in North America. It was all part of a policy of disengagement from the settlement colonies which was largely completed by the time of the withdrawal of the garrisons crisis in 1869–70. If the introduction of responsible government satisfied the cravings of the colonists for local autonomy, the withdrawal of British troops likewise removed for the British people one of the last objections to the 'burden' of the imperial connection. Peter Burroughs places these developments in their proper historical context, beginning with the causes, character and consequences of the American Revolution and concluding with some apt comments on the comparisons between nineteenth-century disengagement from empire and decolonisation in Africa a century later.

Similarly, in the third chapter, on 'India and the British Empire', Robin Moore links events in the late nineteenth century with the coming of independence in the mid-twentieth century. Few would deny the central importance of India to the British empire. After tracing the beginnings of British rule in India and analysing the relationship between economic, political and strategic motives in the extension of British dominion during the years 1800–57 (he remarks in passing that an historiographical battle, perhaps commensurate with that over the partition of Africa, as yet remains unfought), Moore turns to examine the role of India in the British economy, threading his way through a minefield of controversies. His conclusion is clear enough: 'From the Mutiny until the First World War Britain managed India's finances so as to meet the needs of British trade, investment, employment, and imperial defence or expansion'. His final remarks are of equal interest from the point of view of another essay in this volume: from the end of the nineteenth century he sees the British *Raj* 'engaged in the inherently weakening process of buying off the potential enemy within'. In the twentieth century the *Raj* became dependent on Indian collaborators who, finally, declined to play the game.

The historiographical battle over the partition of Africa, to which Robin Moore refers, is dealt with in Chapter 4, in the wider context of 'Britain and the New Imperialism'. In believing the 'new' imperialism to be a legitimate concept, James Sturgis adopts a similar position to that taken by Paul Kennedy in Chapter 1. Further, for the purpose of more detailed analysis, he subdivides the late nineteenth century into three phases reflecting changes in British policy and the political climate of the day which he dubs transitional (1870–82), hesitant (1882–92) and conscious imperialism (1892–1902). He explores these phases both in general terms and in a detailed examination of British policy in the scramble for Africa, mainly north of the Congo river, and concludes the first part of his chapter by discussing the validity of his periodisation when applied to British policy in the Far East. Here, he finds elements of continuity much more important with no significant chronological divide appearing until about 1892 when international competition sharpened. It is interesting to note, however, that British policy in south-east Asia and the Pacific does, in general terms, conform to the suggested pattern. In south-east Asia, the British became worried about French designs from the late 1860s and were forced to react when the French began their conquest of Tonkin in 1884 and established contact with the Burmese. As a result, Upper Burma was annexed by Britain in late 1885. The French advanced again in 1893 when they invaded Siam and Laos and Britain had to make the best bargain she could in 1896 as she was heavily committed elsewhere. In the Pacific, the annexation of the Fiji Islands in 1874, which was intended as a trial case (the Colonial Secretary announced his intention to 'resist the cry for annexation' elsewhere), and the creation of the Western Pacific High Commission in 1877, intended to extend British authority without acquiring further territory, clearly marked a transitional phase in British policy. That British policy was 'hesitant' in the early 1880s is shown by the British veto of the annexation of eastern New Guinea by the colony of Queensland in 1883, and then, following Germany's increased activity in the Pacific, by the subsequent declaration of a British protectorate over the south-eastern shores of New Guinea in 1884. Further agreements were later made with Germany in 1886 and with France in 1888. The final stage of the partition occurred in the late 1890s when the Spanish Pacific empire was dissolved after Spain's disastrous war with the United States over Cuba. Britain took the opportunity to make further rearrangements of territory, principally with Germany.

James Sturgis concludes his chapter with a survey of the various theories and explanations which have been put forward to account for the new imperialism. He feels that an overall consensus is unlikely to emerge and, for the foreseeable future at least, the debate is bound to continue. He regards this as 'a testimony, rather than a rebuke, to the vigour of historical research and writing'.

The vigour with which historical debates are conducted is certainly apparent in Chapter 5. A. E. Atmore's chapter entitled 'The Extra-European Foundations of British Imperialism: Towards a Reassessment' highlights a number of weaknesses in the Robinson–Gallagher theory of collaboration. In many respects it mirrors Oliver Macdonagh's earlier attack on the terminology and universality of the 'imperialism of free trade' thesis. Atmore begins with a case-study of the 'informal phase of collaboration' in the Ottoman empire and quickly demonstrates the ambiguity of the terminology when applied to this region. Should collaboration be equated with modernisation or Westernisation? There were few reactionaries among the Ottoman elite and conservatives as well as gradualists and radicals looked forward to some change in state organisation. But all, traditionalists and Westernisers alike, would almost certainly have regarded themselves as patriots and most of them aimed at establishing a strong centralised state. All may sometime have co-operated with the representatives of European imperialism, but none really deserves the name collaborator and no single group of reformers was singled out by Europeans to perform this function.

A. E. Atmore then turns to examine whether it was the breakdown of collaborative mechanisms that led to European 'take-overs' in West Africa and asks whether the colonial rulers were really dependent on collaborators once European rule had been established. He notes both the scale and the ruthlessness of the original conquests, the wide degree of resistance encountered, and points out that the use of force, or the threat of its use, played a large part in the maintenance of colonial rule. Furthermore, grandiose displays of power, as in the Abyssinian War, seem to have served domestic political ends as well. And why were the most likely group of collaborators, the modernisers (mainly educated Africans), almost universally spurned by the British? As an explanation of the partition of West Africa, the breakdown of collaborating mechanisms is not entirely satisfactory. Atmore concludes that much more rigour and precision need to be used in identifying collaborators and in ascertaining their position in their own societies. Perhaps 'collaboration' also has too many unfortunate connotations and 'co-operation' would be a more neutral term. Perhaps 'the makers of compromises' would best describe the role of the individuals concerned.

Christine Bolt in her essay on 'Race and the Victorians' (Chapter 6) deals with that part of the 'extremist ideology' – overt or implied racism and bogus scientific theorising – which, according to A. E. Atmore, led the British to ignore to their cost the potential of educated Africans as collaborators. She attempts the difficult task, in the words of James Sturgis when trying to assess the impact of Social Darwinism, of bringing 'something "in the air" down to earth'. Her chapter traces the hardening of attitudes towards questions of race in the nineteenth century and attempts to relate domestic and imperial problems and racial opinions. Such opinions are usually said to have loomed large in the minds of late-Victorian imperialists but the significance of the impact of such ideas is rarely spelt out.

However, before entering into any discussion concerning racial attitudes, it is necessary to define certain key terms. The Victorians may not have bothered with such matters but twentieth-century scholars use these terms in a very precise way. In modern discussions, *race* is taken to allude to the biological factor in group difference, *ethnicity* to the cultural element. Members of an ethnic group may be bound by common descent as well as cultural ties; cultural characteristics to which 'social significance' is attached are also attributed to different races. However, the crucial difference between racial and ethnic, and racial and national qualities, is that those belonging to a race – being innate and hereditary – are held to be unchangeable by education or other social influences. It follows that one race, whatever its wishes, cannot be genuinely assimilated by another; racial sentiments will be retained even where contacts permit miscegenation or offer cultural assimilation. *Racism* is a rationalised pseudo-scientific theory that men and women can be divided into higher and lower biological stocks, possessing specific cultural attributes; *ethnocentrism* is a conviction of the invariable cultural superiority of one's own ethnic group, which in its negative aspects becomes a morbid hatred of foreigners, namely xenophobia. Ethnocentric attitudes thus allow for the changing and even assimilation of 'inferiors' by 'superiors' in a way that racist attitudes do not. The term *prejudice* is used to describe a rigid antagonism of mind towards others which may be 'rational' (that is socially-based), or 'irrational' (that is stemming from the peculiarities of the person who expresses it), with both kinds failing to take account of the obvious differences existing between individuals in the despised category; *antipathy* refers to an unfavourable disposition towards a particular group, which may be modified by knowledge or experience. Finally, *stereotypes* are beliefs about the traits of any group which are both over-simplified and embraced regardless of objective factors. They serve as a shorthand way of identifying the groups in question, without the painful probing of reality, and as a means of releasing majority resentments against them. Stereotypes of any group tend to change slowly over time in response to changes in the social thought which supports them. These definitions need to be borne clearly in mind when reading Christine Bolt's careful analysis of the connection between race and Victorian imperialism.

Another thread which came to be of increasing importance in late-Victorian imperial thinking, the 'social question', is discussed by M. E. Chamberlain in Chapter 7. This chapter concentrates on the links between colonial outlets, economic prosperity, social stability at home and the need to improve the living conditions of the working man. The connection between 'Imperialism and Social Reform' is traced from early in the nineteenth century through Disraeli's introduction of a social dimension into Conservative political philosophy to the ideas and activities of Joseph Chamberlain. Particular attention is paid to the remedies suggested for the 'great depression' and to the writings of J. A. Hobson. Finally, the role of empire in the campaign for 'national efficiency' in the early years of the twentieth century is discussed and, while the Co-efficients never achieved their ambition to capture the Liberal party, many of their tenets were incorporated into the political philosophy of the 1905–14 Liberal administration whose programme has been described as a combination of Radical social reform and imperialist foreign and military policy. Improved social conditions were necessary to produce a race capable of defending and governing an empire which, in turn, would assist Great Britain in the struggle to maintain her role in the world both politically and economically, as well as permitting the colonial peoples to take their place in the onward march of mankind.

In the concluding chapter, the editor returns to the discussions concerning continuity with which the volume begins. Here the main concern is not simply attitudes towards empire but the factors which gave it strength and cohesion. After a brief review of one of the more recent interpretations of the role of empire, the results of the researches of the last thirty years into changing British responses to empire throughout the nineteenth century are assessed. Once again problems of definition arise concerning 'separatism' and 'anti-imperialism'. Genuine separatists, who proposed the dismantlement of the empire, were few in number even though anti-empire sentiments could, on occasion, readily appear. The fact that for most of the century the pro-empire supporters were consolidationists or minimalists is also noted and a further distinction is drawn between those who supported dominion overseas and were happy, especially in the late-Victorian period, to see it expanded and those who opposed 'imperialism' yet supported 'empire'. Consequently, it is suggested that one of the strongest sinews of empire – which united both the imperial enthusiasts willing to endorse expansion and the more 'reluctant' imperialists who believed the empire to be a burden of honour – was the sense of mission which was thought by the British to have been given them by Providence. It was the one link in the imperial chain that critics of empire found most difficulty in breaking.

Finally, it must be remembered that while the individual contributors to this volume have endeavoured to outline the current state of historical scholarship in the chosen areas and to present a synthesis of the factors involved, their conclusions are not likely to be accepted by all historians. The debate will certainly not end here. Nor have the eight themes exhausted the many controversial questions concerning British imperialism in the period under discussion. The purpose of the essays is to provide (hopefully a stimulating) introduction to the study of certain aspects of British expansion overseas in the nineteenth century, a subject which has lost none of the vitality Sir John Seeley first breathed into it in his lectures on *The Expansion of England* one hundred years ago.

1. Continuity and Discontinuity in British Imperialism 1815–1914

PAUL KENNEDY*

I

It is difficult to think of a debate in historical scholarship which has not raised problems of continuity. Despite the concentration by historians upon events which they may variously describe as 'turning-points' or 'new eras' or 'revolutions', no writer has ever really meant that *everything* in a particular society was suddenly altered. Although many things changed during a period of political and social turbulence such as the French Revolution or the Great War, others remained the same. Furthermore, even features which appeared at first sight to have been radically transformed often reveal upon closer inspection a less substantial break with the past; the National Socialist 'revolution' of 1933, to take but one example, is nowadays represented by some historians as an alteration of degree, not of kind, with the foreign and domestic policies of Weimar Germany. Change is often less drastic than the contemporary observers of events imagine, and continuities abound even when dramatic shifts of policy seem to be taking place.

So is it also with the debate upon British imperialism in the nineteenth century. To the earliest historians of this topic, the evidence suggested that radically different phases had occurred, the actual 'turning-points' being located in the few decades after 1815, when the age of preclusive colonialism and mercantilism gave way to that of *laissez-faire* and free trade; and again in the early 1870s, when Disraeli's famous Crystal Palace speech and slightly later policies showed that the anti-imperialist era was being replaced by a 'new imperialism' which would last until the First World War itself. This classification of the nineteenth century into a middle period of British aversion towards imperialism, bounded on either side by periods of colonial expansion, was the received version of events until 1953, when two Cambridge historians, John Gallagher and Ronald Robinson, argued in their seminal article 'The Imperialism of Free Trade'[1] that a basic continuity could be detected throughout the entire century. For the past three decades, scholars have taken up positions for and against this reinterpretation, and in the course of a prolonged debate there has emerged a great deal of new and useful information, together with more sophisticated approaches to the study of imperialism. Whether one plumps for the 'continuity thesis' or not, therefore, the whole subject has doubtless benefited from this scholarly controversy.

As with many other disagreements, a great deal depends upon one's definition of, and choice of evidence about, the subject in question – in this case, imperialism. To mid- and late-nineteenth-century observers, with their classical training and fondness for analogies with the Roman empire, the only possible definitions were territorial and juridical: that is to say, an empire consisted of foreign territories possessed by the metropolitan power and in which British laws held sway. Consequently, the early histories of British imperial policy focused only upon those places which were 'painted red on the map' and governed from Whitehall to a greater (India) or lesser (Canada) extent. This was the criterion adopted in J. R. Seeley's famous lectures on *The Expansion of England* (1883), and slightly later in H. E. Egerton's *A Short History of British Colonial Policy* (1897). Seeley, with his consuming interest in 'power-politics', devoted much of his story to the great eighteenth-century wars for empire, and then turned to analyse the nature of Britain's formal, 'military' rule in India. In turn, Egerton, A. P. Newton and A. B. Keith focused upon the various British enactments in the post-Waterloo decades, which permitted responsible government in Canada and the other 'white' colonies.[2] To these scholars, such a loosening of Whitehall's control could only mean that imperialistic policies had been given up by the early-to-mid century.

Such a conclusion was reinforced by important later works like C. A. Bodelsen's *Studies in Mid-Victorian Imperialism* (1924) and R. L. Schuyler's *Fall of the Old Colonial System* (1945), which pointed to two further features of the 1815–70 period: first, the gradual abolition of certain economic measures (protective tariffs, colonial monopolies, the Navigation Acts, and so on), signifying that the preclusive, mercantilistic age had passed away; and secondly, the attacks by politicians and writers against the expenses of running an empire which to them appeared as a collection of 'millstones' around the necks of the British taxpayer. The study of public opinion, in other words, was also held to prove that this was an era of 'anti-imperialism'.

Finally, one should note that the most famous interpretation of all time of what 'imperialism' meant – that which linked colonial wars and annexations with the interests of finance capital – also accepted this division of the nineteenth century into imperialist phases. J. A. Hobson, who during his long career oscillated between a 'socialist' and a *'laissez-faire* Liberal' position, admitted that there was much to applaud in the growth of British overseas trade and in the planting of self-governing, Anglo-Saxon 'stock' in underpopulated temperate zones – for this was, after all, the classical mid-century viewpoint of his hero Cobden. But Hobson also argued, especially in his key work *Imperialism: A Study* (1902), that those 'healthy' tendencies were quite different from what had taken place since 1870:[3] namely, a rash of annexations of tropical territories unsuitable for white settlement and producing little trade, yet acquired with considerable cost of life and money (Hobson composed his book during the Boer War, of which he was a severe critic) and at the urgings of the 'yellow press' and the misled masses.

To Lenin, who differed markedly from Hobson in seeking the collapse rather than the reform of capitalism, the 'periodisation' of imperial policy in the nineteenth century could be even more exactly described by the use of Marxist economic analysis. Repeating the historical orthodoxy that 'between 1840 and

1860, the leading British bourgeois politicians were *opposed* to colonial policy and were of the opinion that the liberation of the colonies, their complete separation from Britain, was inevitable and desirable', Lenin ascribed this disinterest to the existence in mid-century of flourishing industrial competition, of capitalism in a non-monopoly state. After 1876, however, a new process was at work: other countries had industrialised, firms were becoming larger but fewer in number, cartels were forming, and the big banks were increasing their control over industry. 'It is beyond doubt, therefore [Lenin continued], that capitalism's transition to the stage of monopoly capitalism, to finance capital, *is connected* with the intensification of the struggle for the partition of the world'.[4] By around 1900, when almost all of the globe had been parcelled out between the imperialist powers, a further stage was beginning: internally, the era of true monopoly and the undisputed role of the banks; externally, the struggle for the *re*division of the globe and its resources, finally resulting in that 'imperialistic' conflict, the First World War, which was still raging as Lenin wrote his tract *Imperialism, the Highest Stage of Capitalism*, early in 1916.[5] Since, to him and to all who accept the Marxist interpretation, imperialism *was* capitalism at a particular stage, the idea of any continuity in British colonial policy between 1815 and 1914 is absurd; as the economic substructure of the country altered, so correspondingly did its political relationship with the less developed parts of the world.

It is not necessary here to go into the great and prolonged debate about this Marxist analysis. What is important is that both the chief economic interpretations of imperialism *and* the chief non-economic (or territorial-juridical-political) interpretations were united in asserting that the post-1870 period of 'scrambling' for colonies was different from that of mid-century imperial neglect, which in turn was dissimilar from the mercantilist age that had preceded it.

II

It was this cosy consensus which Gallagher and Robinson attacked in their article upon 'The Imperialism of Free Trade'. In their view, imperialism could not simply be defined as the formal annexation of overseas territory; it was better regarded as the *various* ways by which an economically expanding society exerted its influence and protected its interests abroad. With respect to Europe and North America, it was neither necessary (because of their 'civilised' societies) nor wise (because of their military strength) to act imperialistically in the years after 1815. In India, where the circumstances were quite different, the metropolitan power tightened its grip throughout the century. Furthermore – and this was a point which Gallagher and Robinson made much of – in those parts of the globe where the existing native polity occasionally failed to protect or respect British interests (e.g. in Latin America, the Levant, China, and along the African coast), the government in London did not hesitate to use armed force to ensure that protection. Did not this resort to gunboat diplomacy, the pressure exerted by British consuls and naval commanders upon local rulers from Canton to Zanzibar, the signing of trade agreements and the opening of treaty ports, all point to an 'informal imperialism' or 'free trade imperialism' which in many respects was more significant than the formal annexation of territory? Was not the previous 'study of the formal empire alone', they wondered, 'rather like judging the size and character of icebergs solely from the parts above the water-line'?

The two authors also noted that although the British government did not seem to enjoy annexing colonies – given the additional administrative problems, and the reluctance of a parsimonious House of Commons to increase the Colonial Office vote, that was scarcely surprising – it did so *continuously* throughout the nineteenth century. Could the post-1870s imperialism really be described as 'new' when one recalls the judicious strategical annexations in the decades after 1815 (Singapore in 1819, the Falkland Islands in 1833, Aden in 1839, Hong Kong in 1842) and the constant expansion of British settlers and merchants, and the slightly later arrival of British authority, into New Zealand, British Columbia, Lagos, Queensland, Labuan and large parts of India in the 1840s, 1850s and 1860s?

The overall picture, then, was of a British government which used a whole variety of control strategies – whether of formal or informal rule over native societies, or of tighter or looser constitutional strings over Canada – whilst always maintaining the basic aim of preserving national interests. 'By informal means if possible, or by formal annexations when necessary, British paramountcy was steadily upheld'.[6] Consequently, all that was different about the late-nineteenth-century policy, as Robinson and Gallagher went on to argue in their book *Africa and the Victorians* (1961),[7] was that certain conditions now made it less likely that informal rule would work and more likely that formal annexations would have to be resorted to. The incursion of new imperial powers into the tropics, and the fact that African societies were less well equipped to withstand endogenous pressures than, say, the states of Latin America or the Manchu empire, led to a rash of annexations there after the 1870s; but it did not make the late Victorians any more imperialist than their predecessors. Missionary zeal, the intrigues of bondholders and investors, the agitations of the jingo press, could not alter the traditional and cool-headed assessment by the 'official mind' about the real priorities in British world policy. By extension, the public's growing interest in Africa and the concentration by Hobson, Leonard Woolf and other historians upon economic imperialism in that continent, should not blind the reader to the fact that the chief direction for the export of British goods, capital and settlers had been elsewhere: 'in tropical Africa the imperialists were merely scraping the barrel'. And why they even bothered to do so was due less to Africa's attractions *per se* than to the need to secure the flanks to the much more important routes to the Orient. Seen in this larger perspective, British imperialism formed a continuum throughout the nineteenth century, a constant interaction between the expanding metropolis and a host of less developed societies; and the causes and dynamics of this enormous process could never be subsumed under simplistic explanations of 'surplus capital' or gauged solely by the territories painted red on the map.

III

There are several features of Robinson and Gallagher's argumentation which were so plausible and convincing that they have been accepted by many other historians. To regard imperialism as something more complex than the formal acquisition of territory, and to point instead to the whole variety of relationships which may exist between a metropolitan power and less developed societies, surely brings us closer to the tangled realities of international politics. To have also destroyed the myth that a more-or-less instantaneous change in British attitudes and policies towards the empire occurred in 1815 or 1846 or 1872 was a necessary piece of iconoclasm. Instead, we can now see that, with literally dozens of British possessions and spheres of interest scattered around the globe, each at different stages of economic and constitutional development, the very idea that there could be any uniform treatment of the empire consequent upon the state of domestic opinion or changes in the structure of British capitalism is most unlikely. Any 'model' of the dynamics of Victorian imperialism must therefore be a variegated one, taking into account the chronology and circumstances of change *in the specific colonial locality* as well as tendencies in the metropolis. Indeed, in their suggestions about the role of the 'local crisis' and the importance of the 'non-European foundations' of imperialism,[8] Robinson and Gallagher have probably made their most distinctive and valuable contribution to the general theory of the process of Western colonialism. Finally, by pointing to what the British were doing in Latin America and China, by linking Egypt with the Eastern Question and southern Africa with the trade routes to the Orient, and by calling attention to the critical importance of India, the two authors have succeeded in questioning that concentration upon 'the scramble for Africa' which obsessed earlier students of imperialism.

As against these favoured features, however, one should record the large number of objections which have been raised against Robinson and Gallagher's insistence upon the basic continuity of policy. The first cluster of reservations comes from historians of the early-to-mid nineteenth century and concerns that picture of a constantly vigilant, intervention-prone government which is painted in the pages of 'The Imperialism of Free Trade'. In particular, the contention that the politicians of that period 'were no more "anti-imperialist" than their successors' has come in for strong criticism. The belief in free trade was genuine and not calculated, and the yearning to avoid wars and annexations was deeply held by many Britons, and especially by Cobden and the 'Manchester school', as Oliver MacDonagh demonstrated in his article 'The Anti-Imperialism of Free Trade'.[9] The impression given by Gallagher and Robinson of a British government purposefully and systematically providing military and naval assistance in the best Palmerstonian manner to traders in trouble overseas is simply not true, D. C. M. Platt has argued in a number of works. Usually Whitehall stayed aloof from supporting individual commercial enterprises; and many of the annexations which occurred in this period were not the manifestations of a 'free trade imperialism' by Britain but were caused instead by land-hungry settlers, ambitious soldiers, native wars and 'crumbling frontiers'. In addition, Platt notes, the objective requirements of the British economy prior to the 1860s were simply not sufficient to bring less developed areas like the Levant, Africa and China within its orbit, certainly not to the extent that a 'dependency relationship' was created.[10]

While there is much validity in these objections, it is not clear that they have altogether destroyed this part of the Gallagher and Robinson thesis. Whatever Cobden and his followers may have felt about the proper aims of British policy, the fact remains that *they* were not in office; and in any case, as Bernard Semmel has pointed out,[11] many advocates of *laissez-faire* in early-to-mid-Victorian Britain desired the end of the mercantilist system precisely because it would turn the whole world into their oyster. Since quotations from 'free-trade imperialists' can be placed alongside those of the 'anti-imperialists' of that time, it is probably better to judge Britain's imperial policy by what was done, not by what was said.

By the same token, one might concede that while British policy was far less calculated and uniform than Gallagher and Robinson portrayed, there seems little doubt that this was an expanding society, encroaching upon others *at a variety of levels*: pirate kingdoms in north Africa and the East Indies were being attacked by Royal Navy gunboats; pressure was being applied against the slave-traders of Africa and equally against the purchasers of slaves on the other side of the Atlantic and Red Sea; treaty ports were being opened up by *force majeure* in China;

indigenous regimes across the globe were being required to sign treaties of free trade and friendship; explorers, missionaries and concession-hunters were penetrating Arabia and pushing inland from the African coast; settlers were moving across the Great Plains of Canada or the Veldt in search of fresh land; beachcombers, firearms dealers, planters and traders were leaving Australia for the Pacific islands; naval officers were eyeing potential new bases which could act as coaling-stations. By no means was all this activity encouraged and directed from Whitehall: it is easy to agree, therefore, that some overseas entanglements were unwelcome to the British government, that colonial wars and impulsive acts by 'the man on the spot' caused groans in the Colonial Office and indignation in the Commons, and that the decision to stabilise a 'crumbling frontier' by annexation was usually reluctant. It is also possible to concede Professor Platt's claim that many of the less developed societies included within Gallagher and Robinson's analysis were not of central importance to the British economy.

Nonetheless, it surely remains true that after 1815 (and, for that matter, for a long while *before* then) the rest of the world was made increasingly aware of Britain's expanding presence, commercially, navally, militarily, culturally, colonially. The exact form of the interaction between Britain and other societies varied from case to case. Towards Europe and the United States, the British government was 'non-imperialistic'; towards the Punjabis, Maoris, Basutos and many other native societies brought under the Crown, it was very definitively 'imperialistic'. In between these two types there lay another category, of cases where Britain acted in a quasi-imperialistic fashion, by intervening (or threatening to intervene) to protect national interests, but without resorting to the ultimate step of annexation. The frequency and extent of this intervention were also very mixed, so much so that it may be rash to think of British policy towards Latin American states (where Platt's counter-evidence is strongest) as being in the same 'quasi-imperialistic' category as its actions against China and Zanzibar: yet all at some time involved pressure, threats, requests, cajolings by a British government and its citizens upon another polity, the government and citizens of which could never (given the respective balance of forces) respond in the same manner towards Britain. Whether such actions were imperialist or not depends, as always, upon one's original definition and thus one returns to the semantic argument once again. If the term is equal only to formal territorial annexation, then this variety of pressures was not imperialistic; if Gallagher and Robinson's broader (albeit more blurred) definition is accepted, the traditional interpretation of an age which had abjured imperialism looks damaged beyond redemption.

What does seem clear is that the decades between Waterloo and Disraeli's Crystal Palace speech can never again be called *anti*-imperialistic, for that adjective surely implies that the British empire was being dismantled. In reality, during the half-century after 1815 the empire expanded by an average of about 100,000 square miles per annum. Moreover, apart from the Ionian Islands and certain other small areas, no portion of existing British overseas possessions was given up by the government. Bentham's call to 'Emancipate Your Colonies' was echoed in later decades by numerous radicals but was never turned into practice. Even the 1869–70 'crisis' in imperial policy, when Conservative spokesmen and colonial governments (and, later, many historians) asserted that Gladstone and his Colonial Secretary, Lord Granville, were intent upon dissolving the empire, appears on closer inspection to show nothing of the sort. The withdrawal of garrisons from New Zealand and Canada were necessary steps in Cardwell's planned modernisation and restructuring of the British army; and Gladstone's own encouragement of colonial self-reliance was based upon the assumption that white settlers overseas would prefer to be bound to the old country by ties of trade, sentiment and culture rather than by force of arms.[12] Throughout the second half of the century, a considerable body of Liberals were 'minimalists' in that they disapproved of further annexations, wanted cuts in the military and naval budgets, and looked somewhat askance at the imperial federation campaign for tighter ties with the self-governing colonies; but not even those Liberals called for the dissolution of the empire, and they would have been horrified at the very idea of leaving India. That hardly seems an anti-imperialistic stance.

IV

An even larger scholarly debate has concerned Robinson and Gallagher's claim that British imperial policy in the late-nineteenth century was basically a continuation of earlier trends. It should be pointed out, however, that this argument that there was no sharp break in policy around 1870 and that the late Victorians were 'reluctant imperialists' concerned only to preserve the heritage of their predecessors, was most boldly put in the article on 'The Imperialism of Free Trade'. By the time *Africa and the Victorians* appeared in 1961, the authors had become more circumspect and subtly shifted their ground, at least in the conclusion to the book. The features which they stress in this work are offered as *additional* perspectives, and they allow for a *multi-causal* interpretation of Western imperialism in phrases which are a model of caution and balance:

> The moving causes appear to arise from chains of diverse circumstances in Britain, Europe, the Mediterranean, Asia and Africa itself, which interlocked in a set of unique relationships. These disparate situations, appraised by the official mind as a connected whole, were the products of different historical evolutions, some arising from national growth or decay, others from European expansion stretching as far back as the Mercantilist era. All of them were changing at different levels at different speeds. But although their paths were separate, they were destined to cross. There were structural changes taking place in European industry cutting down Britain's lead in commerce. The European balance of power was altering. Not only the emergence of Germany, but the alignment of France with Russia, the century-old opponent of British expansion, lessened the margins of imperial safety. National and racial feelings in Europe, in Egypt and south Africa were becoming more heated, and liberalism everywhere was on the decline. All these movements played some part in the African drama . . .[13]

Nonetheless, no sooner have Robinson and Gallagher conceded this plethora of causes than they again emphasise certain aspects above the others – the importance of the 'official mind' with its traditional concern for security, the lack of any positive impulses towards African annexations, the essential continuity of the habit of preferring informal to formal empire. By stating their preferences, they have tied their flag to the mast – and provoked their critics into counter-arguments.

In one important respect, however, Robinson and Gallagher seem to be pointing to a *dis*continuity in British policy by the last quarter of the nineteenth century. By that time, it appears that the vigorous, 'Palmerstonian' defence of British traders overseas which had characterised the earlier age of free-trade imperialism had somehow been succeeded by a disregard of commercial arguments for empire, apparently because of the disdain shown by the aristocratic statesmen and the strategic experts of the 'official mind' towards mere trade. Indeed, in one later piece, an article upon 'The Partition of Africa', Robinson and Gallagher appear to be mounting a full-scale assault upon virtually *any* economic interpretation of the post-1870 colonial scramble.[14] Aloof, as it seems, from domestic pressures and ideological enthusiasms, concerned primarily with the 'cold rules for national safety handed on from Pitt, Palmerston and Disraeli', the British government lived rather in a world of its own when plotting its imperial policies.

It is precisely this issue of the importance of economic motives during the late-nineteenth-century scramble which forms the first of three major clusters of criticism against the Robinson and Gallagher thesis. As noted above, not only does their disregard of commercial and financial considerations logically suggest a discontinuity in policy as compared with the 'imperialism of free trade' era; but, more substantially, many scholars have also pointed to the evidence of a rising interest in colonial markets shown by British exporters, shippers and chambers of commerce as the 'Great Depression' of 1873–96 checked the mid-Victorian confidence in ever-expanding trade and prosperity. This point only makes sense, of course, if it is linked with the rise in protectionism by Britain's rivals and the latters' colonial drives; but it was precisely in the 1880s that such a challenge arose, eroding the commercial near-monopoly of British traders and, worse still, threatening the future of their business through foreign tariffs. In West Africa especially, as experts such as C. W. Newbury, A. G. Hopkins, H. A. Turner and many others have demonstrated, *economic* motives for the scramble were paramount.[15] But they were also in evidence elsewhere in Africa, in the Pacific, in Burma and especially in China; and even if the benefits which Britain derived from its annexations in those regions had not amounted to much by 1914, the researches of Platt, Hynes and Uzoigwe especially show the marked shift in the mood of British merchants, manufacturers, newspapers *and* politicians when they realised that, if they did not take action, existing trade would be hurt and any potential economic benefits from the overseas world would be seized by others.[16] Even the debate upon the role of bankers, bondholders and their 'surplus capital', which has always been a more difficult economic motive for scholars to prove than that of commerce, is not so open-and-closed a case as Robinson and Gallagher seem to assume, at least in some *specific* examples of colonial conquest.[17]

The second set of objections leads on from the first: just as the 'official mind' appears in Robinson and Gallagher's account to have no ear for the clamour of its traders and manufacturers, so also does it seem unaffected by imperialistic public opinion. This is a difficult point to sustain. Even to those possessing only a general knowledge of the period 1870–1914, its most remarkable features are the changing context within which politicians had to operate. The reform bills of 1867 and 1884 produced a far larger electorate, and in turn led to enormous changes in party organisation and propaganda. Mass elementary education and the coming of a 'popular press' (chiefly of a jingoistic tone) altered the atmosphere of political debates, which could no longer be of concern to a select few. The rise of the so-called 'social question', and the slightly later growth of an organised labour movement, also affected the framework of British politics, throwing up new priorities and questioning the received view of the purposes of government. The world of ideas and culture was in a parallel state of flux; the late-Victorian age showed signs, domestically, of declining religious belief, of Social Darwinism, of incipient socialism, of cultural 'modernism', much of which interacted with a fast-growing concern in many circles about gloomy external tendencies – the loss of the Royal Navy's maritime monopoly, the poor performance of British industry, the threat from foreign tariffs, and the manifold challenges to imperial security and overseas commerce. The cosy mid-century Liberal assumptions about the eternal validity of free trade, liberty before order, low armaments expenditure abroad and a 'night-watchman state' at home, were now under challenge from Egyptian and Irish nationalists, European and American tariffs, the Franco-Russian fleets, trade unionists and Fabians on the Left and 'fair traders' and social-imperialists on the Right. Without exaggerating all these trends, one can nevertheless see that the world in which late-Victorian statesmen operated was in many respects *dis*similar to that occupied by Palmerston and Canning. Salisbury may have regretted the passing of 'the age of equipoise' and sought to delay any changes; but there is little sign that Rosebery, Chamberlain, Curzon and Milner did so. What concerned them, and many more in the country at large, was that the government should respond to these novel conditions by adopting more 'realistic' policies – those of the age of the 'new imperialism'.

The evidence of this changed political and cultural context cannot be provided in this brief essay; but there is now a substantial body of secondary literature[18] pointing to the growing climate of apprehensions and dissolving certainties, especially the fear of being eclipsed economically, navally and in other ways, *which in turn affected British imperial policy*. The country became more defensive, less willing to take chances, much more suspicious of foreign powers and much less tolerant of indigenous peoples; in consequence, much more inclined to take pre-emptive imperial actions, particularly since the government was under considerable pressure from domestic opinion to do so. The clamour to stake out a firm British position in East-Central Africa in 1888–91 against the claims of Portugal and Germany, the agitation to retain Uganda in the early 1890s, the demands for 'firm action' to preserve British interests in China a few years later and the parallel pressure upon Salisbury from the press, backbenchers and even his own Cabinet colleagues to resist France's claims during the Fashoda crisis, are but the most celebrated of the many examples of a British government engaging in imperial actions, *not simply* because of the cool calculations of the 'official mind' but also because it had to show domestic critics that it could act. Late-nineteenth-century imperialism, so far as the British were concerned, was increasingly an imperialism of fear, of *weltpolitische Angst* and a growing 'siege' mentality (albeit superficially hidden behind a Kiplingesque assertiveness) – which makes it altogether different in form from the decades prior to 1870, when the empire's trade and territories were expanding in a power-political vacuum. Robinson and Gallagher hint at this in the concluding pages of *Africa and the Victorians*, but by playing down the role of public opinion and the changes in the intellectual climate, they leave the reader with a somewhat unreal version of the political process.

The third cluster of criticisms need concern us only briefly, because it does not directly relate to the issue of continuity. It is worth remarking, however, that Robinson and Gallagher's theories seem to have little relevance in explaining the imperialist drives of *other* powers. (Although, as mentioned above, their general idea of the 'local crisis' as a way of explaining the dynamics and the timing of an annexationist process *can* usefully be applied to the imperialism of the new powers.) Since the authors were concerned to trace the longer-term tendencies in British policy, their interpretation obviously cannot apply to a European country whose arrival in the tropics was so recent that any idea of continuity is absurd. In addition, the specific references by Robinson and Gallagher to the imperial policies of other states are regarded as the most doubtful parts of the book. Historians of French imperialism, for example, would deny that the territorial partition of West Africa was simply a 'repercussion' of the Egyptian crisis, and point instead to the instigation of a French expansionist policy from 1879–80 onwards.[19] And scholars conversant with the background to 'Bismarck's first bid for colonies' seem nowadays united in asserting that domestic-political, electoral and commercial arguments caused Germany's entry into the colonial field, rather than any 'move in European diplomacy'.[20] Thus, however Robinson and Gallagher's contributions to one's understanding of British imperialism are to be assessed, they seem to offer little to the evaluation of the policies of other states or to a general theory of the 'scramble'.

Nevertheless, reference to the imperialism of other states is of some significance for the debate upon continuity in British policy, since it reminds us again that the world of 1895 was quite different from that of 1825 or even 1865. To a large extent, British imperial policy in those earlier decades had been carried out in a power-political vacuum; the question of whether or not to annex Singapore, or of how to act against some Latin American state, primarily depended upon the relationship between the metropolis and the locality. By the end of the century, the decision whether or not to annex depended upon *three*, not two interacting variables: the situation at home (including the state of public opinion); the nature of the 'local crisis'; *and* the rivalry of third powers, threatening – or at least appearing to threaten – the trade and the military security of the empire. Politicians such as Gladstone and Salisbury may have wished to carry out their foreign and imperial strategies according to the old dispensation; but the blunt fact was that, in an age when Britain had lost its industrial, naval and colonial monopolies, there was no prospect of being able to maintain a continuity in policy. Externally and – as suggested above – internally also, a new and much more troubled political order prevailed.

There is one saving grace which can rescue Robinson and Gallagher from much of this criticism: namely, that in *Africa and the Victorians* (although not in their articles 'The Imperialism of Free Trade' and 'The Partition of Africa'), their real concern was much less with the general problem of British or Western imperialism *per se*, than with the workings of the 'Official Mind of Imperialism', which is the book's subtitle. What interested them most of all, in other words, was how the higher stages of the decision-making process worked when confronted with a plethora of external problems requiring a 'response' from the imperial centre. Consequently, their remarks upon the habits of thought and technique, and the shared *Weltanschauung* of the Whitehall ministries are among the most brilliant parts of their book. At that level, their contribution is a stunning success. Where they may be regarded as going wrong is to suggest, in some of their more extravagant phrases, first, that the 'official mind' was an unvarying factor – as when they claim that its perceptions 'stayed much the same from ministry to ministry, regardless of the ideological stock in trade of the Party in power' (a comment which both Disraeli and Gladstone would have thought outrageous); and secondly, that their approach allows one to understand the imperialist process as a whole – as when they write of policy-making being 'the unified historical field', of 'all roads lead[ing] ineluctably to Downing Street', and of 'official calculations throw[ing] most light on the deeper reasons for imperial expansion . . .'.[21] From being one of the elements in the complex phenomenon of imperialism, the 'official mind' is inexorably promoted by Robinson and Gallagher to be the central factor; and since the *structure* of the British government and the ingrained *habits* of the bureaucratic process did remain reasonably similar throughout the century, the seductive idea of an overall continuity is introduced and expanded upon until it becomes the major, but distorting feature of their interpretation.

V

Is it possible at the end of this debate to produce some synthesis satisfying to all sides? The blunt answer must be 'no', for the simple reason that historians remain divided over the basic definitions. There can be no real agreement about 'the imperialism of free trade' so long as some scholars regard imperialism as the formal annexation of overseas territory, and others prefer a larger but looser definition. Similarly, there can be no argument upon the nature of the 'new imperialism' so long as Marxists equate it with a stage in capitalistic development and non-Marxists define it instead in territorial, political and social terms. Without a breakthrough at the semantic level, the historical debate upon imperialism will always be one of controversy and disagreement.

All that one can do here is to offer a purely personal view of the course of British imperialism in the nineteenth century. When placed in the longer-term context of Britain's history as an independent great power from Tudor times to the Second World War, it seems to this writer that it is possible to regard that particular century in two quite separate ways. The first would be from the perspective of the metropolitan power's relations with non-European societies. Here one could point to a fairly continuous growth of British contacts, trade and influence overseas from the first Virginia settlement in 1607 to the acquisition of the League of Nations mandates in 1919; a growth subjected, admittedly, to variations of tempo and direction, and checked spasmodically by political events at home, challenges by foreign rivals, and rebellions by colonists (Americans, Afrikaners) or native tribes (Afghanis, Sudanese). Nonetheless, British influence and power in the overseas world continued to grow, by fair means or foul, formally and informally, sometimes in a deliberate fashion and at other times 'reluctantly' and almost by accident, in consequence of 'local crises'. Its course and outcome can be measured not simply in the political and constitutional histories of the empire – on this point Robinson and Gallagher were absolutely right – but also in those (now very dated but still significant) geography textbooks which listed the whole variety of raw materials produced and developed in British possessions and other tropical lands for the needs of the home society, from the tobacco of the early Virginia plantations to the oil of the Middle East; and it can be traced further in works upon 'Imperial Military Geography' which detail the strategic bases, coaling stations (Valparaiso and Yokahama as well as Malta and the Cape) and submarine-cable lines by which those many economic interests were buttressed. Despite all the regional and chronological variations, the case for a basic continuity of British expansionism into the 'third world' seems valid.

The second perspective relates to Britain's position *vis-à-vis* its rivals, the other empires and advanced states: that is to say, it concerns the country's *relative* power in the world. Using this criterion, it becomes much more difficult to argue the case for continuity, for the simple reason that a watershed occurred somewhere in the third quarter of the nineteenth century. Before that time, and arguably since as long ago as the War of the Spanish Succession, Britain's strength – strategic, commercial, financial – had been growing relative to that of her rivals; and that strength had been enhanced by the coming of industrialisation, which boosted British productivity and wealth and its ultimate strategic power still further, and which had made it all the easier for this expanding society to press upon less-developed polities overseas in the ways described above. By the final quarter of the nineteenth century, however, a fundamental change had taken place: the transfer of industrial technology to the United States, Imperial Germany, later Russia and Japan, had created new centres of economic and strategic power where previously none had existed. British industry was no longer supreme, its commerce was hit by rival manufacturers and foreign tariffs, its naval supremacy was ebbing away, its empire was much more vulnerable.[22]

Under such pressures from without and the cries of alarm from within, the political managers of the 'weary Titan' sought to buttress their global strategic position, and to protect their trading interests, by a further rash of annexations. Ostensibly, the acquisition of Bechuanaland, the Sudan and Wei-hai-wei look the same as the much earlier seizures of Aden, Natal and New Zealand; but in one basic way they were not. The later actions were those of a country on the retreat, nervous of the future, and deploring the manifold challenges to the global *status quo* which it now preferred to maintain. This was the age of official investigations into the decline of British industrial efficiency and 'the deterioration of the race', of naval scares and invasion alarms, of jingo newspapers and anxious tariff reformers; and what was more, the underlying evidence suggests that such circles were right to be concerned.

In sum, the 'new imperialism' of 1870–1914 witnessed various great powers, confident that the future was theirs, surging forward to take a share of the world's colonial possessions; but it also witnessed one very old great power, far less confident about the future, taking imperialist measures to ward off decline. No greater mistake could be made than to ignore this fundamental difference in world circumstances between British imperialism at Victoria's accession and that which attended her death. To the natives of the Sudan and the Chinese Boxers it was not so obvious, but the advance of Kitchener's army up the Nile and the bombardment of the Taku forts by the Royal Navy's squadrons were the actions of a world power in decline. The confident, expansive imperialism of the *Pax Britannica* had now given way to the defensive reactions of an empire engaged in a struggle for survival.

2. Colonial Self-government

PETER BURROUGHS

Colonial self-government is a central and familiar theme of British imperial history. The issue was first forced on the attention of Englishmen at the time of the American Revolution, when they failed to discover an acceptable means of combining colonial autonomy with imperial unity, with the result that the first empire in America ended in a violent bid for independence. Half a century later the problem again arose in British North America. This time a way was eventually found, through the device of responsible government, to grant the colonists the local autonomy they desired within the framework of empire. This satisfactory resolution of a fundamental and recurring imperial dilemma was applied, where and when appropriate, to other colonies of European settlement in the mid-nineteenth century, and in time proved capable of further extension. Many Victorian politicians and writers hailed the discovery and application of colonial self-government as a triumph of liberal statesmanship, the external counterpart to parliamentary government at home. It thus became firmly incorporated within the Whig tradition of progress and enlightenment. For early imperial historians, the course of Britain's relations with settlement colonies came to be seen as an evolutionary process leading inexorably through representative institutions to local self-government, and later to dominion status when the empire was transmuted into the Commonwealth. Such an interpretation, which viewed colonial communities proceeding inevitably towards nationhood, was equally congenial to nationalist historians, though they emphasised local demands for political liberty rather than the wisdom of British statesmanship as the motivating force of this transformation.

It would be erroneous to suppose, however, that an inescapable conflict of interests existed between colonies and mother country, and that colonists endured an irksome subordination and offered a grudging allegiance. In fact English subjects overseas often cherished their common imperial nationality and evinced a cheerful loyalty. British rule was not imposed by force on peoples striving to form independent states. Even in the progress towards local self-government it was not a question of colonists insistently making political demands which the imperial authorities withstood as long as they could but at last reluctantly conceded. Colonists were not always the aggressors, with Britain on the defensive, fighting a rearguard action to preserve its direct control. Deliberate British disengagement was as influential a force as colonial nationalism in shaping the course of imperial relations at certain crucial moments. Among various techniques for fostering and safeguarding British interests overseas, devolution of authority might sometimes be more effective than centralised supervision.

At the same time, the introduction into settlement colonies of representative institutions patterned after the metropolitan model contained its own constitutional logic. It established a course of political development which, drawing on British precedents and practices, pointed in the direction of local autonomy. As struggles for power sprang up within the framework of these colonial constitutions the imperial relationship was bound to become involved. Home rule was inextricably related to who should rule at home: governing elites might owe their power to acting as imperial agents or collaborators; their opponents might appeal to popular opinion in a way which challenged imperial authority as well as the local oligarchies. Colonial politicians did not readily accept restraints on their power or their ambitions, and British principles of governance could be employed both in local factional contests and to bid for the greater prize of supplanting the imperial authorities. The history of imperial relations is therefore largely the story of periodic attempts to reconcile colonists' aspirations for greater autonomy with the preservation of the unity of the empire. Although colonial self-government was a nineteenth-century discovery, the outcome in particular of Britain's dealings with Canada in the 1830s and 1840s, its origins and character are not fully intelligible without some reference to the earlier British empire in North America and the causes and consequences of the American Revolution.

In 1774 Edmund Burke characterised the old colonial system as a 'state of commercial servitude and civil liberty'.[1] In contrast to centralised, authoritarian French and Spanish practice, Britain's imperial structure incorporated a jumble of inconsistent administrative principles. Metropolitan control, principally in matters of trade, coexisted uneasily with a tradition of local self-management. The colonies were dependencies of the Crown, but they had their own legislative bodies of governor, council and assembly, which broadly reflected the constitution of the parent state, though assemblies had exploited their power of the purse to gain control of the local governments. Given the ineffectiveness and laxity of British supervision, this typically British compromise of economic regulation and political freedom represented a generally acceptable arrangement for about a century. It contained, however, the seeds of potential misunderstanding and discord. It masked an incipient clash between two rival centres of authority. As actual practice increasingly diverged from British theory, differing concepts of empire gradually emerged on opposite sides of the Atlantic. According to the traditional British view, colonies were dependencies whose legislatures were necessarily subordinate to a supreme imperial Parliament, even if this supremacy had in the past been exercised only in the limited sphere of trade and navigation. The colonies, for their part, saw themselves as mature communities long used to managing their own internal affairs without interference from London.

The incompatibility of these views was exposed after 1763. With the conquest of French Canada and the end of the Seven Years' War the exigencies of defence, Indian policy, westward expansion, and above all finance led to closer British supervision of colonial affairs. The government not only tightened up the enforcement of trade regulations, but also sought to raise a revenue in America by means of Parliament's latent authority to tax colonies. This departure from past practice challenged the financial powers long exercised by the colonial legislatures. In response they appealed to the rights of Englishmen and British notions of governance, symbolised by the cry of 'no taxation without representation', and thus turned British constitutional principles against imperial authority. The resulting crisis in imperial relations was deliberately exacer-bated by those American politicians who saw in the outcry against British innovations an opportunity to overthrow ruling groups in the individual colonies and obtain political predominance for themselves.

British ministers were now confronted with the fundamental problem of reconciling metropolitan authority with local autonomy within the framework of the eighteenth-century constitution and concepts of empire. They were not prepared to compromise on the issue of parliamentary supremacy and they could not envisage an empire based on a principle of equal association or partnership. They did not perceive that the answer lay in a devolution of authority to the colonial executives. This would have seemed in the 1770s tantamount to a grant of independence, and the whole drift of imperial policy, then and later, was to preserve the local executives from local control.

The failure of contemporaries to resolve these political and conceptual conundrums necessitated a resort to extreme solutions: outright independence or complete subordination. The Americans were powerful and distant enough to claim independence; it was otherwise when a similar struggle broke out in weak, neighbouring Ireland. At first the British government was prepared under pressure to grant in 1782 Anglo-Irish demands for a parliament with legislative autonomy in internal affairs. This experiment in partnership produced the further demand for Irish ministers to be made accountable to the Irish parliament, a proposition which was fully debated in the 1790s. Whether or not the idea of responsible government eventually percolated to Canada from these Irish discussions,[2] the British government refused to concede an independent executive. It seemed incompatible with British constitutional usage, anomalous within an imperial system, and, in this particular instance, threatened an overthrow of the Protestant ascendancy. The response to revolutionary rumblings in 1798 was the imposition of a legislative union with England in 1801 and the absorption of the Irish parliament into that at Westminster.

While it is a matter of speculation among historians whether American independence hastened or postponed a reappraisal by Britain of its relations with settlement colonies, new policies and practices had to be devised to govern French Canada. The acquisition of a colony peopled by 80,000 non-English settlers with alien institutions, religion and language posed British ministers with novel problems. Should the laws and customs of the French Canadians be preserved or assimilated to those of Britain? Was it appropriate to extend to Quebec the customary system of representative government which existed elsewhere in North America, or was a more authoritarian administration better suited to a conquered colony of French Catholics? Amid the conflicting opinions of local experts, mounting unrest in North America, and instability in domestic politics, British ministers spent ten years after 1763 groping for a policy. At first they assumed that the French must be assimilated through the early introduction of the standard model of representative government. Attempts to adapt the normal political structure to abnormal circumstances, and provide the institutional framework for a gradual 'melting down of the French nation to the English',[3] were defeated by officials on the spot, principally the governor-general, Sir Guy Carleton. He argued persuasively that it would be impracticable and dangerous to place legislative power in the hands either of an ignorant French peasantry of uncertain allegiance or an English merchant oligarchy with selfish ambitions and republican sympathies. More crucially, at a time of growing tension in Britain's relations with the Thirteen Colonies, Carleton wanted for strategic and military reasons to ensure the loyalty of the *Canadiens*. The overriding claims of security necessitated a reaffirmation of the rights guaranteed the French at the conquest and a continuation of conciliar government. Administration by governor and a nominated biracial legislature, formally sanctioned by the Quebec Act of 1774, represented a break with tradition. This constitutional structure, which came to be known as Crown colony government, proved to be a valuable, versatile device for overseas territories inhabited by natives or foreigners, as well as for small strategic bases and convict settlements, where representative institutions seemed wildly inappropriate.

In British North America the experiment in conciliar government was terminated by the influx of the loyalists into Quebec in the 1780s demanding the elective institutions which they had previously enjoyed. British ministers now had to find some way of granting the loyalists English laws and representative government without violently overturning the rights hitherto guaranteed the French Canadians. The answer to this dilemma devised by William Grenville was territorial division and renewed assimilation. The Constitutional Act of 1791 created a British province of Upper Canada with English law and a French province of Lower Canada with French civil law and a privileged Catholic church. It might have been possible to continue conciliar government in the lower province, but in addition to the demands of the English merchants, financial considerations argued against such a course. To relieve the British taxpayer from contributing over £150,000 a year towards the cost of administering Quebec, larger funds had to be raised locally, and ministers had learned enough from the American Revolution to recognise that colonists could not be taxed except by their own elected legislatures. Grenville also hoped that the introduction of representative government would promote the eventual anglicisation of the French Canadians. If they participated as fully as the loyalists in the blessings of British constitutional liberty, surely they would in time adapt themselves to its usages and come to appreciate the superior merits of English laws and institutions.

When Grenville, William Pitt, and their colleagues framed the constitution for the Canadas, their approach was profoundly affected by recent experience with the Thirteen Colonies. They ascribed the loss of the American colonies to the unrestrained growth of democratic, levelling influences which had led to an excess of popular control in the colonial constitutions and an eventual undermining of colonial loyalty. British political institutions apparently underwent a sea-change when they were exported overseas. This tendency to be subverted by democratic forces had to be deliberately counteracted in the remaining colonies in British North America by reinforcing executive power and by assimilating colonial institutions more closely to the metropolitan model. To accomplish this, the constitutions of Upper and Lower Canada each comprised a governor, an executive council, a legislative council and an assembly, representing the colonial counterparts of the British monarch, ministry, House of Lords and House of Commons. This structure departed from previous practice by differentiating between the executive council as the governor's advisers and the legislative council as the upper house of the legislature. According to the architects of the scheme, strong, independent legislative councils, perhaps eventually filled by hereditary colonial peers, would more effectively resist the encroachments of popular assemblies and act not only as a conservative, stabilising force but as a bulwark against republican influences in provinces bordering the United States. Once these constitutions were introduced, it was left to the governor and his advisers to ensure their smooth operation by exerting the same influence over the legislature that the King and his ministers exercised over the British Parliament.

Within two decades, however, tensions and disharmony began to appear and by the 1820s struggles for political power placed increasing strains on the functioning of representative government in the Canadas. To a greater or lesser degree in all the British North American provinces, political control fell into the hands of local oligarchies or 'family compacts' entrenched in the councils. Their hold over government in the Canadas was the stronger because the distinction between executive and legislative councils was not in practice observed. Many individuals sat on both bodies, so that the legislative council failed to achieve the independence and authority its creators had envisaged. Pitt and Grenville secured their colonial elite; but it was an official clique, not a colonial aristocracy with political weight and standing devoted to disinterested public service. The local elites used their power to promote selfish or sectional interests, to overawe governors, and to check the measures and ambitions of the lower houses.

The assemblies naturally responded by asserting their privileges and authority in the time-honoured fashion by exploiting control over the voting of money. They were aided in this campaign by the rising costs of administration and the withdrawal of imperial subsidies, which together made annual appropriations from general provincial revenues unavoidable. Once local executives lost the ability to finance the government's operations by independent Crown revenues, their political powers were endangered. This is what had occurred in Britain, throughout the American colonies and the West Indies, wherever representative institutions flourished: sooner or later assemblies in all the British North American provinces would claim the right to appropriate local sources of revenue in a bid to realise their political ambitions.

Because of variations in local conditions, the timing and pace of this process differed in the individual provinces. In Nova Scotia constitutional harmony was preserved until the 1830s by the willingness of the executive to allow members of the assembly to spend provincial funds on roads and local improvements without enquiring too closely into how the money was actually used. In New Brunswick the loyalist oligarchy and the Saint John lumber merchants captured control of both assembly and council and this for the time being purchased political peace. In Upper Canada the governors managed to maintain executive power and keep the initiative in the legislature until critics of government won a majority in the election of 1824. It was Lower Canada which found itself in the vanguard of political controversy and constitutional advance. By the 1820s the official party had lost control in the assembly. When serious friction occurred, as it did whenever the interests of English and French inhabitants clashed, the governor lacked sufficient patronage and influence to make the constitution operate harmoniously. Indeed, personal inclination encouraged most governors in Lower Canada to use what patronage they did possess to promote the English party, a tendency which created dissatisfaction among leading French-Canadian politicians who wanted to monopolise the patronage themselves. Moreoever, factional fighting acquired a keener edge in Lower Canada because political divisions were accentuated by ethnic antagonisms. Contrary to the original intentions of the British government and early practice under the 1791 constitution, politics in the province soon became polarised with the

English party dominant in the councils and the French dominant in the assembly.

By 1828, when numerously signed petitions of grievance were brought to England by a delegation from the Lower Canadian assembly, the operation of representative government in the Canadas had run into grave difficulties. Behind the immediate protests occasioned by Governor Dalhousie's high-handed actions in his dealings with the assembly, particularly over finance, lay the fundamental problem that gubernatorial influence had not only failed to secure co-operation among the various branches of the legislature, but had created oligarchies and placed councils at loggerheads with assemblies. Councillors could thwart the measures of the lower house without being called to account for their actions; assemblies could protest and bring the machinery of government to a standstill, but they could not effect a change in the personnel or policies of the councils. The two sides acted at cross-purposes with no constitutional method of breaking the deadlock. The petitioners in 1828, and reformers in the Canadas thereafter, put forward two possible remedies for this impasse. The most widely favoured proposal, which harked back to 1791, was to convert the legislative council into a truly independent body, either by improving the selection of nominees or, following the American example, by rendering it elective. The other suggestion was to make the executive council responsible to the provincial legislature for its actions. This eventually proved to be the key to constitutional advance, but in 1828 and the years immediately following reformers in the Canadas placed less emphasis on this proposal and British ministers discovered sundry objections to it. Neither of these changes required a revision of the constitutional structure established in 1791, and the petitioners argued against the intervention of Parliament to resolve the present crisis in Lower Canada, which they attributed to maladministration and Dalhousie's unconstitutional proceedings.

As the House of Commons debate on the petitions in May 1828 strikingly demonstrates, British politicians adopted sharply contrasting approaches to the problems of Canadian government. Radical and liberal Whig MPs ascribed the disputes to political causes, characteristic of representative governments overseas, wherein selfish oligarchies clashed with popular assemblies. Given this diagnosis, the remedy lay in a return to constitutional government and redress of palpable grievances. Tory MPs, on the other hand, blamed the turmoil on the assembly's improper attempts to monopolise power inspired by racial animosity. William Huskisson, the Colonial Secretary, and his deputy Wilmot Horton declaimed against benighted French Canadians seeking to preserve thirteenth-century feudalism. Such unrealistic ambitions had to be strenuously opposed and Parliament might have to amend the 1791 constitution, perhaps reuniting the Canadas along the lines of the bill introduced but hastily withdrawn in 1822.[4]

To allay inconvenient criticism in the Commons, the Tory ministry conceded a select committee, which was no doubt expected to uphold the government's view and recommend suitable constitutional changes. Events belied this expectation. Not only did the assembly's delegation present a convincing case, but liberal Whig members of the committee managed by adroit manoeuvring to secure the adoption of a report highly sympathetic to the assembly's claims. It rejected the Tory argument that French laws and customs were the cause of the colony's ills and should be anglicised by legislative action. The committee endorsed the opinion that recent discontent was essentially the product of maladministration, to be cured by a return to 'an impartial, conciliatory and constitutional system of Government'.[5] Among a catalogue of specific recommendations, the committee urged that the legislative councils be made more representative and independent bodies by the exclusion of office-holders and judges, and that all provincial revenues be surrendered to the assemblies in return for a civil list covering the salaries of the leading officials. Unfortunately for the success of these proposals, two years of fatal inaction followed as British ministers prevaricated. The opportunity for timely, constructive measures was lost. Preoccupied with domestic issues, the Wellington Cabinet and its advisers could not decide what policy to pursue in Canada in the light of a report which they found wholly uncongenial but dared not reject for fear of parliamentary repercussions. This paralysis lasted until a Whig ministry came into office in November 1830.

As reformers at home and overseas, the Whigs seemingly possessed an advantage over their Tory predecessors in attempting to settle the political crisis in the Canadas. Contrary to the assertions of Canadian historians, who have traditionally dismissed British ministers as indifferent to North American affairs and reactionary in their outlook, successive Whig ministries in the early 1830s adopted the select committee's report as their programme of remedial action and deliberately embraced a policy of conciliation. They recognised that in any constitutional struggle in the Canadas the assemblies had valid claims and were bound to win in the long run because of their power of the purse. Moreover, the Whigs maintained that government should be based, in the colonies as at home, on the consent and confidence of the governed. They accordingly withdrew support from the oligarchies, which were no longer employed as the collaborators and agents of imperial authority, and tried to establish good working relations with the lower houses. Whenever the Canadian legislatures became unduly clamorous and extravagant in their demands, the Whigs tended to blame the temporary ascendancy of agitators such as Louis-Joseph Papineau in Lower Canada and William Lyon Mackenzie in Upper Canada, who had misled the people concerning their true interests and were unrepresentative of colonial opinion. Given this congenial explanation, so typical of imperial officials at all times and places, a conciliatory approach was mandatory. While a firm stand on fundamental matters might ultimately be required, until that sticking point had been reached a willingness to meet all reasonable demands was essential if the British government was to appeal successfully to the moderate majority of colonists and neutralise the power of the demagogues.

This balance between firmness and conciliation was subjected to its severest test in Lower Canada, but the interrelated interests of the individual provinces required that a similar constitutional policy be pursued in them all. Furthermore, the Whigs were convinced that good relations with the United States depended on Canadian contentment because the Americans might use political turmoil in the Canadas as a pretext for intervention and indulging an insatiable appetite for territorial aggrandisement. British ministers valued the North American colonies, partly for their commercial potential, partly for accommodating British emigrants, but above all for providing a strategic bulwark against United States expansion and a balance of power on the North American continent. For this reason, Canadian questions and Britain's handling of them were always viewed within the context of Anglo-American relations.

In pursuit of a policy of conciliation, the Whigs introduced a variety of reforms in the early 1830s. To tackle the financial dispute, an imperial act surrendered the customs duties levied under the Quebec Revenue Act of 1774 to the control of the Canadian assemblies and the grant of a civil list was requested in return. The Upper Canadian assembly responded to this gesture of goodwill but its counterpart in the lower province refused to reciprocate because other Crown revenues were not conceded and objections were raised to the personnel and scale of salaries included in the proposed civil list. The Whig ministry also tried to give the legislative councils a more independent, acceptable character by excluding judges and appointing additional members unconnected with the local administration. But this kind of limited tinkering with the councils had little discernible effect over their activities and did nothing to prevent or resolve further clashes with the assemblies. This failure points to the difficulties and limitations to which the Whigs' policy of conciliation was subject. As admirers of the British constitution, they were unwilling to embark on constitutional innovation or experimentation overseas. They refused demands for elective legislative councils, because this would produce upper houses identical in composition to lower houses and in Lower Canada would undermine the political safeguards for the English minority. The proposal to make executive councils responsible to assemblies was rejected because it seemed incompatible with the prevailing concept of empire. A colonial governor had necessarily to take his instructions from London, for if he was to prefer the advice of his local councillors, the colony would be no longer a subordinate, dependent territory but an independent state. Consequently, there were limits to the political changes which the Whigs were prepared to implement, and what they had to offer was insufficient to satisfy the aspirations of colonial politicians.

British policy in Lower Canada was subject to other restraints. By the mid-1830s the Whigs' outlook was increasingly influenced by an antipathy towards the ambitions of the French party. As its leaders flirted with republican ideas and talked of creating an independent state for *la nation canadienne*, British ministers perceived a threat to imperial interests in North America. Any bid to establish a French republic would jeopardise the welfare of English-speaking colonists within Lower Canada, for whom the British government felt a special responsibility, and would almost certainly lead to civil war, since Upper Canadians would not stand idly by lest their outlet to the sea was cut off and the United States would soon become embroiled. It was an ominous, if somewhat melodramatic, scenario but Englishmen recalled the war of 1812 and feared the worst if matters got out of hand in Lower Canada. The *patriote* challenge also aroused latent anti-French sentiments among British ministers. Not only were the French Canadians Catholics, but they were wedded to a backward agrarian society which contrasted sharply and unfavourably with the commercial enterprise of English colonists. In an age of British industrialisation and progress, French Canadian institutions seemed obsolete and retrograde, hardly fitting foundations for a colonial society. Moreover, Whig administrators calculated that even if British emigration did not eventually swamp the French numerically within Lower Canada itself, the latter could not hope to preserve their cultural identity when surrounded on all sides by Anglo-Saxons. Time and historical processes were inexorably leading towards assimilation, and it would therefore be ineffectual as well as misguided to base British policy on any other assumption. Concessions and political advance, which might have been appropriate in other North American provinces, were thus withheld because of the situation in Lower Canada. Indeed, such was the Whig reaction to the challenge of French Canada that by the mid-1830s cultural chauvinism had become a stronger influence over policy than political principle.

During 1836–7 ministers decided that the time had at last

come to take a firm stand. Hitherto they had patiently pursued
a course of constructive procrastination to prevent matters
coming prematurely to a head. While the commission headed
by the Earl of Gosford conducted its inquiries in Canada they
avoided devising a settlement in London and imposing it by
parliamentary authority. Indeed Parliament had been deliberately kept out of the controversy. Most English politicians
agreed that its intervention in American affairs at the time of
the Revolution had been mischievous, and that it should be
held in reserve to adjudicate disputes between colonists and the
British government and give statutory effect to agreements
reached between the parties. By 1837 these constraints ceased
to operate, and the authorities were also faced with the
practical problem that official salaries in Lower Canada had
fallen seriously into arrears because of the assembly's refusal
since 1833 to vote the supplies. The outcome of the ministry's
reappraisal was the resolutions introduced by Lord John
Russell in the Commons in March 1837, which rejected
colonial demands for constitutional changes and threatened to
appropriate provincial revenue by parliamentary authority.

This transformation in Whig policy, as well as the failure of
conciliation to prevent a recourse to violence in 1837, must be
explained in large measure by what had meanwhile occurred in
British North America. The early 1830s in Lower Canada saw
a growing assertiveness on the part of the assembly. As
leadership of the French party shifted from moderates like John
Neilsen to the demagogic Papineau, a new note of stridency and
recalcitrance appeared, symbolised by the refusal to vote the
supplies. Historians have often referred to these developments
as signifying the rise of French Canadian nationalism or of a
reform movement. Papineau emerged at this time as the
spokesman for a beleaguered French community conscious that
its cultural identity was threatened by unsympathetic British
rule and by an influx of British immigrants who brought
cholera with them and who intensified the competition for land
in the province. But the assertiveness of the French leaders also
reflected their frustration and anger at the British government's refusal to capitulate to their political demands. Since
petitions and appeals to London failed to place power in their
hands, they turned to their own resources. In a calculated,

self-interested fashion they appealed to the *habitants* for support by exploiting their discontent, playing on their fears, and whipping up their prejudices. Rural dissatisfaction certainly existed in the 1830s among the *habitants* on the *seigneuries* because of the plight of a backward subsistence agriculture, aggravated in 1836–7 by crop failures and economic depression. Profit-minded *seigneurs* were also putting the squeeze on *habitants* by increasing rents and reserving timber and undeveloped lands. Lest this agrarian unrest get out of hand and undermine the structure of French society, *seigneurs* like Papineau capitalised on popular dissatisfaction and redirected it against the English, who thereby became the scapegoats for the ills of Lower Canada.

This combination of genuine discontent and exploited prejudices provided considerable backing for the French leaders' campaign of non-co-operation with Britain but it unleashed a force which, gathering momentum, carried them almost inexorably towards unconstitutional actions and ulti-mately the violence that some, including Papineau, would have preferred to avoid but dared not repudiate. Behind the slogans and the rhetoric, the appeal to principle, lay a struggle for local power. Contemporaries and later historians might call the malcontents reformers, or even radicals, but apart from some anti-clericalism and a dash of Irish exuberance, their radi-calism consisted of no more than a desire to replace the ruling elite, if necessary by overthrowing British rule. They did not want to restructure society or place power in the hands of the people; rather they wished to preserve traditional society and exercise power themselves. They were socially conservative and politically ambitious. Their eventual assault on British authority made them rebels, but not revolutionaries.

Something of the same explanation accounts for the simul-taneous growth of a so-called reform movement in Upper Canada. There matters were complicated by the assembly majorities alternately enjoyed by conservatives and refor-mers as a result of the quadrennial provincial elections between 1824 and 1836. This provided a partial safety-valve for political discontent and some means of avoiding permanent constitu-tional deadlock. There were also certain points of similarity between these two loose factions, including a common hostility to religious privilege. Though strong partisan feelings were to be expected in an ethnically diverse and multiconfessional society, both the major alignments in the assembly were essentially moderates who had for political purposes to emphasise slender or artificial differences. While specific grievances were aired – over land administration, the predominance of commercial interests, the vast expenditure on canal construction – again the contest was basically a struggle for power. In order to replace the ruling elite, some politicians such as Robert Baldwin advocated the creation of a responsible executive; others recommended an elective legislative council and the superiority of American practice. As in Lower Canada, the imperial government's failure to sanction these demands created dissatisfaction with British rule among frustrated politicians, especially when reformers were trounced at the election in 1836 by a conservative backlash instigated by Lieutenant-Governor Head playing the loyalty card. This was almost the last straw for hotheads such as Mackenzie who, contrary to claims often made, was never the acknowledged leader of a united reform movement in Upper Canada. He was an untypical, eccentric public figure, an Upper Canadian William Cobbett, with an instinctive aversion to the world around him and great talents as a colourful propagandist whom people enjoyed reading but seldom heeded. With such disparate, meagre forces a bid for independence was bound to fail.

When Englishmen heard in December 1837 that rebellion had broken out in Lower Canada, the vast majority, Whig and Tory, ascribed the revolt to racial animosity between French and English. Only radicals persisted with a constitutional explanation and drew a parallel with the earlier American contest for individual rights. The Whig ministry secured an act to suspend the constitution in Lower Canada and sent out Lord Durham to govern with the advice of a special council. A leading politician with avowed liberal sympathies, Durham was a shrewd choice to act as dictator in Canada and for five months he pursued a policy of pacification and reform. But, temperamental and vainglorious, he resigned in a huff when the British government disallowed his ordinance banishing rebels to Bermuda on the ground that he had exceeded his powers. On his return to London he set about writing his *Report on the Affairs of British North America*, which appeared in February 1839.

In his analysis of the causes of colonial conflict, Durham claimed that he had arrived in Lower Canada assuming that discontent had arisen from a quarrel between an assembly contending for popular rights and an executive upholding the prerogative of the Crown. To his surprise he had discovered a profound ethnic enmity which pervaded all aspects of society. 'I expected to find', he wrote in a celebrated remark, 'a contest between a government and a people: I found two nations warring in the bosom of a single state: I found a struggle, not of principles, but of races.'[6] Misleadingly, the rival colonists had been fighting under 'false colours': the French had employed democratic doctrines for conservative purposes and to hide their hostility to everything English; the English had sided with executive authority but were really enlightened reformers attempting to overthrow obsolete French customs and promote commercial enterprise. Given this explanation and the cultural chauvinism of the typical Whig, Durham considered the only sensible long-term policy must be one of assimilation. Without acting oppressively, Britain had to anglicise the French by means of a legislative union of the Canadas in which they would be outnumbered by a vigorous English majority.

In addition to national animosities, Durham attributed political discontent in both the Canadas to the perpetual collision of executive and assembly caused by the combination of representative institutions and irresponsible government. A small clique of governor's advisers had exercised power without regard to the wishes of the people or their representatives, and while the assembly might condemn government policies, it could neither implement its own programme nor replace objectionable advisers. Baulked of this legitimate aspiration, popular leaders had behaved irresponsibly. Durham's solution to this impasse lay in an extension to the colonies of the British constitutional practice of Cabinet government, or what contemporaries called 'responsible government'. The administration of local affairs should be entrusted to executive councillors who could command the confidence of a majority in the assembly. So long as they retained this support, the governor must conduct the government in all internal matters according to their advice, irrespective of his personal views or those of his superiors in London. To avoid a clash of authority, Durham proposed that administrative responsibilities should be divided between colonial and imperial governments, with British control restricted to a few subjects of major imperial concern: the form of government, commercial and foreign relations, and public lands. With this division of jurisdiction and devolution of authority, he believed that the colonists' desire for internal self-government could be successfully reconciled with the preservation of imperial unity.

It was long the accepted view of British and Canadian historians that Durham's *Report* was a document of decisive influence in the history of imperial relations. Durham was accordingly honoured as the saviour of the British empire, because he providentially discovered the secret of responsible government which groping British politicians eagerly embraced. Recent writers have shown that the retrospective claims are exaggerated.[7] The *Report* in fact received an indifferent reception in the British press, and while some contemporaries regarded it as a major contribution to the Canadian debate, the views of ministers were not greatly influenced by its recommendations. They had already concluded independently that some form of Canadian union was necessary, and the Whig Cabinet's eventual preference for a legislative union over a federal union owed more to Russell's advocacy than to Durham's. Because of the exigencies of domestic politics and protests from Upper Canada against a reunion of the provinces, the ministerial measure was postponed until the consent of the Upper Canadians had been obtained, which the new governor-general, Poulett Thomson, accomplished by political adroitness and the promise of a loan. Under union in 1841 elective institutions were restored and equal representation granted the two former provinces in the new assembly, in the false hope that collaboration among English-speaking colonists would ensure their predominance and thereby in time destroy French cultural distinctiveness.

Durham's other recommendation of responsible government was rejected by British ministers in 1839. Although they explicitly disclaimed any desire to govern in opposition to the wishes of the assembly, they were sceptical about endorsing such a vague, theoretical concept. They still found it difficult to reconcile Cabinet government in Canada with the colony's subordinate status, and Durham's division of jurisdiction seemed artificial, unrealistic and certain to be unacceptable to ambitious colonial politicians. Whig ministers preferred to leave future relations between executive and assembly to be settled by time and practical experience. The early 1840s in fact saw the gradual emergence of Cabinet government by coalitions of party groups whose demands governors generally accepted. The government in London, now Tory, acquiesced in these concessions, despite considerable misgivings, most notably in 1842 when Sir Charles Bagot reconstituted his ministry to include French Canadians as well as English reformers. It was not until the Whigs returned to office in 1846 and Earl Grey became Colonial Secretary that the principle of responsible government was formally conceded in Canada.

To explain the reasons and timing of this significant change in colonial policy, historians have offered constitutional and economic explanations. Imperial Whig historians ascribed the transformation exclusively to Durham's influence.[8] This is largely romantic invention, because no-one paid much heed to the *Report* in 1839 and seven years unaccountably elapsed between its publication and the actual revision of policy. It may be that Durham presciently discerned the acceptance in Britain itself of the constitutional convention that a government could not continue in office without a Commons majority. During the 1840s, some writers have argued, Britain achieved 'responsible government' and this recognised practice was automatically transmitted by Grey to suitable colonies like Canada.[9] The difficulty with this plausible explanation is the lack of factual evidence to prove that English politicians recognised by 1846 that this new convention had become irrevocably established practice in Britain and ought to be extended to the North American colonies.

Historians favouring economic explanations have claimed that the acceptance of responsible government was the logical and inevitable consequence of the adoption of free trade in 1846. The downfall of the protectionist system and the relaxation of Britain's economic controls allowed free play at last for liberal notions of colonial government and enabled mature colonies to throw off their subordinate status. To some writers this change of policy reflected a hostility or indifference among Englishmen towards expensive colonial burdens: responsible government represented a device for cutting worthless colonies adrift.[10] Now that historians no longer hold that 'anti-imperialism' characterised mid-Victorian opinion, those who advance economic interpretations regard responsible government as a confident concession made from a position of commercial strength, and as a classic example of the shift from 'formal' to 'informal' methods of pursuing British interests in Canada.[11]

An explanation which is exclusively based on economic factors, and wholly neglects political considerations, fails to reflect the attitudes, priorities, or motives of Whig ministers actually involved in determining Canadian policy in the late 1840s. Their approach to the governance of colonies was fashioned, not by a calculated appraisal of economic interests, but by a desire to give British communities overseas the fullest possible control over their internal affairs that circumstances permitted. By 1846 Grey recognised that Canada had attained sufficient political maturity to warrant, and indeed necessitate, the form of self-government the colonists had long been demanding. He admitted that this was a gamble and his private letters to Lord Elgin, the governor-general, are full of doubts, apprehension, and pessimism. But Grey saw no practicable alternative to trusting to the good sense and forbearance of colonists familiar with British political traditions to harmonise imperial policy with local interests whenever these should come into conflict. By 1846 he no longer considered the French a severe threat to British interests in North America or to the welfare of the English majority. However unreliable his appreciation of Canadian politics under the union, he believed that the challenge of French Canada in its earlier stridently nationalistic and menacingly separatist form had subsided to manageable proportions and could best be left to Canadians themselves to handle.

Grey's attitude to Canadian self-government was also affected by his fears concerning the ambitions of the United States. He dreaded the consequences of permitting Canadian

discent to fester and providing a plausible excuse for
American intervention. Recalling the war of 1812, the border
skirmishes in the aftermath of the rebellions, and American
designs on Oregon, Texas and Mexico, he remained deeply
suspicious of the territorial appetite of the United States and
anxious lest war should break out between the two countries.
Given American might and manpower, he realised that
Canada could not be defended against aggression except by
giving the colonists self-government and fostering a sense of
nationality for which they would be prepared if necessary to
fight. Such self-reliance would not only be decidedly cheaper
for the British taxpayer, whom Grey wanted to relieve of the
financial burden of imperial defence, but would be immeasur-
ably more effective. To uphold British interests on the North
American continent, which demanded the preservation of a
Canadian counterbalance to the United States, Grey appreciated the advantages of a prudential recognition of local
self-government.

Once the process of devolution and autonomy had been
begun in Canada, it was only a matter of time before settlement
colonies in Australia, New Zealand and South Africa
demanded and received similar concessions. The problem
facing imperial administrators was to determine the timing and
pre-conditions of the transfer of power in individual cases. In
the 1830s Whig administrators had mapped out a path of
constitutional progress, whereby Crown colonies might in time
receive representative institutions; lower houses of legislatures
partly elected and partly nominated, as in New South Wales
and Newfoundland by the early 1840s, might be transformed
into fully elective assemblies; and eventually a representative
government supervised from Britain might give way to local
autonomy. The timing and speed of travel along this constitutional highway, as regulated from London, depended on a
colony satisfying certain prerequisites. (Indeed, it was possible
for colonies to retrogress, as Jamaica did after the Morant Bay
uprising in 1865, when the British government implemented its
long-standing threat to abolish the West Indian assemblies and
all the representative colonies, except Barbados, reverted to
Crown colony government.) The criteria for political advance
might include adequate population, economic maturity, finan-

cial self-sufficiency, social or political stability, the absence of religious or ethnic feuds, the abolition of slavery or convict transportation, the equitable treatment of minorities or native peoples. Newfoundland, for example, was refused responsible government until 1854 because the colony was economically backward and politically torn between Protestants and Catholics. Political progress in Australia was delayed until transportation had been abandoned and internal self-government was refused so long as Grey continued to assert British trusteeship over Crown lands. In New Zealand and at the Cape the granting of representative institutions was complicated and postponed by the presence of large, warlike native populations, which raised questions of Britain's responsibility for native policy and of defence expenditure. Grey regarded self-government as a privilege to be earned, not a right, and he thought in terms of a gradual, orderly transfer of power for which the colonists should be properly prepared through a term of political apprenticeship.

Ambitious colonial politicians were impatient of such restraints, and once a breakthrough had been achieved in Canada, they agitated for a similar status. Grey's successors in office in the 1850s put up little resistance to these demands. They recognised their powerlessness to withstand the pressure of colonial nationalism, unless they were willing to confront the kind of frenzied protests Grey's attempt to renew transportation had aroused in Australia, and perhaps repeat the mistakes of the American Revolution. There seemed to be no practicable alternative but to grant self-government, and this was done on an *ad hoc* basis whether individual settlement colonies were prepared for it or not. During the early 1850s the discovery of gold hastened concessions to the Australian colonies (except Western Australia with its convicts), though in this instance it was the British authorities which forced the colonists to accept the principle of responsible government under the 1855 constitutions. In New Zealand representative institutions were introduced in 1854, after a series of postponements, and responsible government was almost at once sanctioned by the acting governor and confirmed in London with a casual alacrity which later seemed foolhardy when the Maori wars broke out in the 1860s. At the Cape representative institutions were launched in 1853, though responsible government was not sought so long as frontier defence remained an imperial charge.

It was during the 1850s, too, that imperial administrators finally recognised that the transfer of political power necessitated Britain's disengagement from the settlement colonies. A paternalist like Grey had been unwilling to admit that relinquishment of supervision over a colony's internal affairs should entail a total surrender of imperial control. A doctrinaire free trader, he believed that Britain had a duty to prevent individual colonies from abandoning an enlightened commercial policy and retrograding to obscurantist ideas of protection. His successors did not entertain such scruples. Canada was allowed to conclude a reciprocity treaty with the United States in 1854 and breached the common policy of free trade in 1859 by imposing duties on British imports. In the sphere of defence the process of imperial withdrawal was even more striking. Grey had first enunciated in 1846 that self-government entailed financial self-reliance and he applied this principle to colonial defence, the last major burden of empire on the British taxpayer. Though discontent in Canada and the annexation crisis in 1849, and later the American civil war and the Maori wars, prevented a rapid and universal application of the policy, the general tendency was to withdraw British garrisons and throw on the colonists the responsibility for internal defence. Here prevailing military theories reinforced financial considerations. From Grey's time until the 1861 Select Committee on Colonial Military Expenditure, the preferred strategy was to concentrate the regular army as much as possible in Britain and India instead of dispersing it in small detachments across the globe.

The logic of the political, economic and military policies of withdrawal was to underline the desirability of nation-building and the promotion of federations. Self-governing territories would be better able to defend themselves if they formed large, viable units and stronger regional communities conscious of a national identity. Unlike their predecessors at the time of the American Revolution, Grey and his contemporaries viewed settlement colonies as developing nations which, according to an evolutionary process of historical growth, would mature and become self-governing at some point. Whether Englishmen regarded the fate of the empire with optimism, pessimism or resignation, they were equally uncertain what Britain's relations would be with settlement colonies once they became independent. But if these former possessions were to be a source of strength and pride to Britain, there was much to be said for encouraging federalism as an antidote to local rivalries and parochialism. Grey himself had no success in persuading Australians of the wisdom of his federal scheme and he considered circumstances in British North America as yet unpropitious. Thereafter federalism fell temporarily out of favour in London until the 1860s, when Canadian demands and continuing problems in South Africa underscored the advantages of federations as a technique of decolonisation, a conviction which persisted intermittently during the next hundred years.

The mid-Victorian disengagement from the settlement colonies was a major development in British colonial policy and an unprecedented transfer of power by an imperial state, comparable in its way with the decolonisation of Africa a century later. Despite certain obvious differences, principally the alien character of British political institutions in African societies and the international context of world war and the Cold War, the similarities between the two processes are striking.[12] Stimulated into action by the Canadian rebellions of 1837–8 and the West Indian riots of 1937–8, the British government on both occasions fully recognised and positively promoted the movement towards colonial self-government. In neither case was it a question of the imperial authorities being caught napping and then fighting a rearguard action against nationalist demands. In the reshaping of imperial policy (the role of Durham and Grey later echoed by Lord Hailey and Malcolm Macdonald), much of the discussion centred on timing and pre-conditions, and on which colonists should be the recipients of the transferred power. While there was much concern with agitators and demagogues, and whether or not they were susceptible to blandishments, the abandonment by Britain of the Canadian elites and attempts to work with assemblies were paralleled by British endeavours to convert elite nationalist movements in Africa into broadly based, popular parties. In both instances Britain released a genie from the bottle, and after one test case in each century – Canada and the Gold Coast – the pace of disengagement quickened and timetables of apprenticeship and preparation were abandoned in an uncontrolled rush to autonomy. On both occasions the rapid process of decolonisation was accomplished with an air of British resignation, followed by a public mood of disillusion with the newly self-governing territories. In neither case was decolonisation a result of British weakness, nor did a direct connection exist between the pace of political advance and the economic relationship of the colonies to Britain. It was a recognition of reality as much as a failure of will, and the attitude is captured by the comments on colonial self-government made to Earl Grey in 1857 by Gordon Gairdner, the senior clerk of the Australian department at the Colonial Office:

Whether it could have been much longer withheld by the Home Government I believe is very doubtful. . . . In fact the agitating colonists pointed to the Canadian Constitution as containing the measure of self Government to which they had a right to look, and their advocates in this country adopted the same tone, without considering that time had matured the societies in the North American Colonies for the enjoyment of that for which the new societies were not fitted; and the Home Government appear simply to have receded before the pressure which they were not prepared to withstand.[13]

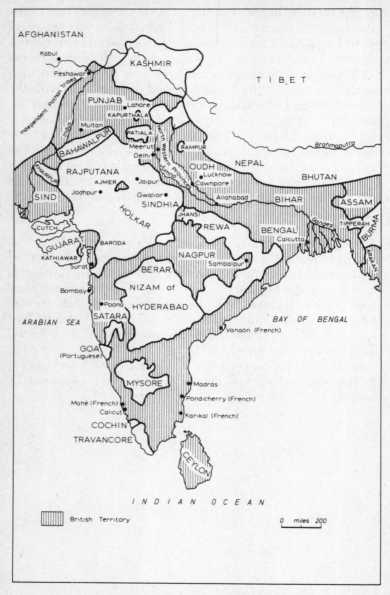

India on the eve of the Indian Mutiny

3. India and the British Empire

R. J. MOORE

I

Until 1813 Britain's trade with India was conducted by the monopolistic East India Company. Surely the most remarkable commercial organisation in history, the company was founded under charter from Elizabeth I. It sent to India the merchants from whose enterprise sprang a massive international and local trade. It also sent out the builders and administrators of a territorial empire that, by the time of the company's demise in 1858, encompassed the entire subcontinent. Reconstructed after the shock of the 1857 Mutiny, the Indian empire remained the rock upon which Britain's prosperity rested until the First World War. It was a secure market for her manufactures, a source of commodities, a safe field for investment, an arsenal for the preservation or extension of interests in Asia and Africa against other European predators. The whole edifice was charged to India's revenues and, beneath a thin British façade, upheld through the agency of Indians themselves.

The sequence of events by which a trading company became a territorial power, and later the paramount power, is clear enough. It must now be adumbrated, as a preliminary to the consideration of its rationale. Formed when Akbar's Mughal empire was in its prime, in the seventeenth century the East India Company acquired licences to establish twenty-odd trading posts on the coasts of India and sovereignty over tiny areas around Madras and Bombay. It then secured rights to collect the revenues from the lands of three villages at present-day Calcutta, to which victory over the Nawab of Bengal at the Battle of Plassey in 1757 added twenty-four *parganas* (revenue subdivisions). In 1765 the company deposed its own puppet Nawab of Bengal and assumed direct administration of his territories and, in consequence of its victories over French forces in southern India, annexed the Northern Circars (coastal districts north of the Krishna river). With these major exceptions, the extension of the company's ascendancy now rested for a quarter of a century mainly upon treaties of subsidiary alliance with Indian rulers. In theory treaties between equals, they bespoke the company's military superiority in their provisions for the company to supply forces to the rulers of Hyderabad and the Carnatic in the south, and Oudh in the north, in return for payments secured against the revenues from the rulers' territories. In the 1790s, wars with Tipu Sultan of Mysore resulted in substantial annexations on the Malabar and Coromandel coasts. In 1801, Lord Wellesley as governor-general (1798–1805) completed the company's hegemony of southern India by annexing the Nawab of the Carnatic's possessions and the Nizam of Hyderabad's territories south of the Krishna, while the reduced states of Mysore and Hyderabad, together with Travancore, remained subsidiary allies under princely rule.

Following his subjugation of the south, Wellesley launched the company upon its secondary phase of imperial growth: the seizure of the half of the territories of the Nawab of Oudh comprising Rohilkhand, Gorakhpur and the lower Doab (plain between the Ganges and the Jumna); and, through wars against the divided Maratha rulers, then the predominant power in terms of territory, the acquisition of Cuttack (thus linking its Bengal and Madras possessions) and, most importantly, the districts of the upper Doab together with the imperial Mughal cities of Delhi and Agra. Wellesley extended the subsidiary alliance system (indeed, he struck a hundred such treaties during his seven years) to include some of the great Maratha rulers. His intended subjugation of the Deccan and central and western India was continued by his successors, especially Lord Hastings (1812–23), and completed with the final reduction of the Marathas in 1818. Now Bombay ceased to be a seaport district and became a major province under direct company rule. Of the Maratha territories a patchwork of subordinate princely states remained – Nagpur, Indore, Gwalior, Baroda and Satara – while paramountcy was extended over the numerous principalities of Rajputana. In Dr Percival Spear's words, 'the settlement of 1818' achieved the establishment of the hegemony of the company throughout India up to the Sutlej river and 'henceforth India was a unit again'.[1]

When a successor to Lord Hastings was appointed in 1823 he was told by the company: 'No further acquisition of territory can be desirable. The extent of empire which you have to govern . . . is such as it would not only be unwise but hardly safe to exceed'.[2] With regard to the company's subordinate princely allies he was to 'preserve as completely as possible . . . the degree of independence which they now enjoy'.[3] Yet after a caesura, and Lord Bentinck's shift (as governor-general, 1828–35), from political and foreign preoccupations to measures of internal reform in administration, the law and education, there followed a tertiary stage of expansion, and fifteen years of conquest that were terminated only by the Mutiny. The annexation of Sind in 1843 and of the Punjab in 1849 extended the frontier beyond the Indus, and the dominions of the major princely states were reduced. Lord Dalhousie (1848–56) assumed direct government of Nagpur in 1853 and Oudh in 1856, assigned the revenues of the Nizam's Berar territories for the payment of the Hyderabad contingent, and abolished several lesser principalities.

The reduction of princely states ended with the Mutiny of 1857. Subsequent administrative disturbances in them produced temporary attachments to British administration but they (and even the pre-Mutiny attachment of Mysore in 1834) were in due course restored to Indian rule. After 1857 there was to be no fourth stage of expansion, only some extension of the north-west frontier into Baluchistan. There was, however, a continuation of the process, begun by the company, of assuming control of territories regarded as necessary to British interests in India or British Indian interests in Asia at large. Thus the annexation of Burma, begun in 1824 and extended in 1852, was completed in 1886. The routes to India, safeguarded by the capture of Capetown in 1795 and Aden in 1839, were further secured by the occupation of Egypt in 1882; access to China, facilitated by Raffles' seizure of Singapore in 1819 and the acquisition of Hong Kong in 1842, was supplemented in 1860 when Kowloon was obtained. There were also post-Mutiny revivals of earlier attempts to assert informal empire, or the ascendancy of British influence, in neighbouring buffer states. The second Afghan war of 1878 matches the first, of 1839, and Lord Curzon's diplomacy (as governor-general, 1899–1905) in Persia and Tibet recalls that of the company towards the former and Nepal in the early nineteenth century.

The interpretation of British expansion in India is complicated, not only by the length of the process but also because the metropolitan authorities were generally too far away to control the 'men on the spot'. The limits of geographical expansion were set prior to the advent of the telegraph, when an exchange of correspondence took several months or even years. Moreover, the authorities in London were often divided among themselves. In 1784 the autonomy of the East India Company was subjected to the surveillance of a Board of Control, over which a minister of the Crown presided. In 1798 Wellesley went to India with secret expansionary instructions from the president, Lord Dundas; in 1805 the company secured his recall because of the extravagance of his foreign policy. Both Wellesley and Lord Hastings undertook large extensions of the company's territories in defiance of its stated policies against annexation. Lord Ellenborough, as President of the Board of Control in 1830, crossed the directors and denied them a voice in foreign policy; in 1844 they effected his recall as governor-general, largely because of his interventionist policies in Gwalior. Yet he had countenanced the annexation of Sind, which, though widely condemned as an immoral undertaking, was irreversible, and the events that would culminate in the absorption of the Punjab were also in train. Though checked periodically because of the immediate costs and difficulties involved, the extension of empire to the geographical limits of the subcontinent was steadily accomplished by the company's servants in India, throughout the century between Plassey and the Mutiny.

II

It was long accepted by historians that the rise of the company as a territorial power in the eighteenth century was the consequence of a determination to keep open the doors to an established trade in the face of two political challenges. From the 1740s the stability necessary to trade was threatened by both the break-up of the Mughal empire and the extension of the Anglo-French wars to Asia. In recent years Professor P. J. Marshall has reappraised these essentially political perspectives for expansion.[4] In view of the findings of some historians that the company and private British entrepreneurs enjoyed remarkable commercial success early in the century, Marshall recognises the possibility that conquest was driven by economic motives. His analysis of the connection between trade and political expansion is supported by his extensive studies not only of the company's operations but also, most notably, of the activities of private individuals.

Marshall distinguishes between an underlying economic dynamism conducive to expansion and the availability of a military capacity to expand. He accepts the traditional view that the provision of the necessary force resulted from the French challenge to British trade. Further, 'neither the British Government nor the Court of Directors believed in using force in India for commercial ends'.[5] The company's main interest lay in the purchase of Indian textiles for European markets, a trade that would suffer through the disruptions of war. In Parliament the prospect of conquest was viewed with repugnance. Yet the conditions of trade in India were such that the company required political concessions from Indian rulers in order to pursue it.[6] Moreover, while the company monopolised trade between Britain and Asia, its own servants and other private individuals (or 'Free Merchants') were engaged in enterprises within Asia. Free Merchants were well established in Calcutta by the mid-eighteenth century, engaged in coastal trades, and also traded at centres well inland, especially in Bengal.

There are difficulties in leaping from the need of the company and private entrepreneurs for political concessions to the conclusion that it was met by the deployment of forces originally sent against the French to campaign for the subjugation of princes and territorial conquest. The evidence does not suggest that there was any 'coherent drive for empire by men actually in India', even such as Robert Clive (1756–60 and 1765–7) and Warren Hastings (1772–85).[7] Nor does it suggest that with the decline of the Mughals local disorder required the intervention of the company in administration. Rather, the readiness to use the newly available forces for limited objectives not thought to be inconsistent with the continuation of Indian states so weakened their rulers that by 1784 Bengal had collapsed and Oudh and the Carnatic had been undermined. The British demands on Indian rulers were sometimes exactions to maintain armies to defeat supposed French designs and sometimes for commercial concessions. In any event, each fresh demand diminished the ruler's prospect of survival.

After Plassey Bengal became the scene of a dramatic transfer of wealth to the hands of the company, its servants, and Free Merchants. While the company's annual Bengal purchases trebled to about £1 million in the 1760s, private remittances averaged an estimated £500,000 a year. Bengal's trade in salt and opium was almost entirely taken over by private traders until the company established monopolies over them. Private entrepreneurs became prominent in indigo, sugar and silk and invested their capital in loans to Indian rulers at exorbitant rates of interest. The Nawab of Oudh owed £300,000 by 1778, the Nawab of the Carnatic £3 million by 1784. Civil and military officers drew fortunes from loot and local influence, with Clive's own fortune reaching £400,000 by 1767. Increasingly the company's own interests shifted from trade to the collection of taxes, as the company undertook to provide troops to local rulers in return for revenue allocations. By 1770 the Bengal army had grown to 4000 Europeans and 26,000 sepoys, and military outran trading expenditure. In the early 1760s districts were annexed to pay for the army until, in 1765, the whole of the Bengal revenue was taken over. The same pattern of securing revenue allocations to support military contingents emerged in Oudh and the Carnatic. In Marshall's words: 'The road from becoming the ally of an independent ruler, to exercising a military protectorate over him, to displacing him altogether, was an easy one. At each stage the needs of the army forced the Company on'.[8]

Marshall considers Wellesley's annexation of part of Oudh against this interplay of economic dynamism and military capacity for expansion.[9] It was a case different from the conquest of coastal provinces whose long-standing production for British agents furnished a strong economic motive for direct control. In the 1780s and early 1790s first Warren Hastings and later Lord Cornwallis (1786–93) resisted the alternative of annexation as a means of obtaining the large subsidy that the Nawab was obliged to pay for company troops. Instead the demands upon him were reduced, and he retained internal autonomy while forfeiting control of defence and foreign policy. In 1800 Wellesley forced the Nawab to reduce his own forces and increase his subsidy for the company's. The next year he demanded the whole of Oudh or the cession of extensive territories, and soon took the latter.

Though British economic interests in Oudh grew apace after the defeat of its ruler and the Mughal Emperor at the battle of Buxar in 1764, Marshall concludes that they 'had little to do' with Wellesley's policy.[10] Traders had soon come from Bengal to sell its wares and those of Britain, to buy Oudh saltpetre, and later to provide piece-goods for the company to export and to engage in the production of indigo and opium. Yet though by 1801 private trade had contributed to Oudh's dependence on the British, it was the company's troops and the subsidy to sustain them that kept the Wazir in subjection. Wellesley did not view the private traders kindly and was not susceptible to their influence. Moreover, the annexation was not necessary to secure the company's military-financial interests. It occurred 'not so much because of developments in Oudh as because of developments in the mind of the Governor-General', reflecting 'a new confidence in British military power in India and in the company's capacity to change Indian society'.[11]

In short, whereas Marshall's analysis suggests that the economic dynamism of British interests was responsible for the use of newly available military resources to extract the concessions that undermined and eventually displaced the rulers of coastal territories, it also suggests that in the case of Wellesley's annexation of Oudh an essentially political subimperialism had come into play.

III

Marshall's close analysis of the relations between the economic and political motives for the beginnings of British rule in India and the secondary spread into Oudh finds no parallel in studies of the completion of hegemony to 1818 or the consolidation of dominion and its extension beyond the Indus by 1857. An historiographical battle, perhaps commensurate with that over the partition of Africa, remains unjoined. The motives for the timing and making of subsidiary alliances, the progression subsequently to direct rule, and the incidence of outright annexation await detailed analysis. Meanwhile scholars have been concerned with the relation between strategy and expansion, in view of the belief that the frontier advanced in response to persistent threats of French and Russian intervention in the subcontinent.

Though the French military presence in India was in fact defeated in 1763, the danger of French intervention remained a prospect until Britain's sovereignty was recognised in the Treaty of Paris in 1814. When during its supremacy in the Mediterranean the French fleet sailed from Toulon for Egypt in 1798 Dundas and Wellesley feared that Napoleon envisaged an overland assault upon India from the north-west. He was known to be in contact with Tipu and a hostile alliance with the Nizam or the Maratha rulers seemed possible. The defence of India thus afforded a 'legitimizing idiom' for Wellesley's campaigns.[12] In 1804 Wellesley was still justifying his Maratha policy by reference to the existence of French commanders at the head of Maratha forces. His governor-generalship had added £20 million to the company's debts by the time of his recall in 1805 and the company was bent on peace. However, in 1807, when Napoleon initiated an intrigue with Persia and achieved peace with Russia, the Board of Control warned Lord Minto (1807–12) that a French attack on British India through

Persia was likely. Though events in Europe now commanded Napoleon's attention and the danger receded, here, in 1807–8, was the beginning of the British attempt to establish an amicable relationship with Persia, which would prevent its becoming the springboard for an attack upon India.[13]

From the late 1820s British fears of an overland invasion of India revived when, after a war with Russia, a defeated Persia ceded certain of her territories and became virtually a client state. Russian influence there could henceforth menace the security of India and the preoccupation of British Indian strategists became security against the prospect of Russian expansion. To establish a counterpoise to the Russo-Persian connection, in 1838 the British attempted to set up a pro-British ruler in Afghanistan. The policy proved an unmitigated and costly disaster. With the purpose of consolidating the frontier at the Indus by direct control, rather than relying upon friendly buffer states, Sind and the Punjab were annexed in the 1840s.

Recent studies of British Indian strategy agree in their tendency to play down the reality of the external threat from France and Russia in the nineteenth century. The danger of actual invasion by either was never strong enough to justify, in itself, the extension of the territorial frontier. Dr Edward Ingram emphasises the role of British moves in the Great Game in Asia in countering Russian influence for the sake of preserving the balance of power in Europe.[14] Dr Malcolm Yapp stresses the propensity of political agents on the frontier to magnify the severity of local crises, for they had a vested interest in territorial expansion.[15] Both believe that the argument for expansion to meet an external threat assumed its most persuasive and influential form when the threat was linked with its implication for internal security. It was not so much that turbulent frontiers and the necessities of defence impelled expansion as that they might encourage rebellion among disaffected Indians within the already subject territories.[16] British rule rested upon a belief in its invincibility, which, if challenged, must needs be demonstrated. Yapp draws out the motif, in his analysis of the annexation of the Punjab.

IV

It is scarcely conceivable that an historical movement on the scale of the progressive British conquest and consolidation of India during the century after Plassey could have proceeded unless it was intimately linked to the needs of the expanding metropolitan economy. The interests of individual entrepreneurs and civil and military officers in India, whether in concessions or exactions from Indian rulers, the spoils of office, or plunder, seem hardly adequate to explain the sustained expansion. Nor is it sufficient to add the yearnings of proconsuls, political agents and soldiers for territorial aggrandisement, expressed in the legitimising idiom of the 'defence of India', linking through Francophobia or Russophobia the otherwise separate spheres of British foreign policy in Europe and British Indian concern with peaceful frontiers and security against the potential enemy within them. The number of campaigns in which British Indian forces were engaged during the century between the wars with Napoleon and the Kaiser is indeed remarkable, and they afforded the important military establishment with almost its only opportunities to experience action. A recent compilation lists some three hundred wars, campaigns or actions.[17]

Professor Eric Stokes has argued that British expansion in India represented a 'reversion to primitive mercantilism, with force itself an economic power', so that 'the political frontier between 1757 and 1818 was flung far ahead of the true economic frontier; and it was not until the 1860s that the two began to be brought into closer correspondence'.[18] The cost of armies was saddled on Indian rulers as a lien on the revenues from their lands. The next step, as in Bengal in 1765, was to assume administration of the ruler's territories, in the belief that British officials would increase the tax collection by bringing 'order and regulation to the decayed indigenous revenue systems'.[19] Stokes comments: 'This was the real reason for what appeared to be the exceptionally rapid assumption of direct administrative responsibility and the abandonment of indirect rule through a protectorate system in all the populous regions of the sub-continent'. The company eliminated Indian intermediaries in order to maximise its revenue receipts, not only at the level of the ruler, but, outside Bengal, down to the subdistrict level: 'its purpose remained mercantilist, to wring a surplus from the Indian revenue' – wherewith to purchase commodities for sale in Europe.[20]

During the half-century following Plassey the emergence of the Indian empire made little contribution to the British economy. Imports from Asia rose from 13 to 21 per cent of the whole. The main import from India, cotton piece-goods, was in decline as Britain's own production of them increased and British manufacturers secured protective tariffs (which were raised twelve times between 1797 and 1819). British commercial opinion began to view India as a market for manufactures.

From 1813, with the abolition of the company's monopoly of the trade with India, British exports to Asia grew apace. By the early 1830s they accounted for some 12 per cent of all exports, a doubling in thirty years. A dramatic increase occurred in cotton goods exports to India: from 800,000 yards in 1814 to 14 million yards in 1820. By 1813 the mainstay of the company's commercial operations had become the import of China tea, which had grown to 26 million pounds (from 6 million in 1784). The purchase of tea was financed by the company's export to China of opium, raw cotton and cotton goods from India. Its sale yielded the company profits of over £1 million a year. The sale of Indian goods to China helped India to finance its purchase of Lancashire cottons. Even after the abolition of the company's China monopoly in 1834, when the company became a purely administrative organisation for the government of India, political force was still used to secure commercial ends, culminating in the Opium Wars of 1841–2.

It is impossible to deny that the possession of India was vitally important in the success of the Lancashire cotton industry, the key to Britain's emergence as the workshop of the mid-nineteenth-century world. Britain's export growth early in the century was dominated by cotton products: they accounted for over half the growth in export values between 1794–6 and 1814–16. By 1804–6 cotton goods accounted for 42 per cent of all British exports and in 1805–7 two-thirds of the cotton industry's output was exported. However, by 1830, when cotton textiles accounted for 51 per cent of all exports by value, Britain was losing its early markets in Europe and the United

States, as the share of total cotton exports going to them fell from 73 per cent in 1820 to 43 per cent in 1850. India helped to fill the gap. Exports of cotton goods to India rose from 6 per cent of all cotton exports in 1820–4 to 15 per cent in 1845–9. They grew by 5.8 per cent per annum between 1820 and 1855 as against an overall growth rate of only 1.7 per cent. Cain and Hopkins sum up: 'None of this could have taken place without British control, which was steadily extended in scope throughout the period'.[21] In common with Stokes and Gallagher and Robinson they see the 1840s and 1850s as a period of commercial aggression with the political arm thrust out to open Indian markets. 'Despite the banner of Free Trade it held aloft', writes Stokes, 'Lancashire broke into the new markets of Asia with all the old-fashioned weapons of earlier mercantilism.'[22] Gallagher and Robinson observe that 'in this supposedly *laissez-faire* period India . . . was subjected to intensive development as an economic colony along the best mercantilist lines'.[23] Moreover, the combination of free trade doctrine and mercantilist state intervention for works of development exacerbated the need to maximise the land revenues.

In the 1850s the Manchester School brought its anti-imperialist and anti-militarist rhetoric to bear against the administration of India by the Peelite Dalhousie, the now non-commercial East India Company, and Lord Aberdeen's Whig-Peelite government. They claimed that wars were got up and annexations undertaken for the sake of aggrandisement and replacing Indian agency by enlarged British civil and military establishments.[24] Thus were emptied the coffers required for roads, railways and public works that would encourage the growth of raw cotton for Lancashire and carry its cotton goods to every corner of India. The debates over the renewal of the company's charter in 1853 were broadly characterised by Marx as between the millocracy on the one side and the bureaucracy/aristocracy on the other. Yet there is an air of shadow-sparring about them. They did not concern the possession of India but rather the best means of exploiting it to Britain's advantage, that is, the direction and limits of British intervention.[25] While Sir Charles Wood at the Board of Control (1853–5) and Dalhousie in India believed in the superiority of British direct, as against Indian princely, rule they were not indiscriminate annexers. Their joint policy towards Afghanistan, Persia and Baluchistan was essentially pacific. When Nagpur and Berar were annexed Dalhousie emphasised their importance as cotton-growing areas. Wood mentioned the point in Parliament and had no difficulty with the Manchester School. At the same time Dalhousie was impressed by the revenues that his annexations would yield. Again, while Wood refused to commit funds on the scale Manchester demanded for the encouragement of cotton-growing, Dalhousie planned and Wood approved the construction of India's great trunk railways by extending a government guarantee of the interest payable on private capital invested.

While a multiplicity of motives operated to extend the Indian empire between the passing of the French threat after the Napoleonic Wars and the Mutiny of 1857 there was a general correlation between the needs of the British economy (and of King Cotton in particular) and the control of India. If there was a determining logic in the progression from treaty relations and indirect rule through Indian princes to annexation and direct administration scholarship has still to reveal it. Dr Robin Jeffrey has recently concluded that there was 'an awesome arbitrariness' about which rulers got treaties in the first place.[26] It depended upon 'the character of the Company's negotiator, the size of the blunderbuss the raja appeared to have, the revenue value of the country, the forces the British had available, and the urgency with which they wished to resolve matters in the area'.[27] If the ruler failed to get a treaty one year his territories might be seized the next; or if he did get one he might survive (as over 500 did) until India's Independence in 1947. Jeffrey argues that 'the whole question of "policy" towards the states at any period is open to doubt' and denies that there was any logical progression.[28] Certainly, even Gallagher and Robinson, who argued the existence of a calculus of imperial expansion, which was characteristically governed in its forms by the doctrine of deploying the minimum of effort, do not suggest the necessity of advances to direct rule in India for the sake of the metropolitan economy. It seems more probable that within the broad context of expansion in India consistent with the needs of an industrial economy there persisted until the Mutiny a Schumpeterian official-military-aristocratic 'power apparatus' (in Stokes's words), pursuing 'its own autonomous goals. As a military machine insatiable for revenue its constant tendency had been overextension of dominion and an obsessive concern for external security at the expense of internal development.'[29]

V

Whilst the tendency of historical research is to emphasise continuities and thereby weaken the periodisation of the past, the Mutiny of 1857 does still appear as a turning-point in relations between the British and their Indian empire.[30] It is not that the abolition of the company and the transfer of its functions to an India Office brought a revolution in government, that policy innovations in the reform of the civil service, education and the law were suddenly introduced, or that having reconquered rebellious India the British now viewed her for the first time as a great national asset to be developed. Changes sometimes associated with post-Mutiny reconstruction had in fact been initiated in the early 1850s.[31] Yet the Mutiny brought major changes in policies towards the remaining Indian rulers in the subsidiary states and intermediaries in the annexed provinces. It had been not only a military disaster but a financial catastrophe, increasing India's public debt by 70 per cent, adding £2 million a year to the interest charges. As it was a condition of empire in India that its costs did not fall on Britain means must be found to ensure peace and economy. As dispossessed *taluqdars* (landed magnates) had been prominent leaders of the civilian rebellion in Oudh they were now re-established, as collaborators of the *Raj*. As descendants of deposed princes had also led the insurrection a moratorium on any further annexation of states was now declared. The *Raj* would be strengthened by the attachment of such prominent collaborators, and they would provide a cheaper form of administration than British officials. Moreover, as the British revenue systems had made rebels of peasants unable to adapt to their demands, attempts were made to secure previously disregarded subordinate rights to land. The discredited military system was totally remodelled, on principles that limited the possibility of its combination for rebellion.

In effect, the post-Mutiny reconstruction ended the operations of an official 'power apparatus' pursuing 'its own autonomous goals'. The links between the metropolitan economy and India, and the role of India in relation to the wider empire, were strengthened.

British reliance on India as a market for manufactured goods, especially cottons, grew steadily. India's 15 per cent share of Britain's cotton goods exports in 1845–9 increased to 20 per cent by 1865–9, 40 per cent by 1890, and 43 per cent in 1913. The value of the cotton goods exports doubled from the 1870s to reach £35 million in 1913, which represented over half of Britain's exports to India and 6.5 per cent of Britain's total exports. Cain and Hopkins observe that cotton piece-goods exports accounted for 28 per cent of Britain's total exports in 1870 and that 'their growth was based upon the rapid development of markets in the newly settled countries and in underdeveloped areas, such as India. . . . By 1914 Britain's export trade had become much too dependent on sales of textiles to India and to a few other empire markets.'[32] Whereas in 1870 India stood third among purchasers of British goods, and in 1890–2 second, in 1913 she stood first, with Britain supplying her with over 60 per cent of her imports. After cotton goods, iron and steel and machinery were the main items, accounting for about a quarter of British exports to India. India's export trade was also important to Britain, but not so much in terms of direct trade. Dr B. R. Tomlinson notes: 'In the late eighteenth and early nineteenth centuries India had supplied opium to China to pay for British purchases of tea. From 1870 to 1914 India formed the vital third leg in a triangular pattern of settlements between Britain and the rest of the world, financing over two-thirds of Britain's balance of payments deficit with Europe and North America.'[33] While Britain's share of India's exports fell from a third to a quarter between 1890 and 1911, the European and United States' share rose from about 30 to 40 per cent.

Britain's control of India enabled her to manipulate Indian tariffs to the advantage of British industry. From 1814 until the Mutiny cotton piece-goods incurred a modest 5 per cent tariff. During the immediate post-Mutiny financial crisis the rate was enhanced in order to raise revenue but unremitting Lancashire pressure for total freedom of trade achieved its return to 5 per cent in 1862 and total abolition in 1882. When a financial crisis resulted in the introduction of a $3\frac{1}{2}$ per cent duty on cotton goods in 1894, an equivalent countervailing excise duty was, in the name of free trade, imposed upon India's cotton manufactures.[34]

British control of India also benefited British investors. Professor L. H. Jenks claimed that it was India that 'made the empire', especially after 1857, when for the eight years to 1865 'the major movement of British capital was towards India, to transform the land with public works'.[35] By 1869, £70 million had been invested in Indian railways and some 50,000 Britons held shares or debentures in them, at government guaranteed rates of interest. Railways, roads, and navigation and irrigation works, strategic to the marketing of British manufactures and the encouragement of Indian cotton-growing for Lancashire, were pushed ahead by British capital secured against the Indian revenues – 'private enterprise at public risk'[36] – during this period of the 'imperialism of free trade'. In 1870, £180 million of a total £785 million British overseas investment was in India. The sum rose to £270 million (out of £1300 million) in 1885 and £380 million (out of £3780 million) in 1913. India was the fourth largest recipient of British overseas investment by 1913. Over 80 per cent of the capital flowed into safe, fixed-interest securities such as the railways or public loans, but most of the remainder financed tea and coffee plantations, mining, banking, and mercantile or managing agency enterprises. The benefit to Britain from such invisible exports as banking, shipping, insurance and broking services defies quantification, as, indeed, does that which accrued from British management of India's currency system and therefore of the terms of India's foreign trade.[37]

By the end of the nineteenth century, when India was paying some £10 million a year in interest to service the national debt (including £6 million for the railways), the annual cost of salaries and pensions paid to the British rulers of India was estimated at a further £10 million. The specialist all-India administrative services were dominated at their senior levels by Britons, and of the thousand members of the Indian Civil Service less than 5 per cent were Indians. Yet by far the largest drain on India's revenues was its military establishments, which accounted for some 40 per cent of the total expenditure. The post-Mutiny ratio of 1:2 British:Indian troops enhanced the pre-Mutiny complement of Europeans from 45,000 to 60,000, whilst reducing the Indians from about a quarter of a million to 120,000. The establishments were maintained not only to secure the *Raj* against the enemy within and guard the existing frontier but also in 'defence' of the empire at large: in a war against Afghanistan (1878), for the annexation of British Baluchistan (1876–9) and Upper Burma (1886), the occupation of Egypt (1882), and East African campaigns of the 1890s. It has sometimes been held that the defence of India and the routes to India was the main motive for British participation in the 'new imperialism' of the late nineteenth century. Certainly contemporary statesmen construed the needs of Indian defence widely, but often, as in the case of Egypt, non-Indian and essentially British interests were substantially responsible for imperialist enterprises. Defence, as in Wellesley's day, supplied a legitimising idiom for expansion and, of course, provided a justification for making India foot at least part of the bills.[38]

From the Mutiny until the First World War Britain managed India's finances so as to meet the needs of British trade, investment, employment, and imperial defence or expansion. The *Raj*'s major income came from the land revenues, which comprised some 40 per cent of the whole, and the monopolistic manufacture and sale of opium and salt, which together accounted for a further 20–25 per cent at the end of the century. In essence, the *Raj* depended upon wringing a surplus from an overwhelmingly agricultural economy, and once the costs of empire were met there was very little left for India's development, or to provide for the contingencies of famine and depression. Tomlinson concludes:

In 1913, then, India still had a large part to play in supporting the British world system of profit and influence, but it was a role less solidly based than it appeared. Bad harvests in India, a depression in world trade, a change in the balance of power in Asia which would place new demands on the Indian army, a decline in the competitiveness of British exports or the emergence of rivals for the

Indian market, a serious disturbance in the exchange rate of the rupee, increasing demands for the protection and encouragement of Indian industries, the need to devote more revenue to buying off the demands of Indian politicians for a share in the resources of government – all these could jeopardize the delicate balance that the Government of India had struck between fulfilling domestic and imperial commitment.[39]

The latter part of the quotation emphasises the need to consider the weakening influence of the *Raj*'s dependence upon Indian collaborators.

VI

In 1872 Disraeli spoke of India as a 'jewel in the Crown of England'. Four years later his government passed the Royal Titles Act, whereby Queen Victoria acquired the style of 'Empress'. The late-Victorian period is frequently seen as the high-noon of empire and the *pax Britannica*. Yet the reconstruction of the *Raj* after 1857 and the terms of the post-Mutiny settlement were inherently weakening. The necessities of economy demanded reliance upon Indian agency to the maximum degree consistent with security. This meant not only attaching princes and magnates to British rule but also enlisting the co-operation of Indians in the machinery of the British administration, as subordinate officials, clerks, teachers, lawyers, etc. By the 1880s these Western-educated 'collaborators' were demanding larger opportunities for advancement, by entry to the higher levels of administration and access to the counsels of government.[40] They demanded, too, a lightening of the land tax in the interests of agricultural improvement and the diversion of expenditure from imperial to national ends: to education, irrigation and industrial development.

From the 1890s the *Raj* responded by shifting the terms of collaboration within an essentially despotic imperial structure. It increasingly admitted aspiring Indian politicians to its consultative circle. In 1861, consistently with the notion of basing its Indian empire on the collaboration of the remaining 'natural leaders' of the people, the *darbar* principle was introduced, providing that when the provincial executive councils met to make laws their British members should be joined by a number of Indian advisers. In 1892 the scheme was extended to provide for the nomination of a larger body of Indians to the legislative councils. Under the administration of Lord Minto as viceroy (1905–10) and Lord Morley as Secretary of State for India (1905–10) the provincial legislatures were very substantially Indianised, but though the principle of representation of interests was acknowledged responsibility was withheld. In the words of a later official report, the Morely–Minto reforms were 'the final outcome of the old conception which made the Government of India a benevolent despotism . . . which might as it saw fit for purposes of enlightenment consult the wishes of its subjects'.[41] The government remained 'a monarch in *darbar*'. At the same time, the princes were again reassured of their status as valued allies. From 1857, the *Raj* responded to Indian demands for association with government by adopting the principle of a mixed constitution (or 'constitutional autocracy', as Minto called it).

During the so-called 'high-noon of empire' the *Raj* was thus engaged in the inherently weakening process of buying off the potential enemy within. In the increasingly dangerous world of great power competition Britain was also engaged in buying off the perceived external enemy: by 1907 she had achieved a defensive accord with both France and Russia. As Victoria's last viceroy, Lord Curzon (1899–1905) opposed concessions to India's politicians, conciliation of the rajas, and the understandings over Persia and Tibet that were essential to the Anglo-Russian agreement. In so doing he was the voice of an anachronistic belief in British strength and self-sufficiency, a Wellesley or a Dalhousie born out of his time.

The First World War exposed the extent of Britain's dependence upon India and thereby strengthened her claims for a new post-war constitutional settlement. At the same time, the war enforced rapid industrialisation upon India, so that her enhanced capacity to supply her own cotton goods precipitated the granting of fiscal autonomy. The consequences were that in the 1920s and 1930s Indians acquired increased association with government and administration and demanded the reconstruction of commercial and financial policies. The impulses to British decolonisation await detailed analysis. It remains matter for debate whether by the twentieth century the demands on the Indian peasant had so impoverished some parts of the countryside that the *Raj* had undermined its own financial basis: the capacity of India to buy British goods and agencies, service the public debt, and maintain the army.[42]

Yet, in the 1930s when India ceased to be of direct advantage to the British economy, in 1939 when Britain had agreed to contribute to the cost of the military establishments, and even in 1946 when the imminence of Independence was apparent, British statesmen continued to plan for a post-imperial presence in India. India was expected to play a critical role in Commonwealth security, and it would be a condition of Independence that she should sign a treaty for the defence of the Indian Ocean area. In the mid-twentieth century the old imperial arsenal would become part of an informal empire for the defence of the oil supply from the Middle East, the rubber revenues in Malaya, and the routes from the Mediterranean to Australasia. It was essentially a role for Indian nationalist collaborators with British imperialism. Not surprisingly, the India of Gandhi and Nehru declined to play it.

4. Britain and the New Imperialism

JAMES STURGIS

I

To J. A. Hobson, steeped in the Cobdenite radical tradition as he was, the Anglo-Boer war seemed a sad travesty of what Britain should stand for in the world. The self-interest of a narrow clique of financiers, it seemed to him, had held sway over the broader interests of the nation. Even more deplorable was the way in which the leading institutions of the state had been infected by a malignant imperial sentiment. Ever since 1870 there had been a 'conscious' policy of imperialism which, although it had not become fully articulate until 1884, had by its rapacity added 4,750,000 square miles of territory and 88 million people to the existing empire. Hobson also noted, besides the innovatory role of finance capital, the number of great powers which had involved themselves in this unprecedented scramble for mainly tropical territories. These developments represented such a break with the past that it justified labelling the period from 1870 to 1902 as that of the new imperialism.

Although Hobson did not coin the phrase it became a part of historical orthodoxy, even if his ideas as to its causation were received more sceptically. Lenin rather reversed the pattern by accepting the central importance of finance capital but not using the actual term, the new imperialism. Nevertheless it could be said that there was a consensus regarding the validity of the concept until 1953 when Robinson and Gallagher, in this as in so many other respects, forced a re-evaluation of British imperialism in the nineteenth century. Making disparaging references to the 'so-called' new imperialism, they saw insufficient evidence to warrant the conclusion that there had been any change in basic British policy or outlook towards expansion during the century. By locating the impulse leading to annexation within the semi-colonial situation itself, Robinson and Gallagher had introduced a whole new way of looking at the period from 1870 to 1914. The continuity which they stressed, in what came to be known as the peripheral approach, clashed with the discontinuity which had always been emphasised by previous writers, in what is called the Eurocentric approach. Since this aspect of the subject is fully examined by Paul Kennedy in Chapter 1, we need only note here that the new imperialism is not a neutral concept and its use implies acceptance of a certain interpretative framework.

Few historians or economists have attempted to account for the new imperialism by the use of a monocausal theory. With some exceptions they have, however much they have given priority to a particular cause, recognised ancillary factors as playing a part. Hobson, for example, analysed the Social Darwinian and humanitarian buttresses to the financial arch of imperialism. Similarly Robinson and Gallagher, while placing greater emphasis on the local origins of annexation, gave due importance to the 'official mind' of imperialism, that is, to those officials who ultimately had to decide on a metropolitan response. Likewise many who uphold an economic interpretation are not unwilling to concede that other motives, perhaps of a political or a religious kind, were at certain times and places of crucial importance.

However, before these general or long-term causes of the new imperialism can be adequately dealt with, it is necessary to consider in specific detail the more immediate context in which the decisions for annexation were reached. This section can do no more than provide an overview of the stages of British expansion and domestic trends. The main focus will be on the scramble north of the Congo river which will allow a closer scrutiny of events prior to the numerous annexations. The chronological divisions, which correspond both with Britain's rate of expansion and with the political climate, are referred to as transitional (1870–82), hesitant (1882–92) and conscious (1892–1902). A fourth period from 1902 to 1914, which cannot be examined here, sees Britain trying to cut its colonial commitments by alliances and to rescue its own people and institutions from the enervation of the past.

Transitional seems the appropriate description for the period from 1870 to 1882 during which many of the presumptions of the mid-Victorian years proved to be unworkable. At the beginning there was a desire to follow a policy in West Africa which had been advocated by the parliamentary select committee of 1865, an injunction against further commitments and, as far as was practicable, an objective to withdraw from all coastal enclaves except Sierra Leone. But by 1882 this policy was in ruins. In the same year Britain suffered the additional shock of the French sanctioning de Brazza's treaties on the Congo, thus posing a threat to Britain's trade. In North Africa, from a situation in 1869 when the Suez Canal opened under French control, events had reached such a stage by 1882 that the 'reluctant' imperialists were sending British forces to occupy Egypt. Crucial in both West and North Africa were men on the spot who pressed for an imperial initiative. A further contradiction within this period is the caution and pragmatism of most Secretaries of State for the Colonies when contrasted with the imperial bombast of Knatchbull-Hugessen (Parliamentary Under-Secretary, 1871–4) and the imperial rhetoric and vision of Lord Carnarvon (Colonial Secretary, 1874–8) whose policies in southern Africa led to the annexation of the Transvaal in 1877. These men were probably the exception rather than the rule and the prevailing outlook was an uncertainty both of imperial ends and of means.

Carnarvon's extensions of British control in 1874 over Fiji, the Malay States and the Gold Coast were in line with the consolidationist policy of the previous Liberal government. W. D. McIntyre, who has made a study of all three areas, concluded that protection of trade was the main motive in the Gold Coast, the preservation of trading routes in the Malay States and humanitarian concern in Fiji. He also insisted that these developments did not signal any new imperialism but were minor adjustments in a continuing policy of consolidation and restraint.[1] Nevertheless it might be argued that Disraeli did seek to project the image of a more 'romantic' empire to the new electorate. Disraeli's first two choices for the Colonial

Office, Lord John Manners and Lord Carnarvon, both fitted this mould. When Carnarvon was eventually selected his imperial vision was revealed by his willingness to envisage a kind of British Monroe Doctrine extending over the whole of Africa. Two qualifications have to be made, however. One is that Disraeli, despite public speeches to the contrary, took no more personal interest in colonial affairs than he did in social reform. His preoccupation was with foreign affairs and the maintenance of British power through the hold over India. Hence his purchase of the Suez Canal shares in 1875 and the gaining of the right to occupy Cyprus from Turkey in 1878. Secondly, the most characteristic form of imperial expansion in this period resulted from the uncontrolled actions of imperial agents on the periphery. In Malaya two successive governors exceeded instructions to the extent that the residential system was extended to three of the states. This pattern was repeated in southern Africa where Sir Bartle Frere's wilful pursuit of federation eventuated in the disastrous confrontation with the Zulus in 1878. Similarly, Lord Lytton (Viceroy of India, 1876–80) defied instructions, thus dragging Britain into war with Afghanistan. As a result an opening was created for Gladstone to exploit during his Midlothian campaign of 1879–80.

It was during this 1880 election that imperialism, and the word was now first used in its modern sense, became a subject of public debate. The Liberals gave vent to their fears that imperialism endangered the moral character and liberal traditions of Britain. They conjured up the picture of 'Beaconsfieldism' as a coherent system which would inevitably drag the country into the depths of autocratic repression. The riposte of the Conservatives was to expatiate on the noble and altruistic aspects of accepting imperial responsibilities. As one writer has recently put it, 'the strategic and economic imperatives which underlay Britain's extensive involvement in the New Imperialism were clothed in the righteous garb of the civilising mission'.[2] Important to note here is how the echoes of this clash could still be heard two decades later in the conflict between Hobson and the imperialists.

It was bitterly ironical then that it should be a government headed by Gladstone that took the decision to occupy Egypt. This in itself should be a warning against discounting the powerful forces at work and emphasises the inability of individuals to deal with them. There is no generally accepted view on why Britain intervened. Basically, the disagreement is between those who see the 'police action' as reflecting the demands of the bondholders and those who view it as deriving from strategic concern for the Suez Canal. Historians among the latter group do not deny that the source of the problem was the financial profligacy of successive khedives and the extortions of European moneylenders. However, in their view the Dual Control, imposed on Egypt in 1879, had proven itself effective in ensuring repayments of debt. What changed the minds of British ministers was the threat posed to internal stability and the canal by the machinations of the nationalist leader, Arabi Pasha. In the end Gladstone, anxious to save his Irish policies, had to defer to his more hawkish colleagues. Upholders of the economic interpretation point to the long period of association between Egypt and Europe during which a financial straitjacket had gradually restricted Egypt's freedom of movement. Men on the spot, with the interests of the bondholders at heart, fed distorted information to the government. As the crisis worsened, it was at a very late date, and almost as an afterthought for public consumption, that any reference was made by Liberal ministers to the dangers posed to the canal. However, this argument, persuasive as it is, does lose sight of the long-standing British strategic concern with the Levant; Palmerston, who had tried to block the building of the canal, always realised how much control in the area by one nation would upset the balance of power.[3]

During the period of what we have called hesitant imperialism (1882–92), an awareness of the realities of the European dimension of imperialism impressed itself on successive ministries which, however reluctant they were to assume control, were forced to act for fear of losing valuable markets and strategic footholds. Gladstone followed a zig-zag course – sometimes adhering to the tenets of Midlothian and at other times responding to the demands of official, mercantile or public opinion. Salisbury's governments became increasingly imperialistic but were constrained by fear of another Mid-lothian, Treasury disapproval or parliamentary resistance. As a result this was the period of 'imperialism on the cheap' when chartered companies were set up as proxies of the Foreign Office or, almost literally, as holding companies for long-term interests. Another aspect of this approach was the frequent recourse to declaring protectorates over new territories thereby incurring fewer costs and responsibilities. In other words, Salisbury came to have a shrewd notion of the ends but could not see his way clear to will the means.

Heightened European activity in West Africa between 1883 and 1885 must be seen against a backdrop of European economic crisis and rising tariffs. This had a knock-on effect in West Africa where lower prices for palm oil led to increased tension between traders and African middlemen, the one anxious to gain control of trade into the interior from the other. Further disturbances to the equilibrium were the French moves on the Congo and initiatives from Senegal towards the western Sudan and the Upper Niger. Thus fears were also created for the continuance of Britain's informal paramountcy in the Oil and Niger rivers. By 1882 the British presence there was dominated by the National African Company headed by George Taubman Goldie. Inspired by the example of a charter granted to the North Borneo Company in 1881, Goldie bought out his French rivals in order, he hoped, to secure consent for his own chartered company.

However complacent Gladstone was regarding the French challenge, this was less true of the Foreign Office officials and agents. The consul for the Bights of Benin and Biafra, E. H. Hewett, demanded action. So did Percy Anderson, the head of the new African department within the Foreign Office, whose diagnosis was that France had a blueprint for action which, if successful, would utterly stifle British commerce. As a conse-quence British resistance stiffened with Hewett declaring a protectorate over the Oil and Lower Niger rivers in July 1884. This was combined with an attempt to block French designs on the Congo by the ruse of recognising the historic claims of Portugal to the mouth of the river.

When Bismarck made his fitful appearance upon the African stage during 1884–5 by the annexations of South-West Africa,

Togoland, the Cameroons and Tanganyika it elicited a different British response. The basic reasons were that Anderson's bias was Francophobic, a frank recognition that Germany was bound to enter the lists at some point and, most importantly, a need for Germany's friendship. This derived from Gladstone's insistence that Britain's occupation of Egypt was only temporary and that international agreement was needed for its financial arrangements. Therefore Britain also had to swallow Bismarck's refusal to accept the Anglo-Portuguese treaty regarding the Congo and his demand for a conference at Berlin to discuss outstanding African issues. Anderson, the dominant British personality at the conference, was willing to recognise French and Belgian claims on the Congo and the new German possessions. In return he secured consent for the Niger protectorate and the principle of free trade on the Congo.

After this there was a pause in European activity as Bismarck lost interest and Ferry was defeated in France. Britain, however, did not relax its grip on the Niger for, as *The Times* claimed, it was, and had been 'for nearly a hundred years, practically a British river'. Practical effect was given to this sentiment in 1886 when the government granted a charter to Goldie's renamed Royal Niger Company. By an elaborate set of commercial regulations, the company soon began the process of creating a monopoly for itself in the Middle Niger region. Though Britain did not enter whole-heartedly into the paper chase for African signatures into the interior of West Africa, there were obviously certain parts, such as Yorubaland and the Upper Niger, about which she was concerned. In Yorubaland, where there had been a disastrous series of civil wars, there was both missionary and mercantile interest. The Church Missionary Society and the Liverpool Chamber of Commerce were two bodies whose members put pressure on the government to take more resolute action to restore stability. By 1893 a protectorate had been declared over the area. There was less willingness to defend the hinterlands of the Gold Coast (except the Ashanti region), Sierra Leone and the Gambia which were all eventually lost to France. The question for the future was whether the Upper Niger would go the same way.

European attention switched to East Africa in the late 1880s. Because of their traditional and growing influence over the sultan of Zanzibar, who also exercised a vague overlordship over much of the mainland, the British had been surprised by Bismarck's move in 1885. The government tried to calm public fears and in 1886 concluded an agreement with Germany which, on paper at least, protected Britain's sphere of influence in the northern half of the sultan's territory. There was still much apprehension, however, on the part of isolated individuals regarding Britain's loose claims in Uganda and the reappearance in the Lakes region in 1887 of the German adventurer, Carl Peters. The British consul in Zanzibar, Sir John Kirk, conspired with Sir William Mackinnon, a rich Scottish businessman and British imperial patriot, in the setting up of a chartered company to protect British interests. To this Anderson and the permanent officials were receptive but the chief obstacle was Salisbury, who still saw the area as one of mainly commerical concern where traders should accept due risk. Salisbury also failed to warm to Mackinnon personally, either to his anti-German outlook or to his imperial visions. Nevertheless the officials succeeded in getting the green light for Mackinnon to sign treaties in the interior at the same time as the realms of high finance, imperial interests and philanthropic bodies were shaken down to provide an impressive list of subscribers for the proposed company. By 1888 Salisbury's diffidence was overcome, allowing the Imperial British East Africa Company to receive its charter.

This step proved to be a fortuitous one for Salisbury because by 1889 he had decided that the British occupation of Egypt would have to be permanent. This implied a whole new strategic priority for the area north of Lake Victoria. Mackinnon, with more patriotic zeal than commercial acumen, needed little prodding from the government to send an expedition under Frederick Lugard into the interior. At the same time Salisbury opened diplomatic negotiations with the Germans and by the Agreement of 1890 extended the westward limits of Germany's exclusion, thus removing any threat from that quarter to either Uganda or the upper Nile. Unfortunately for Mackinnon, however, the expenses of Lugard's expedition so depleted the company's finances that its days were numbered unless a subsidy could be arranged.

Within Britain during this decade imperial sentiment was

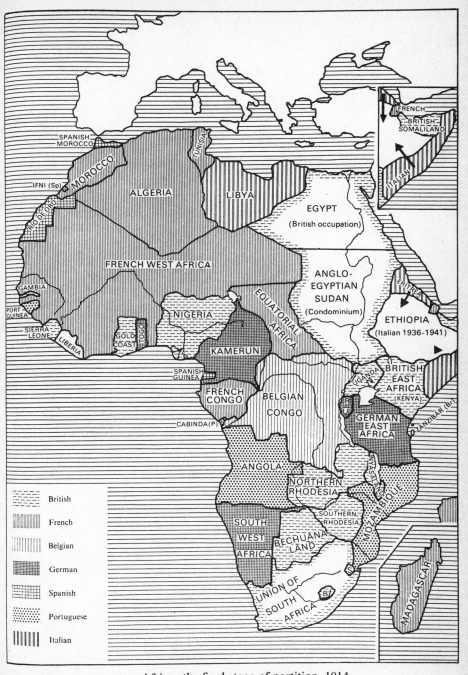

Africa: the final stage of partition, 1914

fanned most of all by the failure of Gladstone to uphold British interests abroad,[4] the most flagrant instance of which was Gordon's death in the Sudan. Imperial feelings, admittedly, oscillated between the poles of jingoistic outbursts and domestic introspection. Nevertheless once the Liberal leader's conversion to Irish Home Rule became known, in the very same month that the Indian National Congress was formed, it seemed to confirm the threat posed to imperial unity by Gladstonianism. Salisbury required no such warning as these events provided, although his very aloofness and distrust of *demos* inhibited any approach towards popular involvement. Neither was he willing to break with financial orthodoxy. Only when he saw a problem in terms of grand national strategy did he seem to come alive.

Hobson's phrase, conscious imperialism, is most appropriately applied to the period from 1892 to 1902. Upon Gladstone's return to office, he was elbowed out of the way by his own Foreign Secretary, Lord Rosebery, whose advocacy of continuity in foreign and imperial policy represented an attempt to remove such matters from inter-party conflict. The vagaries of party politics should not be allowed to endanger Britain's imperial destiny. The demise of the chartered companies coincided with an intention by both Rosebery and Chamberlain to assert greater vigour from the centre. The British South Africa Company, it is true, did survive. But after the debacle of the Jameson raid the imperial factor dropped its mask, leaving Rhodes with considerable time to fight the Matabele and revise his will. There was now for the first time a near congruence of imperial means and ends.

The downfall of Mackinnon's company was precipitated by its headlong rush into Uganda where Lugard had to contend against Muslim and Catholic opposition. Mackinnon, preferring to reside in the south of France, was neither on the spot nor as ruthless as Rhodes. That the difficulties arose in part as the result of governmental pressure caused bitterness but, in truth, it was the imperial quixotry of Mackinnon which brought the company to its knees. Rosebery absolutely refused to grant it a new lease of life, despite the injection of money from the Church Missionary Society which prolonged its stay of execution for a while. Rosebery then, in a quite Machiavellian fashion so far as honesty with the rest of his Cabinet colleagues was concerned, engineered an imperial take-over in Uganda in 1894. A similar fate awaited Goldie's Royal Niger Company. Chamberlain became exasperated with its failure to meet the French challenge in the Upper Niger and Sokoto. Anxious to develop 'the imperial estates', Chamberlain was a man in a hurry. He bypassed the company by setting up the West African Frontier Force which enabled Britain to gain substantially what it sought from the Anglo-French Convention of 1899. The company, mortally wounded, staggered on until 1900, its last years marked by disputes over compensation. An amazing transformation had taken place, writes Professor Flint, by the fact that 'now it seemed that it was the Imperial Government which was prepared to spend money and assume responsibility, and the chartered company which counted pennies and shirked responsibility'.[5]

The 1890s witnessed one punitive action after another against recalcitrant tribes, the successful outcome of which allowed administrators to administer and contractors to build railways. Chamberlain's forthright attitude led to an expedition against the Ashanti in 1895 and the consolidation of British control in the outlying areas of the Gold Coast. It was the confrontation between General Kitchener and Colonel Marchand at Fashoda in 1898, however, which displayed the new resolve most impressively. There was no question of a tepid reaction from Salisbury, under fire as he was for his compliant reaction to the Russian occupation of Port Arthur. Without doubt there were important strategic interests at stake, but ultimately the quarrel was about national honour and prestige, considerations which largely concealed the comic opera qualities of the drama. Against the backdrop of an aggressive British public reaction, the stark choice for the French was between war and retreat. That combat was averted in this instance as in others has beguiled a few historians into seeing the scramble as at heart a co-operative European venture, which it was not, but it was not worth war either.

From this examination of Africa the difficulty of generalising about the causes or timing of the scramble can be appreciated. When other areas are considered, problems increase. In the Far East, for instance, elements of continuity seem much more important with the result that no significant chronological divide appears until about 1892. Britain clearly had a continuing commercial interest there which dated from the late eighteenth century and which had resulted in the acquisition of key positions such as Singapore and Hong Kong. This was an expression of the capitalist drive and ethic which refused to accept closed cities and ports. Accompanying it was the missionary impulse which refused to accept closed hearts and minds. Of note is the way Richard Cobden in mid-century expressed his profound regret that missionaries were such firebrands and that his former mercantile allies in the campaign for free trade had become fixated by the prospect of rich markets if China could be forced open. Cobden remarked too on the willingness of the constituencies with the widest electorates to applaud the bellicose and chauvinistic utterances and actions of Lord Palmerston, as during the punitive action against China in 1857. The ingredients of the new imperialism were thus present. Yet from a governmental point of view, realism dictated that in a situation where Britain had overwhelming commercial superiority as a result of the wars of 1839–42 and 1856–8 the *status quo* should be maintained for as long as possible. Only when international competition sharpened in the 1890s was a change in course required. In 1893 Britain checked a possible French threat emanating from Indo-China to her commercial predominance in the Yangtze Valley by signing an agreement with them to respect the independence of Siam. The turning point in China was the Japanese victory in war in 1894 which compelled Britain, under severe pressure from consular officials and trading interests, to engage both in the struggle for a 'sphere of influence' (via railway concessions and encouragement of British firms) and in as much of the Open Door (via cooperation with the United States and the Anglo-Japanese Alliance) as was feasible.

During this period the imperial ideology established something close to hegemony over British cultural life. One area where this was most evident was the press. Symbolic of the new imperialism was the manner in which the rectitude and altruism of David Livingstone was linked with the adventurism and self-seeking of H. M. Stanley via a newspaper's drive for circulation. Newspapers no longer acted mainly as mere purveyors of official opinion but as conduits of public opinion. Alfred Harmsworth, who founded the *Daily Mail* in 1896, 'gloried in the vulgarity of the New Imperialism' and tapped a new market by his paper 'written by office boys for office boys'. It was, however, a barometer of a gradual change which conformed to the almost monolithic imperialist stance of the metropolitan press in 1900.[6] To what extent the imperial faith filtered down to the masses is still a debating point, but that it saturated the lower middle class is without doubt. One measure of its political advance was the development of the Liberal Imperialist wing of the Liberal party. In 1892 the Imperialists constituted one-eighth of the parliamentary party but by 1905, having increased their numbers steadily at every election, they comprised one-third of MPs. The areas of Britain most susceptible included Scotland and the English borders where Rosebery's influence counted for a lot. There was a further concentration of Liberal Imperialists in steel-making constituencies centred on Sheffield. They were also strong in seaports, dockyards and shipbuilding towns.[7] Dissent from imperialism could now only express itself from one side of the Liberal party. Within the Conservative party Chamberlain, who had always appreciated the leverage which a supportive public could provide, tried to cultivate public opinion in favour of imperialism by means of his South African policies. In the end he became the prisoner of the over-simplification of the issues which this involved.[8] Once the Boer War was under way no amount of management could quieten the voices of protest. Civil disquiet, Hobson's book, setbacks on the Veld and 'methods of barbarism' all touched off the soul-searching and intimations of decline which marked the period after 1902.

II

Some historians, preferring to remain anchored within the empirical tradition, have chosen not to speculate on the general causation of the new imperialism. They see, as it were, numerous partitions rather than a 'Partition', the clues to each having to be unlocked by their own specificity. On the other

hand a majority, even if they fight shy of using the word
'theory', have constructed a general interpretation which could
be subsumed within the meaning of that word. In the belief that
historians should deal with such problems, this section will
examine some of the recent attempts at general explanations.
With due regard to the risk involved, these approaches have
been combined under three main headings – economic, great
power theory and peripheral.

Economic interpretations of the new imperialism postulate
that industrialism was the single most important factor
explaining the transformation of power relationships. The
spread of this system meant an intensified competition for
markets and goods, worsened by the onset of economic
'depression' from the early 1870s and the turning away from
free trade by Britain's rivals. Declining prices spurred on the
search for a steady and cheap supply of raw materials,
especially palm oil and cotton. An impressive list of contemporary figures – Keltie, Dilke, Lugard, Johnston and
Goldie – can be pointed to who testified to the importance of
finding new markets and sources of raw materials. A variant of
the economic approach, because it sees the problems arising
from industrialism as the key, is social imperialism. Overseas
expansion, it is argued, arose less from any need for markets
than from the urgency of coping with social tensions at home by
the spurious appeal to class unity which it provided. Finally, it
should be mentioned that few researchers have been willing to
follow the full rigours of Hobson's financial and conspiratorial
analysis. This is not to say that his identification of a *rentier* class
in south-east England increasingly looking for profitable
overseas investments has not had modern resonance. The City
was a more prestigious entity than either industry or commerce.

The most thorough statement of the economic causes of
British expansion has come from P. J. Cain and A. G. Hopkins,
who argue that the relative failure of the British economy and
the rise of efficient competitors after 1870 provoked a new
search for markets. They are concerned with the way in which
Britain's informal influences could be manipulated to advantage or even lead to formal annexation. For example, they see
the Egyptian affair as the result of the attempt to impose

financial 'law and order'. Since the time of the agricultural revolution a link is evident between British expansion and the phases of the development of the economy. Their conclusion is that: 'From being an adjunct to the interests of the landed gentry and City financiers in the mid-eighteenth century, Britain's overseas concerns expanded as modernisation proceeded until, by the time of the First World War, they were crucial not only to particular powerful financial and industrial goods but also to overall economic growth, to internal stability, and to great-power status'.[9] For the economic argument to have weight it must be possible to show that governments were attentive to commercial considerations. The research of D. C. M. Platt has shown how, after 1882, the traditional policy of the Foreign Office to seek no special favour for British traders changed when the shortcomings of *laissez-faire* began to be realised. The result was that 'anticipatory annexations for safeguarding of markets played at least some part in the scramble for Africa'.[10] Recent studies by W. G. Hynes have highlighted the degree to which chambers of commerce after 1881, especially when panicked by bouts of severe recession, lobbied for greater protection for trade and annexation of territory.[11] The difficulty inherent in this approach is establishing to what extent commercial bodies had an impact on official opinion and policy. A sympathetic audience at the Foreign Office was no guarantee that subsequent action was grounded on similar premises. Or, even if Anderson or others might be convinced, could the splendid isolation of Salisbury be broken down? On the other hand, even Salisbury recognised that much of the partition resulted from the failure to ensure free trade in the undeveloped world.

The case for the new imperialism as the result of the need for raw materials in a renewed era of mercantilism has been vigorously put by C. C. Wrigley. The attraction of the mercantilist model is that it almost totally dissolves the line between the state and the economy. Wrigley puts politics further into eclipse by the argument that, although European diplomacy determined the exact timing of the scramble, the process was advanced only by a few years since 'the planet was visibly contracting and claims on its still unclaimed riches would have to be pegged out sooner or later'. Even if, Wrigley maintains, some of the new annexations were deficient in natural resources, the prospect was that in time they would prove their worth and in the meantime must be held in reserve.[12] The fact that Britain so stubbornly adhered to free trade might cause some scepticism regarding her inclusion within such a framework. However, a systematic study of West Africa by A. G. Hopkins reveals how the British drive to acquire palm oil at lower prices, itself a result of the economic 'depression', led to far-ranging political changes, especially when faced with an equal African determination to maintain existing price levels. Demands were made upon the government to cut the African middleman down to size, to counteract French encroachment and to establish law and order.[13] In other words, a long-established set of relationships along the coast could be overturned by the impact of new economic priorities and conditions in Europe.

Although the relevance of social imperialism has been hotly debated in connection with Bismarck's bid for colonies, the only use of the idea in the British context has been for the period after 1895. The idea bears a resemblance to the views of Joseph Schumpeter, who had stated the case for imperialism being the result of the attempt of the old ruling class to resolve class conflict and to maintain itself in power by imperialistic power and pomp. Lately, Dr Freda Harcourt has tried to apply a variation of this approach to Britain in the late 1860s. Her argument is based upon the contention that the new imperialism emerged as the result of a number of crises: financial collapse in 1866; reform riots; working-class distress; failure of nerve on the frontiers of empire; and revived militarism in Europe. She then proceeds to the view that 'the idea of enhancing Britain's imperial status was seized upon by Disraeli in 1866 as the obvious, indeed, the only way of confirming Britain's position as a great power in a rapidly changing world. He acted on the belief that the trappings of imperialism might have as wide an appeal as they did elsewhere. . . .' An account is then offered of the enormous expense and elaborate military planning which went into the Abyssinian campaign of 1867, the purpose of which was to retrieve a few British captives by a force of 12,000 men. It was the success of this venture, accompanied by a blaze of publicity, which gave Disraeli the confidence to make his pan-class appeal in 1872 at Crystal Palace.[14] This is shrewdly suggestive of the way in which imperialists were always seeking a way to bend down and involve the masses. There is similar evidence of Conservative and City encouragement of the outbreak of jingoism in 1877–8.[15] One question which must be asked, however, is whether Harcourt has not exaggerated the fears of the governing classes in 1866–8; surely one of the reasons for the extension of the franchise was that the working classes were now considered 'safe'.

As with the economic interpretation, great power rivalry has a long ancestry as an explanation of the new imperialism. This category is intended to convey more than the idea of the diplomatic quarrels of Europe being extended beyond its borders, the argument of A. J. P. Taylor, but is meant to include the domestic fuelling of these urges by nationalism and Social Darwinism. Again, the starting point is that of crisis, the defeat of France in 1870 and the gradual collapse of the Concert system. Pent-up nationalistic feeling in France expressed itself in the attempted restoration of prestige by the accumulation of a great deal of what Salisbury was facetiously to call 'light soil'. Where the other powers might dismiss King Leopold's initiative on the Congo as an eccentricity, they could not help but react to France's imperial boldness after 1879. In other accounts the actual starting point varies, sometimes Britain's seeking after paramountcy in the 1870s is cited, sometimes Leopold's actions, and often Germany's annexations in 1884–5. British 'reluctance' to extend her formal commitments derived from the fact that she was a 'conservative' power with more to lose by the expansion of others than to gain by the extension of her own frontiers. British statesmen were alive to the necessity of maintaining power and prestige and hence the retention of India was vital. In the end, after considerable vacillation, Britain had to intervene to protect her essential interests. One significant advantage of this approach is its plausibility for explaining both what happened and what did not happen. For example, it was in the interests of the great powers to prohibit the total carve-up of China. In addition, it is also a refinement of this model which provides the most satisfactory explanation for the outbreak of war in 1914.

One recent restatement of the great power thesis has been made by Winfried Baumgart who sees the new imperialism as growing out of a traditional concern for the balance of power. The prime difference in the post-1870 period was the collapse of the Ottoman Empire which eventually necessitated the introduction of this principle into the division of its territories. When additional extensions were made further afield the same principle was incorporated into the process. He believes that, while the scramble was touched off by Egypt, the most decisive change was the translation of Anglo-French rivalry into a multinational one. And once under way, there was a stampeding effect that partook of the irrational.[16] Baumgart, it should be added, opposes any monocausal explanation but does give greatest weight to great power rivalry. His account has the merit of showing how the conflicts engendered by partition could be kept within safe bounds. Another interpretation bearing a somewhat similar hallmark is Tony Smith's *The Pattern of Imperialism* (1981), except that he is of the opinion that great power rivalry was ignited by economic 'depression'. In the 1870s free trade imperialism transformed itself into a political rivalry which culminated in the takeover of African and Asian societies, already weakened by the corrosive effects of European capital and culture. He concludes that: 'Imperialism thus emerges as a multiform process whose pattern was determined in the course of British hegemony (though not exclusively) by the agents of capitalist industrial expansion, by the momentum of great power rivalries, and by the [in]capacity of southern governments to deal with these forces'.[17]

One arm of the great power approach, upheld by Robinson and Gallagher, is the reliance upon the strategic interests of 'the official mind'. To those who say that strategy was but one remove from economics, their reply is that India was more than an assured market but also a means of maintaining Britain's credibility and capability as a great power. They make much of the contrast between the relative British diffidence towards West Africa compared with the determination shown in East Africa after 1889. The chief difficulty with 'the official mind' as a concept is its extremely self-enclosed nature; it is hard to accept any model of decision-making which operates within a vacuum. Even elites have grassroots, however rarified they might be.

In order to explain attitudes towards other nationalities and ethnic groupings, Social Darwinism is often imported into great power theories. So far no satisfactory general treatment is available, but anyone wishing to sample such ideas need only consult Dilke's *Greater Britain* (1868), Bagehot's *Physics and Politics* (1872), Froude's *The English and the West Indies* (1882) or Kidd's *Social Evolution* (1894). A misinterpretation of Darwin's writings allowed an existing ethnocentrism to be wrapped in a covering of pseudo-scientific certainty. Ideas regarding the necessity for the struggle for 'racial' survival were endemic among late-Victorians. Introducing a hardness into thinking about war and race, they could justify the imposition of rule over the 'child' races. The impact of Social Darwinism upon the thought of Salisbury and Rhodes, to name but two, is well known. The overall difficulty is, of course, to bring something 'in the air' down to earth.

The writings of the classic theorists of imperialism were dominated by ideas of European capitalism, social class or national rivalries. It was Robinson and Gallagher who broke with this tradition by adopting the peripheral approach. In fact, the phrase was actually coined by D. K. Fieldhouse, who argued for its validity within a worldwide framework. His is an interesting case because in his earlier works, where his main concern had been to repudiate the determinism of Lenin, he had upheld the great power rivalry outlook. But in *Economics and Empire 1830–1914* (1973) he developed the argument that annexations were the result of a pragmatic response to intractable problems as they arose in the margins of European influence or control. Nearly always, it seemed, the impulse towards expansion originated within the periphery. As problems arose, whether economic in origin or not, they had to be 'politicised' before government would consider annexation. This line of reasoning owed much to Robinson's theory of collaboration which showed how, in situations of informal empire, governments by necessity had to work through native elites. Often the result was that impossible demands were made of these collaborators to the extent that the resulting alienation and social ferment necessitated the imposition of formal rule. One other aspect of the peripheral approach is the idea of subimperialism whereby partly-sponsored but largely unmanageable figures such as Cecil Rhodes could pursue their own ambitions. In the Pacific, Australia and New Zealand effectively practised subimperialism.[18]

One of several advantages of the peripheral approach is the way it invites closer scrutiny of numerous groups of Europeans overseas – consuls, missionaries, traders and adventurers – who, on any reading of events, played such an important role in expansion. Often emanating from backgrounds of relatively low social status, they were ambitious and careerist. When this was mixed with an enhanced patriotism and a genuine enthusiasm for the value of a new possession, the resulting alloy was puzzling to the mandarins in Whitehall. Another advantage is the need which is created for the study of the effects of European contact upon indigenous society. Missionaries were prone to setting up a state within a state, thus producing collaborators and modernisers within the local society. Fourah Bay College in Sierra Leone became in a way the seminary of partition.

The main defect of peripheralism is that it threatens to wrench partition completely away from its metropolitan moorings. By reducing Eurocentrism to a motive of deliberate calculation, the complicity or sheathed sword of the powers in the background can be lost sight of. In many instances the man on the spot was emboldened by the knowledge that redress from the centre was possible. Nor is it easy to explain, without reference to European political or economic conditions, why there should have been so many local crises to contend with after 1870. There is also the difficulty of explaining how imperial takeover could be engineered from the centre, as was the case with Upper Burma in 1885. Lord Randolph Churchill and his officials at the India Office rode rough-shod over the doubts expressed by the viceroy of India and his officials, including an accurate forecast of the military difficulties which were sure to be met. Churchill, anxious to attract urban and business interests to the Conservative cause, paid close heed to the frequent deputations from chambers of commerce urging a forward policy. In the end his only regret was that confirmation of the new possession arrived too late to benefit the Tory party in the election of that year.[19] What may be reasonably expected in future is a synthesis of the Eurocentric and peripheral approaches. Professor J. D. Hargreaves has given due balance to both European and African conditions in his *West Africa Partitioned* (1974). In explaining the events after 1880 he writes:

> . . . governments began to face these [local] crises in a new spirit; not merely did the emergencies seem to require more drastic action, but there were elements within European nations which demanded more positive uses of the power of their state. It is true that these elements did not always win; but their strength and influence during the 1880s seems to be unduly discounted by Robinson and Gallagher.[20]

III

The new imperialism is a legitimate concept to use to describe the period from 1870 to 1902. There were both quantitative and qualitative changes of importance, especially when seen in the full European context. The former is most dramatically reflected in the increased pace of partition. The latter is shown by the emergence of new political and economic pressures and priorities, culminating in the gradual and wide acceptance of an imperial ideology. The period after 1870 did not just face the problems arising from a breakdown in collaborative arrangements on the frontier, although these were obviously more likely to affect existing imperial powers like Britain or France, but also those which were engendered by new European and domestic instabilities. Britain confronted a more hostile and aggressive world, where rivals were unwilling to play the game by the old rules, which directly challenged her supremacy. With self-confidence already sapped, new strategies were forced upon political leaders by economic setbacks and increased electorates. Party leaders strove to find a unifying issue and the attempts to do so can be traced at least to Disraeli's Crystal Palace speech. Not to be outdone, the Liberal party was inundated by imperialism, even if Rosebery insisted that his brand be called 'sane imperialism'. Parish pump and imperial pomp merged together. Gladstone's second government was much damaged in public esteem by its overseas failures. Salisbury's remark that Irish Home Rule awoke 'the slumbering genius of English imperialism' is a reminder of how internal dynamics could have wide ramifications.

Any study of the new imperialism must concern itself with the culture of the state. However muted it was at the time, the imperial ideology shaped itself well before the 1890s. Jingoism appeared in the 1870s and any British victory or setback might call it forth – the chairman of the local Conservative party in Kensington in 1882 was quoted as saying 'that the bombardment of Alexandria was a roar of the British lion that made him feel two feet higher than he had done for several years'. The public schools and the universities, the music halls and the press, became agencies of the new imperialism. The 'stiff upper lip' was not a traditional British posture but something purposefully inculcated in the young. The patriotic songs emanating from the music halls were far from being free of social control and manipulation. And one publication, the *Pall Mall Gazette*, almost solely led the campaign for Gordon's mission to the Sudan in 1884.

It is not realistic to expect that any overall consensus regarding the new imperialism will ever prove acceptable. Of course, specific points of agreement will undoubtedly appear – such as the inapplicability of the Hobsonian model or the economic bases for annexation in West Africa. New research will continue to upset seemingly settled judgements. But more importantly, differences of perception and values among historians will preclude the possibility of concurrence. The lens through which we look at the past is clouded by our own experiences and beliefs. The new imperialism will remain a seminal debating issue. That this is so is really a testimony, rather than a rebuke, to the vigour of historical research and writing.

5. The Extra-European Foundations of British Imperialism: Towards a Reassessment

A. E. ATMORE

I

In a justly acclaimed article published in 1972, entitled 'The Non-European Foundations of European Imperialism', Dr Ronald Robinson deftly produced a 'sketch' for a theory of collaboration. 'The theory of collaboration', he wrote, 'suggests that at every stage from external imperialism [or informal empire] to decolonisation, the working of imperialism was determined by the indigenous collaborative systems connecting its European and Afro-Asian components. It was as much and often more a function of Afro-Asian politics than of European politics and economics'.[1] In conclusion, he enumerates the five main stages or periods of collaboration:

At the outset it depended on the absence or presence of effective indigenous collaborators, and the character of indigenous society, whether imperialist invasions of Africa and Asia were practicable or not. Secondly, the transition from one phase of imperialism to the next was governed by the need to reconstruct and uphold a collaborative system that was breaking down. The breakdown of indigenous collaboration in many instances necessitated the deeper imperial intervention that led to imperial takeover. Thirdly, the choice of indigenous collaboration, more than anything else, determined the organisation and character of colonial rule. . . . Fourthly, when the colonial rulers had run out of indigenous collaboration, they either chose to leave or were compelled to go. . . . Lastly, since anticolonial movements emerged as coalitions of non-collaboration out of the collaborative equations of colonial rule and the transfer of power, the elements and character of Afro-Asian national parties and governments in the first era of independence projected a kind of mirror image of collaboration under imperialism.[2]

A first reaction to this basically simple set of propositions is one of wonder at the breadth of its scope. It covers both formal and informal empire in the long period of the expansion of European mercantile capitalism up to the middle of the nineteenth century. It covers the high-noon of nineteenth-century imperialism, and resistance to it (it should be noted that at every stage the theory of collaboration can be inverted to explain non-collaboration or outright resistance). It covers twentieth-century colonisation, nationalism, neo-colonialism and neo-imperialism, development, underdevelopment and non-development. Dr Robinson's theory of collaboration has turned out to be a veritable Pandora's Box, into which a vast range of problematic elements have been crammed.

The theory has been widely accepted by historians and other scholars. It has become a major part of the conventional wisdom in writings on aspects of imperialism, made use of by Marxist and non-Marxist historians alike. This chapter will examine two 'case histories' which illustrate different stages of the theory. The first, the response of the Ottoman empire to European pressure and intervention, relates to the period of informal empire and also suggests the reasons why there was not a European carve-up of the empire until after the First World War. The second case examines the European conquest of West Africa (with a brief excursion into Ethiopia). It will describe the military and violent nature of this conquest and will pose (if not answer) the query, was this conquest an outcome of the breakdown of the collaborative mechanisms in that region? In conclusion, a few general points will be made about collaboration and resistance.

II

Dr Robinson cites the Ottoman empire as an example of what he terms the external or informal phase of collaboration. He notes that 'if the Turkish collaborators were eventually ineffective, European statesmen and bankers who dealt them a bad hand to play in Ottoman politics were largely to blame'.[3] This conclusion deserves further examination, because it is such a striking twist in the story of collaboration. An outcome like this suggests a high degree of consciousness and articulation over the motives and intentions of both sides of the relationship between Ottomans and Europeans. But was the reality as clear-cut as this neat turn of phrase implies?

The ambivalence, ambiguity and complexity of relations between the European capitalist states and the extra-European world are well illustrated by the history of the Ottoman empire in the nineteenth century. European-Ottoman relationships were ambivalent because there were elements of love and hate in them. They were ambiguous because they contained much obscurity and incomprehension, and because at any time between the 1830s and 1914 their outcome was uncertain. They were complex because there were so many different and often competing elements on both sides. Moreover nineteenth-century European-Ottoman relationships were conditioned, to a lesser or a greater extent, by over four centuries of close contact. Indeed, so intimate was the contact, in the Balkans, the Black Sea, the Mediterranean, the Levant and the Fertile Crescent, that Europeans tended to regard the Ottoman empire as another, albeit extremely backward, European state – the Sick Man of Europe, as it was termed. Yet the intimacy was itself ambiguous, because it contained large areas of mutual incomprehension; geopolitical intimacy could be possible in situations where actual contact was minimal.

The Ottoman empire was in many ways different at the end of the nineteenth century from what it had been before the first wave of reforms in the 1830s.[4] Then it was an unwieldy collection of provinces with archaic structures – social, economic and political – all of which were largely autonomous. The state was so weak that it existed only in a rudimentary form. The main centralising factor was the army, and even this was fragmentary and rebellious. By 1900 – certainly by the time of the revolution of 1908 – some of these structures survived, but most had undergone radical change. They had largely lost their autonomous character. The economic structures had been penetrated by European commercial and industrial capitalism.

The social structures of the Ottoman empire were least amenable to change, but even these had lost their rigidity by the beginning of the twentieth century. The empire survived the loss of most of its European provinces, to the heady forces of Balkan nationalism. The archaic political structures had been undermined by the Ottoman state. Centralisation is the major theme of nineteenth-century Ottoman political development, and centralisation was the outcome (if not the intention) of reformers and Westernisers. They were attempting to regain control of the political organs of the empire, and power over largely autonomous provinces, and to modernise most aspects of Ottoman life: fiscal, administrative, judicial, military, educational. In many cases they were encouraged, if not persuaded, by those European politicians who concerned themselves with Ottoman affairs. Many of the models copied were French. Their activities led to a reaction from Muslim traditionalists, who came to power in the early 1860s and again in 1878. But the traditionalists did little to reverse the modernising processes, and during the regime of the reactionary Sultan Abdulhamid many of these were accelerated. The real gainer of the Ottoman reforms was the state system, which was never as strong as it was at the end of the nineteenth century. Paradoxically, as the empire was becoming increasingly under the sway of European capitalism, it was becoming politically stronger. The institutional and ideological transformations, achieved by Westernisers and traditionalists alike, resulted in a state system strong enough to withstand direct European aggrandisement. In the development of Ottoman-European relationships during the nineteenth century, the position and role of collaborators and collaborating groups was uncertain in the extreme.

At the outset, problems of definition arise. In the Ottoman context, is the general term 'collaboration' to be equated with the equally general terms 'modernisation' and 'Westernisation'? Were all modernisers, collaborators? This is not an easy question to answer. The modernisers were members of the ruling political, administrative and religious elite of the Ottoman empire. They were Turkish-speakers, if not being ethnic Turks. In the provinces members of this elite shared power, in different proportions, with native ruling groups. It could be maintained that the government of the empire itself depended upon the support of collaborating and co-operating groups. The Ottoman ruling elite was largely separate from commercial and manufacturing petty bourgeois elements, to an even greater extent than were the rulers of the *anciens régimes* of Europe.

In the course of the nineteenth century a number of different attitudes to modernisation became apparent among this political ruling elite. There were conservatives who wanted to adapt change to existing modes of life. There were gradualists who wanted to use reforming legislation to channel the current of Ottoman historical development in more modern directions. There were radicals who dreamt of revolutionary transformations of all aspects of Ottoman life. There were few if any reactionaries, people intent upon a complete isolation from things European. None of these attitudes to change were exclusive: most people revealed different attitudes at different times (and in different places). It would be difficult, however, to find anyone, certainly among the Ottoman ruling elite, who intended to sell the empire to the foreigners, who was prepared to assist in some kind of territorial dismemberment. Nearly all members of this group would have considered themselves to be patriots, though the object of their patriotism would have differed.

There were three main peaks in the range of nineteenth-century reforms, the rescripts or decrees of 1839 and 1856, which paved the way for reforms, and the constitution of 1876. The 1839 decree was issued in the shadow of the threat of Muhammad Ali, and that of 1856 at the end of the Crimean war. The 1840s and 1850s were the great reforming decades, known as the *Tanzimat* (Reorganisation). The 1876 constitution was promulgated on the eve of an international conference at Istanbul, convened to try to prevent a Balkan war between the Ottoman empire and Russia, and after the government announced suspension of interest on the Ottoman debt. But to see these focal points of reform merely as a response to heightened European concern with the Ottoman empire gravely over-simplifies the issue. Certainly many critical Europeans dismissed Ottoman reforms as window-dressing, to obscure the real circumstances of the Christian and other subjects of the empire, on whose behalf Britain, France and Russia threatened to intervene. Such critics, however, were themselves largely blinded by prejudice and ignorance, and failed to appreciate the changes that were taking place in the empire. Behind the rhetoric of the reformers (and they did indulge in vivid flights of verbosity) there was always substantial institutional and political movement, the accompaniment of the economic and social changes.

The Ottoman constitution was promulgated at the end of 1876. Within weeks the chief instigator of this ostensibly liberal democratic innovation, Midhat Pasha, was removed by Abdulhamid, the new sultan. The first Ottoman parliament met once, before being dissolved by Abdulhamid early in 1877. For the next thirty years the sultan ruled as an autocrat, a regime more readily adopted following the disastrous war with Russia in 1878. Seemingly a pattern of events had been enacted: reforms followed by reaction. But a closer examination of the activities and ideas of the main participants suggests that the situation was less cut and dried and more amorphous. The regimes of both the reactionary periods – from the 1860s to 1875, and after 1877 – continued to modernise and to reform. It was during Abdulhamid's reign that much of the basic infrastructure of modernisation was constructed. The only reform of note that was 'smothered at birth'[5] was the constitution of 1876, and this was a dubious measure: the Hamidian regime was certainly 'illiberal', in the nineteenth-century western European sense of the word, but then how liberal were the constitution-makers? The constitution provided for a bicameral parliament to share (within limits) the legislative powers of the sultan. This was the first and last constitution of the Ottoman empire: it was suspended in 1878, soon after the election of the parliament, and was restored after the revolution of 1908.

All the *Tanzimat* reformers were authoritarian. There was no way – at least until the first parliamentary elections – that the rulers of the empire could be democratic. The reforms were authoritarian in two respects. They were imposed on the people of the empire and, despite their liberal wording (and no doubt intentions), they made it more possible for a centralising government to be effective. Even the constitution was authoritarian. It was in the form of a concession from the sultan, with no kind of democratic agreement. It enumerated but did not exhaust the sultan's prerogative, and gave future governments wide powers in the proclamation of martial law. Centralisation and authoritarianism emerge as the dominant trends in the nineteenth-century history of the Ottoman empire.

After the collapse of the constitution, the *Tanzimat*, the first great period of Ottoman reform, seemed to have come to an end. The radical Young Ottoman movement was sharply critical of the generation of *Tanzimat* reformers. It accused them (with justification) of being arbitrary and absolutist. The Young Ottomans had an abiding faith in constitutional and parliamentary government as the remedy for the ills suffered by the empire. They were anything but unpatriotic. The Young Turks grew out of the Young Ottomans. They were more aggressively nationalistic, both in relation to the European states and to the empire's subject peoples. They espoused both pan-Turkish and pan-Islamic ideals – thus having an appeal to peoples beyond the empire's borders. But within months of their revolution of 1908 the more liberal revolutionaries had been overwhelmed by the authoritarian and hard-line Turkish nationalists. The 1876 constitution was restored, but by the middle of 1909 the Committee of Union and Progress had become the dominant force in the empire, and from 1913 a triumvirate of army officers governed in what was virtually a military dictatorship.

One of the main accusations against the *Tanzimat* reforms by the Young Ottomans was that the policies and practices of the reformers had opened the gates of the empire to a flood of European capitalist intervention. Europeans were enabled to own land in the empire and, by the second half of the century, European capitalism had made deep inroads into the fabric of the empire. By the 1850s the production of textiles had been severely disrupted by the importation of European (especially British) cotton and woollen goods. It has been argued that the Ottoman empire had been reduced to a peripheral area of international capitalism,[6] so that (for one thing) 'craft production entered a period of structural crisis'.[7] But the breakdown was not as complete as this analysis (and the inference of the Young Ottomans) suggests. For one thing (and it is a not unimportant element) it was not the *policy* of the Ottoman establishment to allow the agents of European capitalism to undermine the economy. They introduced fiscal policies of free trade, an ideology imported from Britain. It was these liberal policies which smoothed the way for European capitalism, but this was not their immediate intent. Even within the urban areas of the Balkans, Anatolia and the Levant there remained considerable economic activity which was maintained irrespective of European capitalist intervention and exploitation, and a more outlying province such as Iraq was largely free of any such involvement.

To what extent, then, were the Ottoman reformers and the Greek and other merchants collaborators in the expansion of European imperialism? How well does this brief description of Ottoman establishment politicians, autocratic sultans, reforming ministers, and a radical and nationalist intelligentsia, fit into the Robinson theory of collaboration and resistance? In the first place, it does not appear that any group of reformers, or individual reformers, was singled out in any specific or conscious way by Europeans, certainly not at the diplomatic or political levels. European merchants and capitalists sought out Greek or Levantine merchants, and this was a long-established practice. Spokesmen of European Christian sects were in contact with the leading figures of the Christian groups in the empire. European politicians and bureaucrats brought pressure to bear on Ottoman governments in general, making little differentiation between the various contenders for power in the empire. This pressure consisted of particular and spasmodic diplomatic exchanges, in the forms of notes passed to Ottoman envoys in Europe, or, more usually, passed from European ambassadors at Istanbul to the sultan's government. The international conference of 1877 was exceptional. For the rest, 'influence' was of a personal kind, the amicable relationships between individual diplomats and members of the Ottoman elite. Over and above commercial and political influence and intervention was the aura of European ideas and technology. It is difficult to appreciate the significance of these ideological and cultural inputs. It must remain an open question as to whether or not they softened up the empire in its relation to European capitalist and political power.

It seems that the European states related politically to the empire irrespective of the personalities in government or the type of regime in power. Britain maintained a predominant relationship until the last quarter of the century. France had strong ties with the empire, especially after 1841, when Muhammad Ali ceased to be a major threat, and until the defeat in the Franco-Prussian war in 1870. After this time Germany became much more influential politically, and expanded economically into the empire. German politicians, military men and industrialists operated as successfully with the regime of Abdulhamid as their British counterparts had done with the *Tanzimat* governments: and they continued so to operate after the Young Turks revolution of 1908. It could be argued that the British naturally sought out liberal governments while the Germans got on well with autocratic and military regimes. Equally it could be argued that after 1870 Germany overtook Britain (and France) in the economic penetration of Eastern Europe and the Balkans – the 'Drive to the East' down the Danube valley – and the Ottoman empire was the geopolitical extension of these areas. But in both cases the main reasons for this shift in political and economic predominance lie much more in the situation of Europe than in the internal dynamics of the Ottoman empire. It was a question of the European capitalist powers relating to the empire in a manner that changed according to circumstances within Europe, and the Ottoman state apparatus and mercantile capitalists relating in a similarly circumstantial manner. To label any of the groups within the empire as collaborators seems to beg the premises that lay behind this set of suppositions. All important elements within the Ottoman hotchpotch of communities and groups (let alone classes) found it useful and at times necessary to co-operate with the representatives of European imperialism.

III

Dr Robinson's theory of collaboration maintains that it was the breakdown of such collaborative mechanisms in extra-European polities, 'which hitherto had provided [the European powers] with adequate opportunity and protection', but which resulted in the 'takeovers' by the imperialists of Africa and parts of Asia. Eurocentric theory, according to Dr Robinson, 'exaggerates the break with previous collaborative processes that colonial rule involved'. In the transition to formal empire he acknowledges that 'the shooting was real enough'. Thereafter 'the amount of force at the disposal of colonial rulers locally seemed tiny in comparison with the possibility of disaffection and revolt'. The colonialists 'still had to work through indigenous collaborators and political processes'.[8] In what perforce are a couple of paragraphs, Dr Robinson encompasses the complex history of the European conquests of Africa and African resistance to this gigantic expansion of imperialism. Other scholars of imperialism also tend to overlook the scale and ruthlessness of this conquest and the resistance to it. The partition of Africa by Europe was achieved only by the use of military muscle and other resorts to aggression, as well as to psychological pressures and blandishments.

The maintenance of colonial rule was likewise based on force. It is true that most of the units of colonial police and armies were small in number, but they were excellently trained and extremely well armed. There was some measure of continuity between these units and the pre-colonial forces of law and order. Many African rulers had relied, for keeping their peace (a highly ideologically tainted concept, as is that of law and order) and the collection of taxes and tribute, upon relatively tiny military forces: the cavalry of the Sudanic states, the royal hunter-warriors of the savanna kingdoms. Also in the colonial period, there might seem to be endless possibilities, under the heel of alien rule, for disaffection and revolt. There was much disaffection and a few revolts, but these were contained and vigorously suppressed. That they were not far more widespread is in part due to the mediation of collaborating groups, but in part also due to the deployment of well-armed police and soldiers. One of the first acts of colonial regimes was to establish a police force, followed soon by army contingents, these generally on a pan-colonial basis (such as the King's African Rifles in East Africa, and the West African Frontier Force). The police-cum-military had great potential power relative to any conceivable disaffection. This power was both real and symbolic. One of the first edifices constructed by the white rulers of African and other tropical dependencies was a gallows, an instrument of force (and terror) that typified both functions. There was an extremely strong ideological rein-forcement of the new colonial law and order mechanisms, in religion and in education, with explicit reference to divine law and to the *Pax Britannica*. Again, there were many echoes in all of this of the practices and ideologies of African polities. But to return to the prior stage of colonialism – even a summary examination of the conquest of Africa indicates its crucial technological and military dimensions.

The reasons for such demonstrations of violence and aggres-sion can be found to some extent in the kinds of breakdowns of established mechanisms of collaboration described by Dr Robinson. These breakdowns in West Africa were, it is claimed, accompanied by increasing violence on the coasts of this arena of informal empire. But they were also a response to the increasing competition and resulting rivalry and insecurity among the European imperialist states. There was in addition a large element of force unprovoked either on the imperial peripheries or at its metropolitan centres. This almost certainly had its origins in the assertive materialist and racialist ideologies which were coming to the fore in the metropoles.

This European propensity for the use of military force to achieve imperial ends in the latter part of the nineteenth century was not, however, a new departure, although some features of it made it significantly different from what went on before. The history of the European mercantilist colonial empires in the Americas, India and Indonesia is strewn with armed conflicts (but as much against fellow Europeans as against indigenous peoples). After the 1850s these imperialist conflicts were on the one hand made much more effective by the use of more technologically advanced weapons (reliable breech-loading rifles and artillery guns, well before the introduction of the machine-gun in the 1890s) and of more disciplined military forces. On the other hand the later Victorians inclined towards grandiose displays of power on a wholly disproportionate scale. The rapid-fire rifles in the hands of well-trained soldiers went side-by-side with the showing of the flag by warships decked with all the panoply of naval might in the baroque style of high imperialism.

Moreover, the actions of professional soldiers and the manifestations of impressive armed forces did not serve only to promote colonial enterprises and to warn off imperialist rivals. Militarism in the advance of imperialist goals equally well served domestic political ends in the metropolitan countries. In an era of rapid development in liberal parliamentary democracy, imperialist aggression was deemed to be popular and to be politically sound tactics. These critical links between domestic politics and colonial wars were in the second half of the nineteenth century most apparent in the contexts of Africa and to an obviously lesser extent on the seas surrounding the Pacific islands, but they were also manifest by further expansion and 'frontier wars' in India.

The earlier nineteenth-century displays of British might in Africa were perhaps geared more to bourgeois than to a wider popular appeal. The British naval anti-slave patrols off the coasts of West Africa and the consequent gunboat diplomacy made the use of violence in West Africa acceptable to philanthropic opinion, by appealing to high moral principle. With the exception of these patrols and of the exploits of Napoleon in Egypt and the British at the Cape, the French invasion of Algeria in 1830 was the first large-scale deployment of military force by a European state on the continent of Africa. Algeria proved to be the nursery for French expansion in tropical Africa. Practically all the military men and the technocrats who became involved in the colonial wars in West Africa and on Madagascar (as well as in Indo-China) had served in Algeria, including the energetic Faidherbe, governor of Senegal from 1854–65. But before the big thrust of the French into the western Sudan got under way, Britain entered into two flamboyant tropical African military campaigns.

In 1868 the British invaded Ethiopia with a large expedition, undertaken at enormous expense, to force the emperor

Theodorus to release a few captives who were British subjects. It has been argued that this expedition was undertaken largely for the purposes of Disraeli's manipulation of domestic politics.[9] To heighten its imperial significance the expedition, unlike previous overseas campaigns, was conducted in a blaze of publicity. The force of 12,000 men was drawn from British and Indian regiments, under the command of Sir Robert Napier. The army of Theodorus was defeated; the emperor committed suicide, and his citadel, Magdala, was destroyed. Napier then withdrew, first to the coast and then to India. A great blow had been struck for British imperial prestige. This new imperialist ideology of Disraeli and the Conservatives in 1866–8 was too attractive politically to be ignored by the Liberals. It was Gladstone's administration which embarked on the Asante war of 1873–4. This costly expedition, under the command of Sir Garnet Wolseley, achieved little more than the Napier campaign. Asante armies were defeated, but the empire was not conquered. After an occupation of thirty-one hours of the capital, Kumasi, Wolseley withdrew his forces. Even more than the Ethiopian expedition, the Asante war was widely publicised in British newspapers, 'by a surprisingly large and talented group of war correspondents'.[10]

Once the partition got under way, the British had to use force to invade and occupy territory in the Gold Coast, Nigeria and Sierra Leone. Between 1895 and 1900 a series of wars were fought to bring Asante under British control. In 1892 an expedition was sent against the Ijebu in eastern Yorubaland, to ensure the freedom of passage for British goods in the hinterland of Lagos. After the campaign the independence of the Yoruba city states crumbled, and in 1893 most of Yoruba-land became a British protectorate, attached to the colony of Lagos. In 1894 a combined naval and army expedition was launched against Nana, the ruler of the Itsekiri city state of Ebrohimi, as a result of which the British gained control of the Niger coast and its profitable trade. In 1897 it was the turn of the ancient city of Benin, which was burnt to the ground.

British expeditions against the Ibo, in the hinterland of the eastern Niger coast, were more protracted, lasting from 1896 to 1909; Ibo unrest lasted until the bitter revolt in Udi in 1914. The Tiv people of the Benue valley put up an equally protracted resistance, which dragged on into the 1900s. Only a more humane and gradualist administrative approach brought peace to the troubled region. The biggest campaign the British waged in West Africa was against the emirates of the Sokoto caliphate. This commenced in 1897, and ranged all over the caliphate, until the final defeat of the sultan's followers at Burmi in 1903. The war of 1898 against the Temne of northern Sierra Leone, under their leader Bai Bureh, was one of the most difficult undertaken by the British in West Africa.[11]

These were the most prominent of the military campaigns waged by the British in the conquest of their portions of West Africa. Thousands of British, West Indian and African troops were used, and a great deal of modern weapons and equipment. The military operations of the French in West Africa (as also in Algeria, Tonkin and Madagascar) were on an even larger scale. From the late 1870s to the late 1890s the French military were almost in total control of the policies for territorial expansion. The *officiers soudanais* (who had served in the great *Armée d'Afrique* of Algeria) commanded the highly disciplined and well-equipped *tirailleurs* and the wilder *spahis*. Their conquest of the western Sudan, fighting against African leaders of the stature of Sultan Ahmadu and Samori, has been chronicled by A. S. Kanya-Forstner.[12] Some 4000 to 5000 French African troops were employed in the western Sudan. Likewise, the French waged a bitter war against King Behanzin of Dahomey in 1892–3, with a 2000-strong expeditionary force, mainly comprised of *tirailleurs sénégalais*.[13] The Germans had to battle their way into northern Togo, and had to conquer large parts of Cameroun, particularly the western grassland areas. The story of military conquest, of the use of ruthless force, can be repeated throughout the continent, from Morocco and Tripolitania to the Transkei, with the Ethiopian victory over the Italian expeditionary force at Adowa in 1896 being the only definitive defeat of the European invaders. There was plenty of criticism of and opposition to the use of military force in the pursuit of imperialist ends in the metropolitan countries (if for no other reason than that these wars were generally costly). But there was also much support for militarism. Public opinion (however defined) was as often as not vocally jingoistic and militaristic in Western Europe at the end of the nineteenth century. From the

1870s to the outbreak of the 1914 war in Europe, Africa was conquered and partitioned by force of arms. The oft-repeated couplet of Hilaire Belloc has become the adage of European imperialism in Africa: Western technology produced the Maxim machine-gun, and Western-type military forces knew how to use it.

There is a postscript to these histories of imperialist wars in West Africa which is of significance in an examination of the problematic of collaboration and resistance. Alongside the build-up of informal empire – before the age of military violence – on the coasts of West Africa by Britain and France (Senegal and Freetown being the main exceptions) went movements towards political and ideological modernisation. The modernisers were Africans, mostly recaptured or returned slaves, or the descendants of such ex-slaves. Some, in Senegal and on the Gold Coast, were of non-slave origin. A few of these African modernisers had been educated in Britain, France or America, but most were surprisingly well educated in European-type schools in coastal West Africa. These English- and French-speaking Africans played a large part in the trading networks of West Africa which were engaged in exporting to and importing from the European world economic system. Others were fervent Christians, who carried the new religion to their former home countries. Others yet again became involved in political affairs in Senegal, Sierra Leone, the Gold Coast and Yoruba-land, in particular Abeokuta.

One noteworthy feature of the African modernisation was not so much the process itself but the British and French response to it. These late-nineteenth-century Africans were uniquely suited for the role of collaborators. Many of them identified with Europe and its culture. They were whole-hearted proponents of Western technology. They generally accepted the British and French ideological attitudes to Africa; they looked forward to a future along the lines of Christianity and civilisation, in the contemporary sense of those terms. They were willing agents of capitalist commerce and production. On the other hand they retained close ties with the traditional West African elites. Yet they were spurned by the British almost absolutely after the 1860s and by the French very largely; the French were more prepared to accommodate culturally assimilated Africans, but repelled economic competition – in some respects the opposite to the British response. The British attitude to the 'trousered blacks' in West Africa had its counterpart in imperial British and European colonist attitudes to educated Africans in South Africa.[14] The colonists extended to this distinguished group of people only the minimum of cultural and political recognition. The British almost totally ignored their value as potential 'collaborators'.

The reasons for this rejection of the West African modernisers were complex. They lay deep in the ideological and psycho-social processes of nineteenth-century Britain and France. In Britain there was an ideological contradiction between morality and culture. The bourgeois (often petit bourgeois) philanthropists' moral environment was countered by the cultural superiority of the establishment, the great British aristocracy and upper middle class. The contradiction was elaborated intellectually in the latter part of the century, when overt or implied racism provided the pretext for prejudice overcoming morality. Technological advance and bogus scientific theorising rigidified attitudes of superiority. They were also the baggage of the strident militarism of the *fin de siècle*.

The rejection of the modernising elite of West Africa had profound effects upon the region's subsequent history. The groups who were chosen by the Europeans to be co-operators, the handmaidens of empire, were drawn from the traditional ruling classes, kings, chiefs and headmen, emirs and holy men. They were shorn of most of their political power, and then forced to play the part of middlemen (or mediators) between the colonial rulers and subjects. This difficult situation further eroded their positions (positions which were undermined but not collapsed; some traditional rulers were adept at manipulating the colonial situation to their advantage). The modernisers and Westernisers rapidly fell to criticising and attacking the colonial administrations, and indeed, the very notion of colonisation (which some of them had earlier advocated). By the end of the nineteenth century this opposition was extremely vocal. It cannot be maintained that the modernisers, if they had been given the opportunity of becoming co-operators, would have not turned to opponents of empire. But in providing these early African nationalists with a heaven-sent anti-colonial case, the imperialists paid a heavy price for the adherence to an extremist ideology.

IV

The notion of collaboration between the European imperialists and certain groups of people in the regions of the world open to this expansionist movement has been widely accepted by historians of imperialism and its effects. Dr Edward Steinhart, for example, in a study of western Uganda, is categorical in his use of the term:

> The means by which . . . external forces were accommodated to the domestic political scene by the leaders of the local African polity is the process I have termed collaboration. It is clear that collaboration as I have used it does not mean submission, defeat or resignation. On the contrary, it is an active policy of co-operation and compromise. In the African context, freed from the derogatory connotations and nuances of moral corruption assumed by the term in the wake of the European experience of Quisling and Pétain, collaboration can be understood as one option among several others open to African leadership in the situation of crisis and conflict engendered by the scramble for African territory and the colonisation of the continent by the European powers.[15]

So diffused has the notion become that in many cases it is used without direct reference to Dr Robinson's essay, and it even seems that it is used by some scholars unconscious of this seminal piece. As has been noted in the introductory remarks, the theory of collaboration has become part of the conventional wisdom of the historiography of imperialism. It will remain an indispensable tool of the trade of these historians, if for no other reason than that its arguments are eminently sensible or even self-evident. Now, however – a decade after Dr Robinson's essay appeared in print (and twenty years since the publication of *Africa and the Victorians*,[16] which contains the germ of the notion of collaboration) – seems an opportune time to raise a number of points about the theory of collaboration.

The theory says little about the position of the collaborators in their own societies. This point was raised in the discussion at the Oxford Theories of Imperialism seminar to which Dr Robinson contributed his paper, and which is printed in the Owen and Sutcliffe volume.[17] Dr Robinson, it was claimed, 'gave little guidance' as to how 'collaborating groups were to be identified and defined'. His reply at the time did not advance the argument very far: 'In a number of cases they [the collaborators] were to be found not as groups but as collections of people of different kinds, at different levels, who were drawn into collaboration as a result of the creation of European types of institutions within their societies'.[18] I have been similarly guilty of using vague nomenclature in this essay. I talk of groups, political elites, establishments, petty bourgeoisie, and use such terms as mechanisms or processes of collaboration. What is required is much more rigour and precision, with an old-fashioned class analysis of each specific society, by scholars of all hues and complexions. Otherwise there is the danger that the theory will be as Eurocentric as the extension of European politics and economic theories, from which Dr Robinson resolves to escape. The theory of collaboration (and its obverse, resistance) can still be Eurocentric, if scholars rather haphazardly project European political and economic processes on to extra-European societies. To be of value in unfolding the histories of extra-European countries or peoples, we must know the social, economic and political positions of collaborators (and of resisters). Many such analyses of extra-European societies have been or are being attempted (the task is generally very difficult). One essay into this minefield, by John Lonsdale and Bruce Berman, neatly side-steps the problem of who the collaborators are by using the phrase 'politics of collaboration'.[19]

Another, more minor point, but not unimportant historiographically, is whether we call collaborators those 'groups of people' who in their own estimation and/or in the sight of the imperialists, were 'allies', 'friendly people' 'honest merchants', etc., or whether we extend the term to all groups whom we, the historians, judge to be collaborators. This can mean almost everybody who did not outwardly oppose the forces of imperialism. In fact there must be gradations along a continuum, with the great majority of people in the middle, neither collaborators nor resisters. Indeed, some historians have rejected the 'bipolar axis' of resistance and collaboration as an explanatory model of the colonial experience. Dr Gwyn Prins, in a remarkable study of the Lozi people of western Zambia, argues that by instituting a 'spectrum of the intensity of power . . . we can add precision to our statement that, in Bulozi, whites possessed neither the will nor the force to dispose of a high intensity of power'. The Lozi elite drew 'upon concealed resources of power in order to extract from the late-nineteenth-century colonial encounter tactical advantages which their European protagonists never understood'.[20]

I have been in part responsible for applying the term collaborators to groups who would not have considered themselves to be such, nor were so considered by the imperial power. In South Africa just prior to the Anglo-Boer war there were very few groups of outright collaborators with British imperialism, the most notable being the South African League. Yet the British government (in the persons of Chamberlain and Milner) was well aware that it could no more rely on this small, unrepresentative group for allies in South Africa than it could on President Kruger's Afrikaners.[21] Likewise, after the war, the 'patriotic', pro-imperialist bodies in South Africa were small in number. The British governments, and High Commissioners Milner and Selborne, had to make a series of major adjustments to representative white parties or groups in South Africa in order to produce any kind of situation acceptable to British imperialist interests. Dr Shula Marks and I have concluded that 'Britain has found in South Africa's white governments entirely satisfactory collaborators in safeguarding imperial interests'.[22] But is it historically correct to extend the meaning of the term collaboration to groups which were, if anything, unfriendly towards and unco-operative with British imperialism? In the case of South Africa we are dealing with a vast process of compromises, on all sides. Perhaps we should talk of the makers of compromises rather than of collaborating parties.

In spite of Dr Robinson's assertion, and those of writers such as Edward Steinhart, about the neutral position of the term collaborator, some scholars – and perhaps a wider public – have found the word distasteful, too loaded with unfortunate connotations. A distinction between collaboration and co-operation has been made, for instance, by Professor Robert Gregory in an article on Asians in East Africa:

> During the period of British colonial rule in East Africa, enterprising traders from South Asia co-operated and collaborated to their mutual advantage in the economic development of the whole region. Co-operation, which is readily apparent in the historical record, presents few problems for the historian. 'Collaboration', however, entails an element of secrecy that militates against its being adequately described and understood ... collaboration denotes an association with government by one who benefits personally at the expense of the community he represents.[23]

In this essay, I have tried to show how extremely ambiguous the term collaboration is when applied to such a complex society as the Ottoman empire; no doubt it is ambiguous when applied to less complex societies. I have also tried to show that in the case of West Africa (and by implication much of the rest of tropical Africa) the notion of the break-down of collaborating mechanisms ushering in the partition is not entirely satisfactory. Previously there were not many collaborating groups, and geographically their range was limited. Much of West Africa – and the rest of the continent – was conquered by brute force, the ultimate responsibility for which lay in the internal and external political, social and economic processes of the major European capitalist states. Perhaps then we should be a little more cautious in the use of the term collaboration – we should apply it more to groups who really did collaborate, in Professor Gregory's definition of the term. Mediation (mediator), alliances (ally) and agency (agent) are – or should be – also specific terms. Co-operation is perhaps the term least open to misuse and misunderstanding. What we are so frequently talking about were groups of people who muddled and lurched from one compromise to another in their relations with the legions of imperialism; and the imperialists themselves had to dodge from one compromise to another, when they were not using brute force. Imperialism was essentially a messy business, which it is difficult to reduce to neat historiographical patterns.

6. Race and the Victorians

CHRISTINE BOLT

hardly two persons use such an important word as race in the same sense.

> James Hunt, President of the
> Anthropological Society of London

(In the ancient world) distinctions of race were not of that odious and fantastic character which they have been in modern times.

> Matthew Arnold

I

These two quotations neatly summarise the main problems associated with Victorian pronouncements on race: that is, their frequent imprecision yet their obvious importance and unpleasant implications. While the words race, racism, ethnocentrism, stereotype and prejudice will be used here according to the modern definitions offered in the editor's *Introduction*, it should be borne in mind that nineteenth-century observers generally simply spoke of race and races. Nor did they perceive the same models and patterns of race relations as recent scholars, despite the Victorian passion for elaborate racial and linguistic hierarchies. Instead, race often became merely a vague but potent force; an explanation of differences and antagonisms between human groups, and a concept whose importance was understandably debated by Britons who had little acquaintance with 'inferior' races at home but controlled, with minimal numbers, a greatly extended empire overseas.

It will be the purpose of this chapter to show that, though the British empire and hostile British attitudes to other races had been evolving long before the Victorian era, racial attitudes changed and hardened during that era. In seeking to explain these changes, attention will first be paid to the declining influence of the anti-slavery movement by mid-century, to the connection of abolitionists and missionaries with empire, and to the racial views of both. The importance of the dissemination of new scientific ideas on race at about the same time will then be assessed. Lastly, an attempt will be made to relate domestic and imperial problems and racial opinions. Particular scrutiny will be given to the reactions encountered by 'alien' groups in Britain, and to the role of educational and class assumptions, sexual mores, and the Victorians' growing national pride in shaping what Barzun and Arendt have termed 'race-thinking'.

II

Until the 1870s, slavery and its aftermath regularly aroused public interest, though responses to the institution and its opponents were not static. During the 1790s, abolitionism had suffered in the political reaction provoked by the French Revolution and the successful slave revolt in St Domingue. These shocks in turn helped to replace the Enlightenment view of the 'savage' as a rational but antithetical indictment of civilisation, with the Romantic conception of children of nature, marked by their sensibilities but enslaved to passion and all the cruel, slothful features of the natural world. When the anti-slavery cause recovered from the doldrums, its Evangelical exponents on both sides of the Atlantic helped to popularise this derogatory image of 'primitive' peoples. In what has been described as a romantic form of racism, they celebrated 'concepts of inbred national character and genius' in a cosmopolitan fashion and, though accepting Anglo-Saxon superiority, acknowledged the debilitating effects of the slave environment and the complementary and compensatory qualities of blacks.[1] Such patronising attitudes could, in Britain, readily extend to Irishmen and Highlanders.

Yet the abolitionists' environmentalist arguments were not

adequately refashioned to cope with the continuing decline of the West Indian economy and the agricultural problems of the American South after slave emancipation. As Temperley and others have demonstrated, in terms of popular support and the zeal of its members, the British anti-slavery movement was a diminished force by the mid-Victorian years.[2] The missionary societies of that time experienced similar difficulties. Since reformers facing intractable poverty in Britain had begun to feel that only the deserving poor could or should be assisted, it is easy to see how able-bodied blacks, who might have been 'deserving' in slavery, could in poverty-stricken freedom be dismissed by sceptical Victorians as just another part of the massive undeserving poor. And for their life style, as presented in Romantic and missionary literature, they might be disparaged as a profoundly unrespectable part.

In an attempt to reassert their influence, and perhaps indicating disillusionment with the results of earlier tactics, missionaries and abolitionists alike supported British territorial expansion and intervention overseas for humanitarian ends. A number of historians have noted this imperialistic thrust, discussing the various bodies making up 'philanthropy' as just one of several lobbies seeking to affect colonial policies in the later Victorian period. Its members exerted pressure on the Colonial Office for, among other things, the acquisition of Fiji, New Guinea, Yorubaland, Nyasaland and Uganda, the suppression of the Polynesian 'slave' trade, prevention of the cession of the Gambia and withdrawal from the Gold Coast. But the humanitarians' impact was offset by many other influences on policy-making, as well as threatened by opponents within their own ranks.[3]

The position of the missionary in the field was controversial in additional respects. On the one hand, he acknowledged the abstract equality and capacity for progress of all men, which the genuine racist denied. In both India and the West Indies, evangelists were not unfairly blamed by the local and London governments for inspiring unruly behaviour and subversive aspirations among their converts. Their stress on the value of native recruits in running the church abroad and the importance of learning the vernacular made many missionaries unusual agents of imperialism. Among non-whites, there were some who appreciated what the mission schools offered, albeit the bias towards vocational education might imply that converts could never attain the intellectual heights of their teachers. On the other hand, to justify constant appeals for funds and possibly to differentiate the faults detected in the unredeemed overseas from those diagnosed in the targets for home missions, evangelists laboured the worst features of 'savage' societies as they saw them, thereby strengthening the unflattering stereotypes which Britons already entertained of the inhabitants of 'heathen' lands.

By the middle of the nineteenth century, when early Victorian philanthropy was thus checked and changing, another challenge to humanitarianism came from the alternative and apparently plausible racial theories being advanced by ethnologists and anthropologists.[4] A variety of disputes and differences served to disrupt the Ethnological Society, formed in 1843, and a breakaway Anthropological Society of London was founded in 1863, though the two groups eventually reunited in 1871 as the Anthropological Institute of Great Britain and Ireland. Rejecting the Englightenment stress on the similarity of men's bodies, the new society's president, Dr James Hunt, and his followers endeavoured (not without opposition) to prove the inferiority of blacks by means of craniology and comparative anatomy. This element clearly wished to see some practical application for their findings, challenged propositions in favour of the equality of races, and advanced a racist position regarding the behaviour and condition of blacks in the United States and the West Indies, who were widely held to be retrogressing in freedom. Other methods of classifying men used in the second half of the century, whether they relied on physical or cultural characteristics, or a mixture of both, also resulted in the placing of Europeans at the top of the racial hierarchy.

Such an outcome was partly achieved by selective comparisons between the most advanced Western cultures and the least advanced elsewhere. The Victorians' preoccupation with the achievements of their own age did not, however, involve contempt for the past. On the contrary, the scientific discoveries which altered their knowledge of the age of earth and man, together with their awareness of the accelerating pace of change, made them intensely interested in what they saw as the organic simplicity of the medieval world or the high culture of the Ancients. What they could not admire were societies which, in the state of knowledge prevailing for most of the century, might have an exotic fascination but were thought to have no history: no law, no great towns, monuments or artefacts.

Commentators who emphasised the gulf existing between white and non-white races took fresh heart at mid-century from the writings of Charles Darwin. Darwin only reluctantly accepted the application of his doctrines to man, and in scientific terms they obviously undermined the arguments supporting polygenesis: that is, that races constituted separate species with separate origins. And yet because the theory of natural selection, as popularised by Herbert Spencer, stressed the differences between human varieties and the inevitable destruction of those least equipped to survive, it further weakened Christian environmentalism and brought Britain more into line with thinking abroad which elevated the influence of heredity. Although Victorian faith in social evolution was fed from many sources and Social Darwinist doctrines were espoused by men with varied views on politics and empire, once in the hands of popularisers they could be – and were – used to justify both class rule and race discrimination.

Of course Darwin did not finally demonstrate which races were stronger, more intelligent and better suited to succeed than others. The fate of aboriginal tribes apparently did, and was taken up with new relish. Additional debate was stimulated by those racial interpretations of history which had been appearing from around the 1840s in Britain as part of the growth of Romantic nationalism, and were destined to become so common at the end of the nineteenth century and during the first decades of the twentieth. And since a universally acceptable definition of the Aryan race remained elusive, the British, French and Germans all continued to claim to be the only true descendants of the original Aryans, and therefore pre-eminent among races. In other words, the internationalist implications of the theory of a unified Aryan race were undermined by ethnocentric, nationalist attempts to monopolise this ingenious proof of virtue. Hence race became a useful tool in distinguishing between the ostensibly similar white peoples of Europe, for the differences between the various racial components of Britain and Europe could assume as much significance in the Victorian mind as those between the white and coloured races.

But if certain Victorian scientists were racists, the confusion of race and culture and the delight in measurement and classification infected many Victorians whose writings were too unsystematic to be classified as racist. It would likewise be wrong to suggest that most of those who contributed to the scientific debate were motivated simply or largely by prejudice. Hunt and company did believe that 'the success of our colonisation depend(s) on the deductions of our science' and that 'the composition of harmonious nations (was) entirely a question of race'. It was another matter to secure the implementations of these ideas, owing to their initially limited political value. Britain did not contain the large and 'threatening' ethnic groups to be found in the United States, and even there scholars differ about the application of scientific racism. By the end of the century, anthropologists had gained ground in both countries, but 'applied anthropology' did not emerge for some years on either side of the Atlantic and the discipline continued to be criticised as amateurish in methods and antiquarian in bent. However, the work of the scientists was important because it gave the weight associated with ordered, empirical data to widely circulating ideas which seemed to conform to Victorian domestic realities and experience of the wider world. It appeared to confirm the inevitability of racial conflict, the validity of generalising about group characteristics, the desirability of racial purity, the need to control 'inferior' elements in any race, and the justice of imposing European civilisation on the hunting economies and cultural crudities of 'savagery'.

We must now sketch in the other influences which shaped the racial attitudes Britons took abroad with them, and which affected both the domestic discussion of empire and race relations within the colonies. It should be stressed at the outset that many of the available records – private papers, periodicals, newspapers, official documents, the memoirs of traders, soldiers, travellers, settlers – largely reveal the ignorance or particular interest of the individuals commenting. Naturally, there were principled, educated and sensitive exceptions to this rule. But most Victorians did not have first-hand experience of black and other ethnic groups in Britain, while the majority of those who visited imperial outposts stayed too briefly abroad or were too insulated from native culture by their transplanted institutions to penetrate below the surface of things. The frequently alarmist tone of the British and colonial press on matters pertaining to race may have been designed in part to sell copy or may have reflected predominantly middle-class anxieties, even when a journal was ostensibly speaking for labour. Indeed, a real difficulty is posed by the scarcity of working-class documents which illuminate racial attitudes. Neither British labour newspapers nor the ballads and poems enjoyed by the working class displayed much interest in racial themes, though exotic and Oriental tales had a certain attraction. We are consequently heavily dependent on studying the *behaviour* of this class for indications of its thinking about race.

On the other hand, literary sources (including literature for children) and the evidence contained in minstrelsy, cartoons, illustrations and advertisements, though they do not explain changes in British racial attitudes or the forces shaping them, are an excellent guide to the racial stereotypes that all kinds of Victorians found acceptable. Where an author's works were bestsellers, as for example in the case of G. A. Henty, they as much as factual reports may actually have shaped the views of individuals who subsequently went out to empire or helped to frame imperial policy.[5] All the same, caution should be employed in judging the impact of popular fiction on racial opinions because, more than is the case with most literary materials, we do not know what readers absorbed and what they ignored. The 'nigger minstrel' shows which were particularly popular from the 1840s to the 1870s have also been seen as reinforcing disparaging stereotypes of blacks among the Anglo-American Victorian public at large, and it is highly probable that they did so, despite the minstrels' presentation of plantation life in both sympathetic and comic terms. Yet it seems equally sensible to assume that some of the minstrels' patrons merely went to stare and did not ponder what they had seen, and that some were primarily impressed by the good-humoured foolery, spirited music and evocation of a vanishing rural world that the performances afforded.

Victorian attitudes to race were profoundly affected by the presence in Britain of other non-white visitors, as well as established communities of non-whites and of white immigrants. Antipathies towards strangers did not simply depend upon a considerable 'alien' presence, for such aversion, fed by fear and fancy, may grow as easily in a population where outsiders are little known as in areas where they are numerous. Unfortunately, while much new work is in progress, there are still large gaps in our knowledge about the lives and racial opinions of the Chinese, Indian and black Britons located mainly in the cities, army, navy and merchant marine. It is similarly hard to present a complete picture of the non-white visitors to Britain during the nineteenth century: the ex-slaves turned orator or clergyman, African and West Indian students, imperial dignitaries, black minstrels and North American Indians. Some evidence suggests that even visitors who were kindly received appeared to have been respected for political reasons or enjoyed as exotic reminders of a simpler age. Many were not happy with their reception.

Lorimer has argued, with regard to the black strangers, that before about the 1860s their social standing had determined the treatment they received in Britain, but that from then onwards, as a result primarily of changes in English society, 'the idea of a "black gentleman" became a contradiction in terms'.[6] We also know that black Britons suffered from the loss of the aristocratic white patronage they had enjoyed in the eighteenth century, and possibly from a decline in community solidarity.[7] Although non-whites were never sufficiently numerous to provoke legal discrimination, anti-miscegenation laws or race riots on the American pattern, it would be unwise to assume from existing evidence that the degree of mutual toleration which persisted in Victorian Britain could have survived any large non-white influx. This pessimism would appear to be further justified by the experiences of nineteenth-century white immigrants.

The impact of such immigrants on British society is an extremely complicated one. The most strident pronouncements on race were to be found in London and the south of England, as a result of the concentration of 'aliens', newspapers and anthropological inquiry in the capital, and the high representation of Conservatives and retired colonials in the region as a whole. The lives of strangers in the provinces could prove very different, though not necessarily better. In the main, however, attitudes towards settlers stiffened when they became numerous – the Irish from the 1830s, the Jewish immigrants from the 1880s. They did not improve until the dislocations caused by their arrival had eased, and the newcomers were meanwhile denounced as degraded, un-English competitors for scarce resources. Culture-shock was often eased for both sides by the native Britons' habit of preaching assimilation but practising residential segregation, a pattern easily transplanted to and extended in the colonies, where whites, though the invaders, were determined to preserve both their distinctiveness and their vaunted superiority.

So far the case seems clear for explaining British aversion to strangers in terms of tangible social factors, but there was an extra racial dimension involved in Victorian responses to immigrants. Accordingly the English levied racial slights against the Germans, Irish and Jews, and the Scots against the Irish and Lithuanians in their midst. And if the English conviction of the inferiority of Irish 'Celts' may have been exaggerated, while part of the stereotype of 'Paddy' was fostered by the Irish themselves, the resentments these slurs produced in many Irishmen played no little part in nourishing Irish nationalism and a hatred of English racial pretensions, wherever they were manifested in the world.[8]

Of course in the end all these groups, being white, could be and were assimilated fairly quickly into British society. The racial vein in ethnocentrism, like ethnocentrism itself, fluctuated according to changing economic and political circumstances and could vanish altogether if the circumstances were right. By contrast, the frequent existence of contradictory stereotypes regarding any race did not undermine belief in the basically immutable qualities of its members, or in its fixed status within the contemporary racial hierarchy. Moreover, British ethnocentrism could manifest itself as easily in Francophobia or Russophobia as in any form of racism, and paralleled the similar expressions of vanity which burgeoning

nationalism was encouraging in America and continental
Europe. But when every reservation has been noted, the
Victorian acquaintance with strangers at home could only
serve to strengthen their dislike, on racial and other grounds, of
'alien' races encountered overseas.

What it did not do, because of the limited number of
non-whites in Britain, was to create a clear political interest in
racial discrimination such as that primarily represented by the
Democratic party in the United States for much of the
nineteenth century. In both countries, nevertheless, political
parties were quick to take account of the presence of minority
groups who were potential voters or against whose presence
other voters might be mobilised. In both countries, anti-
Catholic sentiments were very useful to politicians looking for
votes. Notable are the efforts of British Conservatives to rally
anti-Irish opinion in the 1840s, and in Lancashire and Cheshire
in the 1860s. This ability to activate ethnic resentments,
particularly strong in the mid-Victorian period, relates to the
comparative decline of class conflict as well as the growing
interest in race. It was once more apparent when, to the
backdrop of 'new imperialism', clamour mounted to restrict the
'alien invasion'. And again it was the Conservatives who chiefly
manipulated ethnocentric fears to procure working-class support and Jewish exclusion, while Liberals, Radicals and
Labour Members of Parliament argued that the problems
associated with immigration could be cured by other means
and were anyway exaggerated.[9]

We see here another of the many connections between
domestic and colonial attitudes to race and empire. Ethnic
groups in Britain were not drawn into politics via the boss
system, as they were in the United States. Yet it was
increasingly difficult for Victorian leaders of the Liberal-
Radical 'left', which needed the support of nonconformist and
nationality groups, including the Irish, to endorse either
political appeals to ethnocentrism within Britain or support for
colonies in which 'Anglo-Saxon' minorities ruled over native
majorities in the pride of racial conquest. The embarrassments
which this vital connection created for the left are perhaps best
seen, outside the Home Rule conflicts, in the Irish Nationalist

opposition to the Boer War, with denunciations being made of the British army and prayers offered that God might 'strengthen Boer resistance'.[10]

The British educational system, self-image, class assumptions and sexual mores were all comparably important in their influence on 'race-thinking' at home and in the empire. The absence in Africa especially of the institutions associated in Britain with civilisation was put down to the racial deficiencies of blacks. The colonised were condemned because they lacked culture, as Britons understood it, but the assumptions of the colonisers, fashioned in part at school, implied the impossibility of its development among foreigners. Various scholars have noted that at British public schools, by the third quarter of the nineteenth century, ambitious men acquired genteel status and an outlook which revered group loyalty rather than the sentimental individualism of the Evangelical era.[11] When their graduates went out to serve the empire or make their way, their strongly held values linked them to each other more firmly than uncomfortable exiles might normally have been, and made them peculiarly unresponsive to contrasting qualities in white 'outsiders' and 'alien' races. Thus if the culture of black peoples was crudely misinterpreted, even Indian groups – notably the Hindus – were disparagingly depicted as the antithesis of the British public school ideal: namely unduly pious, complacent, effeminate, easily led and treacherous. The Indians, however, were at least accorded more diversity than black peoples.[12]

Victorians applied this ethnocentric yardstick in a number of ways. They could, for instance, admire Indian races who showed some of their own combative instincts, and recruited these 'martial' races into the Indian army. In Africa, too, Britons distinguished between timid and warlike tribes, seeking to recruit from the latter the native troops they needed to help sustain a presence there. Similarly, using alleged British attributes as the norm, the inhabitants of China and India were more acceptable than those of Africa because, whatever their suspected deceitfulness, they had none of the supposed indolence of blacks. In fact, while Asian 'coolie' labour was meant to be the answer to the problems of the West Indian planters, the legendary diligence of the vast Chinese population eventually became a cause for white concern. The response to the Chinese abroad offers a salutary reminder that even favourable racial stereotypes could be ignored if economic and social circumstances seemed threatening to the white majority. Indian minorities overseas, though useful, were likewise feared as a disturbing example to other non-whites and a threat to white supremacy.[13] Many Britons in Africa and elsewhere were themselves indolent: sometimes because of the effects of a tropical climate, sometimes exploiting others to avoid severe exertion on their own part and thus scarcely measuring up to the Victorians' Christian code. But they were unwilling to deny the benefits of that code to their 'inferiors'; 'steady industry', the *Spectator* remarked, 'in English opinion, is the single virtue, except reverence for white faces, to be demanded of black men'.

Having become so self-conscious about their own attributes, Victorians reacted still more unfavourably to the appearance of black people. In India, conversely, if Englishmen had some harsh things to say about the dark southern tribes, other sections of the population measured up to European standards of beauty. The Aryans of the north, as politician and administrator Sir George Campbell put it, were often 'magnificently handsome', with features of an English cast and a gratifying inclination to revere a pale skin. Queen Victoria, whose views on race were liberal, and who was anxious that '*all* her Colonial Governors should *know* her feelings on this subject', was most insistent that Indians should not be called black men.

The black individual was also displeasing to whites, so the prominent lecturer Robert Knox maintained, because he was to be feared: his brute energy 'is considerable; aided by the sun, he repels the white invader'. This kind of judgement gained a wide currency in Britain because of the public taste – fostered or catered to by a sensationalist popular press – for heroic exploits in which the British army or pioneers engaged a savage foe, preferably despite daunting odds. It worked against the respect for 'martial' races which we have noted, and was further encouraged by the fact that imperial military crises provoked heated discussion in the 'serious' papers, as well as among outraged conservatives and the 'non-serious' novelists of empire whose 'adventure tales', as Martin Green among others has argued, 'formed the . . . energizing myth of English imperialism'.[14] And although these writers might stress the ferocity of such enemies as the Zulus, one has the feeling that they did so in part to throw the achievements of the British into romantic relief. Black 'savagery' was demonstrated by the endemic native wars in South Africa and what the historian Thomas Carlyle described as 'miserable mad seditions' like the Jamaica revolt of 1865. Indian groups were, on the whole, less suspiciously regarded, and the Indian Mutiny was felt to be less a product of innate sepoy brutality, albeit there was much initial uproar along these lines, than of the interference by Britain with established local customs. Yet the validity of 'might is right' was seldom questioned where blacks were involved. According to a white colonist writing in *The Times* during the 1860s, strong rule over such 'savages [was] vital or we shall not be in existence to be ruled at all'.

Here we see another major difference between Indians and blacks, to the Victorian mind. Long before the end of the nineteenth century, many Victorian colonisers evidently expected that they would be misunderstood. Nonetheless, the Indian middle class apparently displayed its appreciation of British rule by an initial acceptance of English education, language and literature. And Cohen has shown that in the Indian army the development of this gratitude was not left to chance. Rather, great care was taken to preserve and go beyond the dependent relationship by appealing to caste pride and combining a hierarchical organisation with 'a rough public-school variety of equalitarianism'. Even during the Mutiny the existence of loyal sepoys was celebrated, and of course the faithful native retainer was a favourite device in fiction dealing with empire.[15] Unfortunately the ruling race failed to see that genuine gratitude is only possible between acknowledged equals, and that dependent status too often comes to be regarded by those who experience it as inferior status. Unlike the Indians, blacks in various parts of Africa and the West Indies were felt to be largely unappreciative of British efforts among them, and the resentment this produced did much to unite colonist and domestic taxpayer.

However, whereas Victorians distinguished between African and West Indian blacks on the one hand, and Indians and Chinese on the other, there is little to show that they acted upon these distinctions in Britain. Moreover, they did not fully acknowledge the civilised attainments of the latter groups. No dominant people has ever avoided convictions about the superiority – social, racial or both – of its representatives. Therefore while the British recognised Indian cultural achievements and the Aryan tie between themselves and their Indian subjects, Indian decadence was emphasised long before the Mutiny, and the British presence was justified with references to the stranglehold of caste or the pitfalls of sensual religious practices. The progress for which the Anglo-Saxons were famous was denied to Indians, since they themselves despised it; and so, because an end to British rule could not be envisaged in the foreseeable future, increasingly all that mattered was British power.

Apart from the historic colour prejudice which it greatly strengthened, of all the features of nineteenth-century racial thought, possibly the most influential in its relation to imperialism, was this increased association of certain races with unfitness for self-government. It was an association destined to prove as fateful for the Irish 'Celts' as for African and Indian peoples. And it led to the minimising of individual affronts committed by Europeans against non-whites in the empire, which inflamed native opinion, in the comfortable belief that such incidents were scarcely credible aberrations in a ruling race.[16] It seems to relate both to a genuine belief in the merits of the British system of government, which was not confined to Britons, and to various less pleasing sensations. If, as middle-class power and morality apparently triumphed, there was an intensification of upper-class awareness that its distinguishing features were becoming blurred, the middle class itself entertained misgivings about the new business, and increasingly independent, professional groups, as well as about the decline in those opportunities for upward mobility on which a stable class system rested.[17] Such anxieties, noticeable in mid-Victorian times, were intensified by the economic, immigrant and imperial challenges at the end of the century. In this context 'race-thinking' in Britain was evidently cultivated as part of a general search for group certainty in a fast-changing society, just as technology was valued for reassuringly taming the natural world about which so much unsettling new knowledge was being accumulated, and as exposure of the evils of primitive religions appealed to men whose own faith was far from secure.

Imbued with a disturbing sense of change, and dismayed by democratic political pressures on both sides of the Atlantic, Victorians plainly responded to the American Civil War and Reconstruction, and to the Jamaica revolt of 1865, according to what Huxley termed their 'deepest political convictions'. These in turn reflected their class position, with only Radicals and labour spokesmen displaying much anxiety about military rule or semi-despotic government for 'alien' races and their possible link with opposition to the expansion of working-class rights at home. Under such circumstances, it is not surprising to find that authoritarian political and racial views not only became more attractive by mid-century but tended to go together for many middle-class commentators within Britain, as one can particularly clearly see in the reporting of these crises by the conservative press. Ironically, though Victorians justified strong government over 'inferiors', they deplored – while often supporting – native autocracy in India, West Africa and the tropics.

When Englishmen went abroad, they found that the racial component helped to justify 'dominant minority'[18] status and provide additional assurance, when 'aliens' were unwelcoming, that the Englishman had an innate status which need not be earned. The assertion of racial superiority thus classically became a justification for avoiding social intercourse with the poor or disreputable and a means of resisting any challenge to minority privileges. Colour consciousness was buttressed by class bias especially strongly in Africa and the West Indies, where invariable poverty and consequent low status made the coloured population an obvious target of contempt for whites, whether of the middle or upper class, who were accustomed to despise uneducated working-men of their own race and to equate black and white 'savages' at home. Middle-class bias in turn had an unfortunate effect upon working-class Victorians.

Although generally proclaiming themselves to be anti-slavery, labour leaders in Britain were not necessarily pro-black, resisting any equation of 'the pallid toiler and the negro chattel', despite the eventual extension of union protection to the country's ethnic minorities. Working-men also resented

any concern for subject races in the empire which diverted
attention from pressing domestic ills. As the question was
posed during the Boer War, 'what does it matter to me what is
being done . . . amongst the blacks anywhere? All I want is
victuals'.[19] We know comparatively little about the racial
opinions of working-class Englishmen overseas. As far as
behaviour is concerned, there is some evidence that they were
the worst offenders against the weakest sections of native
populations. Certainly in England, her colonies, and the
American South alike, the ruling elites liked to think that racial
'excesses' were confined to the lowest elements in white society.
And equally plainly some aristocratic Britons – including
Canning, Curzon, Lytton and Salisbury – tried to restrain
expressions of race prejudice. It would seem that their belief in
the importance of 'breeding' in people as well as animals could
be beneficial for all kinds of 'inferiors', in so far as it invoked the
kind of paternalism which gentlemen should exercise over
servants.[20] On the other hand, the scarce records reveal
scattered expressions of working-class sympathy with non-
whites they encountered in the empire. Private soldiers in the
Indian army, for example, might stress the superiority of white
troops and deplore the cruelty and poverty of the sepoys, but
could admire the beauty of India's women, the glamour and
good looks of its princes, the bravery of the native troops, and
the diligence and simplicity of Indian peasants.

After the Mutiny, there are signs that the British rank-and-
file shared with their officers an indignant hatred of the native
population, who were described as 'fiends' and 'brutes', or
(sarcastically) 'sable friends' and 'gallant black sons of Mars'.
As Queen Victoria feared, Indians had become 'niggers' to
whites (in India *and* Britain) who might once have distinguished them as superior to blacks, and Indian army camp
followers were quick to perceive this. Even so, there remained
the same soldierly dislike of extreme brutality towards the
enemy as there was of officers who despised their men 'as the
lowest class of animal'. And such feelings could survive within
the stereotyped common soldier who, as presented in the
person of G. A. Henty's Tim Kelly in *With Clive in India* (1884),
believed that natives were black heathens who ought to learn
English but meanwhile should understand if shouted at. In

some ways the more rigid insistence of the white middle class upon proper respect, and its successful recreation of English institutions in an alien setting, provoked as much resentment as the blunter rejection of foreign ways by the working-class section of the Victorian presence.

Indeed, racial and class prejudices were so intertwined in Victorian times that it is hard to separate them. Suffice it to say that London officials frequently looked suspiciously on all colonists with a personal economic stake in the empire, or snobbishly at their civil servants overseas. Administrators in the colonies might be patronising towards colonial whites or critical of missionaries, and many Victorians were censorious of British employers of native labour. Members of settled expatriate communities, some of whom saw themselves as engaged in social reform comparable to that going forward in Britain, looked down on the birds of passage, fleeing from a shady past or openly in search of a windfall. But all these whites, from private soldier to district commissioner, had the same basic interest in claiming the deference due to the British race, even if they did not personally epitomise its achievements or sustain such solidarity at home. Their race did set them together and apart from all kinds of non-whites. This distancing increased over time throughout the empire, sometimes as part of a struggle by white ex-slaveholders to reassert a once unquestioned dominance; sometimes because of growing numbers of whites, including women; sometimes as a result of native aversion, which Western education only marginally broke down. Another influential factor was the increasing frequency of home visits, facilitated by improved transport, a point made by Lord Northbrook to Queen Victoria in explaining post-Mutiny tensions, though death and ill-health had caused regular changes in imperial personnel long before.

The arrival of white women is seen as causing a rift between white and Indian society by the middle of the nineteenth century, with signs of strain evident much earlier. In Africa, the comfortable era of native mistresses came to an end for many European men by the end of the century. Undoubtedly the memoirs of empire left by Victorian *memsahibs* do not suggest that they were any more sympathetic to 'feminine races' there than they could afford to be at home. Some inter-racial sex and marriage took place in Victorian Britain, primarily involving white women. It was deplored by middle-class white men whose sentimental image of the opposite sex could not allow for civilised women co-habiting with 'lesser breeds', and who generally denounced the corrupting or democratising effects of sex between individuals of unequal rank. And this despite the prostitution which existed in Britain on a massive scale, providing a powerful link between the respectable classes and the disreputable poor. While such attitudes prevailed, the only proper role for white women in relation to non-whites was as supporters of philanthropy which operated at a safe distance from its object.

Women overseas, whatever the effect on them of these taboos, struggled to force entry into a masculine world, to 'manage' servants reluctant to take orders from women, and to survive without most of the sophisticated cultural amenities or the strong family network that were supposed to be their special province. They might in the process show much curiosity about native peoples, and the *noblesse oblige* towards social inferiors which would be expected in Britain. But there was little to stimulate cultural relativism in a group of female dependents or subordinates, who were concerned not to be hampered by association with other dependent groups. They were normally wary of incurring the disapproval of their menfolk, and had no wish to 'sink' to what was seen as the utterly inferior status of non-white women, at a time when the position of women was taken as one of the measurements of the degree of civilisation attained by any society. The situation of the Victorian *memsahibs* was also not unlike that of white women in the American South, in that they were aware of the sexual liaisons between their menfolk and native women, a nice reversal of the situation in Britain. They were aware, too, that the very 'inferiority' of such women – allegedly shown by their sensuality and 'easiness' – could be an attraction seldom openly acknowledged but nevertheless touched on by novelists and other writers. Under these circumstances it might be as appealing as propagandists hoped it would for white women to proclaim themselves the rearers and preservers of the imperial British race.

The one area where the customary underlay of white unity

abroad did not prevail was in and regarding South Africa. There the race situation was complicated by the presence of Eurafricans as well as Africans, and a minority of both English- and Afrikaans-speaking whites. When conflict eventually broke out between the latter in the Anglo-Boer War, fought between whites for control of the region for nationalist and trade reasons, British racial assumptions were to be a source of weakness rather than strength. For while Victorians claimed not to be tainted by the race prejudice of the Boers and to be determined to abandon neither the natives nor the *uitlanders* to Afrikaner 'oppression', their military victories against 'lesser breeds' had given them a false notion of what the British could achieve. And they could not see the similarities between English and Boer settler defences of white behaviour in South Africa. Consequently, many were able to persuade themselves – before events proved otherwise, and notwithstanding the existence of some sympathy for the Afrikaners as fellow whites – that the Boers were an inferior race, savage and indolent, over whom victory was inevitable.

III

Can we draw some broad conclusions about these Victorian observations on race, at home and abroad, and present them as in some sense an expression of Victorian imperialism? It is tempting to tidy Victorian prejudice into neat generalities, and prejudice and imperialism alike into 'periods'. This, however, can be distorting. For just as we can see fundamental continuities in African, West Indian and Indian social patterns, despite colonial rule, so we can see similar continuities in racial ideas, despite the mid-century lurch towards racism, given an additional impetus by the later scramble for Africa in which philanthropic pressures played no small part. Thus throughout the nineteenth century, racial stereotypes allowed 'inferiors' some good qualities, notably simplicity, spontaneity, intuition. They were permitted, no doubt, as a reminder to the civilised world of what it had lost or as a demonstration of the tolerance for which the British race was said to be famous: permitted nonetheless.[21] Victorians were prepared to exercise candour a little further and admit faults in the British people, particularly displayed abroad. Miscegenation was one obvious example.

A couple more illustrations may suffice to show why we should avoid simple 'overviews'. In India, the eighteenth- and nineteenth-century accommodation of the British to their subjects is acknowledged to have been halted by the desire of Evangelical and Utilitarian reformers to refashion major aspects of Oriental society in the Western image, in order to improve Britain's administration of the continent. Yet even so influential an Orientalist as Sir William Jones – attacked by James Mill as an uncritical romantic – did not claim that Indian civilisation was better than European. Indeed he justified absolute rule by whites in India, was mistrustful of ordinary people there and at home, and never treated his Indian contacts as equals.[22] The Mutiny produced an intense degree of racial hatred among the British which took years to diminish, led to harsh reprisals and a spate of novels designed, in Singh's judgement, to reassure Victorians that all would again be well within the empire because of British courage and ingenuity. But there were, according to Greenberger, no real signs of melancholy or insecurity in Victorian fiction concerning India. In certain respects race relations were worse in the 1880s, following the Ilbert Bill proposing that Indian judges should be allowed to try European British subjects, and the formation of the Indian Congress Party. And though the old Orientalism had vanished, the post-Mutiny period saw its resurgence in a revised form as a means of enhancing British power over the native population.[23]

Finally, despite their fear and dislike of the educated, Westernised native, the British employed Asian immigrants in positions of responsibility throughout East Africa. Even the reduction of opportunities for educated Africans in the administration of West Africa by the end of the nineteenth century can be explained not only as a result of growing prejudice, but also as a consequence of higher educational standards and the appearance of a large supply of British graduates who possessed them, whereas the African applicants frequently did not.[24]

The relationship between Victorian racial opinions and the formal justifications of empire is also far from clear, beyond the fact that both upheld the expansive superiority of British civilisation. What the state of scholarship at the moment would suggest is that there is no demonstrable *causal* relationship between racism, expansionism and colonial policy, especially in the 'pragmatic' mid-Victorian period. Moreover, it is widely accepted that after 1870 the majority of British acquisitions were designed to strengthen existing possessions, while in the imperialism of the late nineteenth century economic motives played a more prominent role. Although racial views as such hardened fairly steadily in the second half of the nineteenth century, that form of imperialism represented by Dilke and Chamberlain, which emphasised the global destiny of the Anglo-Saxon race and saw its British branch as, in Chamberlain's words, the 'greatest of governing races that the world has ever seen', had been overshadowed by the end of the century by the rather different emphases of Liberal empire, and of the glorifiers of the nation state and the 'market view' of empire.[25] Equally apparent is the fact that Victorian anti-imperialists, some of whom were strongly critical of British treatment of native races, did not contribute fundamentally to the abandonment of empire, but rather to the acceptance of indirect rule as a means of modifying, without abandoning, existing responsibilities.[26]

Acknowledging these difficulties, the connection between race and imperialism would seem to be roughly as follows. One definition of imperialism is that it constitutes the sustained assertion of power over others, and the development of justifications for its assertion. Political power, in Stokes' words, might tend 'to deposit itself in the hands of a natural aristocracy', but that power had, ostensibly at least, to be exercised with justice and mercy. British rule overseas was defended as paternalistic not racist, through the extension to the colonised of the benefits of British civilisation. Race would initially appear to have been an expression of Victorian imperialism in so far as the attributes of the British race and British civilisation were invariably confused, and the claimed superiority of the Anglo-Saxon race was used to reassure Britons that they had a humane mission, that their power abroad would be well used.[27] As the growth of the empire and of opposition among the colonised suggested that imperial responsibilities would last longer and weigh heavier than was once supposed, the ideology of Anglo-Saxon supremacy more than ever served as a guide and comfort to the colonisers and as a rationale for coercion of their troublesome subjects. Race is therefore less the moving force behind British imperialism, or the key to understanding its forms, than its variable though invaluable adjunct.

7. Imperialism and Social Reform

M. E. CHAMBERLAIN

'The Empire is a bread and butter question', Cecil John Rhodes declared in 1895. He had just attended a meeting of the unemployed in the East End of London and his journalist friend, W. T. Stead, recorded his impressions. 'I listened', said Rhodes,

> to the wild speeches, which were just a cry for 'bread! bread!' and on my way home I pondered over the scene and I became more than ever convinced of the importance of imperialism. . . . My cherished idea is a solution for the social problem, i.e., in order to save the 40,000,000 inhabitants of the United Kingdom from a bloody civil war, we colonial statesmen must acquire new lands to settle the surplus population, to provide new markets for the goods produced in the factories and mines.

V. I. Lenin noted the quotation and used it in his *Imperialism, the Highest Stage of Capitalism*, published in 1917.[1] The close connection between imperialism and what they called 'the social question' at home, was very clear both to the advocates and to the opponents of colonial expansion.

The mid-Victorian period, the 1850s and 1860s, had been an exceptionally prosperous one in Britain but, in 1873, a crash on the Vienna money market heralded the beginning of a long depression which affected the whole of western Europe to a greater or lesser extent. In Britain agriculture came under severe pressure from the new grain imports from North America and meat imports from South America and Australia.

There was chronic over-capacity in many industries, notably in iron and steel. The slump seemed to be of the type which some economists would now refer to as L-shaped. For a long period there were no signs, or only false signs, of recovery. By 1879 both British and continental economists were becoming seriously worried. In 1885 the British government agreed to the setting up of a Royal Commission to investigate the 'Depression of Trade and Industry'. The options before the British government seemed, however, to be strictly limited. The last serious depression they had known had been that of the 1840s. Almost everyone believed that that had been cured by the adoption of free trade and, more particularly, by the abolition of the Corn Laws in 1846. Protectionism was associated with 'dear bread' and the depression of the economy. Only a very bold man would advocate a return to that discredited policy.

The Royal Commission sat for two years and collected a massive amount of evidence, from chambers of commerce, trade associations of various kinds, trade unions, and both British and foreign experts. One of the few books which makes any attempt to analyse the significance of its findings for a study of imperial expansion is J. E. Tyler's *The Struggle for Imperial Unity*, published as long ago as 1938. On some points the evidence before the Royal Commission was almost unanimous. There was a serious depression, affecting most trades and industries, characterised by surplus production, low prices, poor investment opportunities and unemployment. Furthermore, the depression had been going on for a long time and there were few signs of an up-turn. When it came to suggesting causes or remedies, there was more disagreement. Interestingly, few employers suggested that the fault lay with their own workmen. In reply to direct questions, they tended to dismiss the idea that the problem arose from wage levels or demands for shorter hours. But many did believe that the problem was foreign competition. By the 1880s it was clear that Britain was no longer alone in the industrial field. Germany and the United States were becoming formidable competitors and even France posed some threat. The United States had had high tariffs since the Civil War, while Germany had imposed a protectionist tariff in 1879 and France in 1882. It would have been flying in the face of all economic orthodoxy in Britain at the time to suggest that British industry could not defend its share of the world market in conditions of free competition, but the argument did begin to be heard that these were not conditions of free competition and that foreign industries were being artificially boosted and favoured by their governments. A number of chambers of commerce, in reply to the commissioners' questions, emphasised the need to keep foreign markets open to British trade and to find new markets. A few even spoke specifically of new colonial markets, especially in Africa.

The members of the commission were unable to agree on their report and eventually produced a majority and a minority report. The majority report restated all the orthodox free trade arguments and advocated very little action. The minority report was signed by the Earl of Dunraven, Nevile Lubbock, W. Farrer Ecroyd and Philip Muntz. Lubbock was a director of the Colonial Bank and a vice-president of the Royal Colonial Institute. Farrer Ecroyd was the Conservative MP for the textile town of Preston and Philip Muntz for Tamworth. Lord Dunraven is best known for his attempts to find a compromise solution to the Irish problem in the early twentieth century but in the 1880s he was a rising young politician, with a particular interest in colonial affairs, who was twice to serve as Parliamentary Under-Secretary at the Colonial Office. In May 1881 Dunraven had become the first president of the Fair Trade League, of which Lubbock, Ecroyd and Muntz were also members. The League had been formed to demand protection, or as they would have preferred to say 'fair play', for British industry and the British working-man against foreign competitors and their government backers. Orthodox economists were scandalised but the League won a considerable working-class following from those who flocked to their meetings from Bermondsey to Sheffield.[2]

The minority report came near to advocating a system of imperial preference. Britain's colonies, they insisted, provided her safest market. In 1884, three million Australians had purchased £23 million of British goods while fifty-five million Americans had bought only £24 million worth. India was even more important. Comparing the quinquennium 1880–4 with that of 1870–4, exports of worsted and woollen manufactures and yarns had decreased by 30 per cent and those of cotton manufactures and yarns by only 1 per cent. The difference was almost entirely accounted for by the Indian market, which had taken an additional £30 million worth of cotton goods, while exports to other places had declined by £26 million. The proposition that the possession of a colonial empire cushioned Britain and Holland from the worst effects of the recession was one which was also familiar to German writers and played a significant part in the propaganda for the establishment of a German colonial empire.

On this argument colonial outlets were necessary for economic stability at home and on economic stability rested social stability. European governments had good reason to be frightened of the forces which they saw rising up round them. Population was increasing at an unprecedented rate. In Britain the population had risen from 12 million in 1801 to 21 million in 1851 and to nearly 42 million in 1901. Continental figures were comparable. As long ago as 1798 Thomas Malthus had drawn attention to the dire consequences of the population increase outrunning the means of subsistence, which always increased more slowly. Malthus based his estimates on the best statistics then available and his arguments carried conviction. The idea of limiting the population by birth control was anathema to most nineteenth-century writers – and the means available were generally unsatisfactory and unreliable. Emigration therefore seemed to provide the only safety valve. This consideration made a number of anti-colonial thinkers in the early nineteenth century, including even Jeremy Bentham, pause in their wholesale condemnation of colonies.

Population pressure is one of the oldest revolutionary forces in human history and in the nineteenth century it took some particularly ominous forms. In Britain a high proportion of the population was now herded together in the new manufacturing towns. Housing conditions were often bad; the amenities of life poor. Literacy was more widespread. Revolutionary philosophies, including communism and socialism – nineteenth-century conservatives tended not to distinguish between them – had a better chance than ever before of gaining a hearing.

To distract malcontents at home by spectacular successes

abroad is an ancient device of nervous governments. It might be expected that an imperial policy would be peculiarly well adapted for this. The government could appeal not only to the patriotism of the workers to postpone their demands but, more subtly, to their vanity. Their wages might be low and their housing conditions unpleasant but they could take comfort from the fact that they were part of a governing race. In France Napoleon III embarked on his Mexican adventure in 1861, as Charles X had embarked on his Algerian adventure over thirty years earlier, as just such a distraction. H.-U. Wehler in his *Bismarck und der Imperialismus* (summarised in his 'Bismarck's Imperialism, 1862–1890' in *Past and Present*, 48 (1970), 119–55) suggests that this kind of 'Bonapartism' played some part in Bismarck's policy. The idea is also briefly discussed in Bernard Semmel's *Imperialism and Social Reform* (1960). One of the most influential critics of imperialism, J. A. Hobson, believed that the newly literate British public was peculiarly vulnerable to such propaganda. 'Popular education', he wrote in *Imperialism, a Study*, 'instead of serving as a defence, is an incitement towards Imperialism: it has opened up a panorama of vulgar pride and crude sensationalism to a great inert mass who see current history and the tangled maze of world movements with dim, bewildered eyes.'[3]

This 'Bonapartist' element has not generally been regarded as very important in the development of British imperialism. In France the Napoleonic legend of a victorious foreign policy was a genuinely potent myth. In nineteenth-century Britain, foreign policy only intermittently roused much interest – and imperial policy even less. T. B. Macauley complained, when the British empire in India was near its height, that an Indian debate emptied the House of Commons quicker than the dinner bell. But it may be necessary to revise this judgement in the light of Freda Harcourt's thought-provoking article on 'Disraeli's Imperialism, 1866–1868: a question of timing', in which she argues that, at the time of the extension of the franchise in the Second Reform Act, Disraeli quite deliberately invoked imperialism as a national objective to distract attention from the increasing class conflicts at home. On this analysis the Abyssinian campaign of 1867–8 becomes an exact parallel with Charles X's Algerian adventure of 1830.[4]

But many politicians, both British and continental (and Benjamin Disraeli was probably among their number) espoused the imperial idea, not because they thought it would provide a distraction from the social question but because they genuinely believed that it offered a potential solution. Cecil Rhodes, quoted at the beginning of this chapter, was a convert to this view. Rhodes was unusual in that he was interested first in British possessions overseas and only subsequently in their importance for solving social problems at home. Most men came to this conclusion by the other route, deep concern for social evils at home, followed by the grasping of a possible solution in the empire.

The idea that the colonies and the mother country should play complementary roles in each other's economy was, of course, a very old one. It underlay the whole concept of eighteenth-century mercantilist empires but it also survived in various forms the apparently anti-colonial sentiments of the early nineteenth century. Sir H. Wilmot Horton had argued for giving paupers a new start in the colonies. Archbishop Whately had linked the idea of assisted emigration with that of encouraging British capital to go to British colonies and building up markets there which would be of benefit to British industry. Edward Gibbon Wakefield's ambitious schemes for systematic colonisation rested essentially on the concept of bringing together the surplus capital and surplus labour of the mother country and the surplus land of the undeveloped colony.

Benjamin Disraeli never actually used the phrase '*imperium et sanitas*' but the popular memory which credited him with it was not badly astray. By '*sanitas*', a word he did use, he meant not, as his Liberal critics derisively suggested, 'a policy of sewage', but the whole social question and the condition of the working classes. Disraeli had begun his political life as a radical and a radical strand always remained in his thought. He introduced a social dimension into Conservative political philosophy, which was conspicuously lacking in contemporary Liberalism. By the standards of the times his administration of 1874–80 had a quite remarkable record in social legislation, with important acts on public health, workers' housing, pure food and the trade unions. His administration was even better remembered for its imperial policy, although 'imperial' in this context tended to mean the defence of India and the route to India, rather than any deep understanding of the empire, including the empire of settlement, as a whole. Whether Disraeli's conversion to the imperial cause was sincere or a cynical election manoeuvre, whether indeed he was 'converted' at all, or whether he had always had a high regard for the empire, must remain controversial. But he taught his party to believe that Britain's greatness and prosperity were linked with her empire and his party included a great many of the newly enfranchised working-men, who saw more concern for their problems among the Conservatives than among the Liberals.

But the man who combined imperialism and social reform *par excellence* was Joseph Chamberlain. There is little doubt by what route Chamberlain came to imperialism. His original concern had been the social question. He had been Radical Joe, the reforming mayor of Birmingham, long before he entered national politics at all. It is not easy to date when Chamberlain first became interested in imperial questions. Some writers, such as Peter Fraser in his *Joseph Chamberlain* (1966), have suggested, as others have of Disraeli, that there was no real moment of conversion and that interest in empire was implicit even in his earlier thought but his official biographer, J. L. Garvin, makes a good case for saying that, as a younger man, Chamberlain's views were really those of a Palmerstonian patriot, and that it was only in the late 1880s that he came to embrace 'imperialism' as the word is usually understood in that period.

If Chamberlain became an imperialist in the late 1880s, there is plenty of evidence that only a few years earlier he had not only believed that Britain was facing a revolutionary situation, but, in the eyes of many, was himself one of the principal actors in it. On 5 January 1885 he had launched his 'unauthorised programme' at a working-men's demonstration at Birmingham Town Hall with his notorious 'ransom' speech. The context was the new parliamentary reform Act but Chamberlain went far beyond the orthodox Liberal line. He told his audience: 'Two millions of men will enter for the first time into the full enjoyment of their political rights . . . and for the first time the toilers and spinners will have a majority of votes and the control, if they desire it, of the Government of the country'. They would demand, he suspected, legislation 'more directed to what are called social subjects than has hitherto been the case'. The measures he had in mind were modest enough: free education, local government reforms, better workers' housing, the provision of allotments and properly directed investments. What alarmed his contemporaries was the searing contrast he drew between the misery of the farm labourer and the urban worker and the privileged life of the propertied classes. 'What ransom', he asked, 'will property pay for the security it enjoys?' His proposals for financing his projected reforms were again modest enough by modern standards – differential income tax, death duties, special taxes on unearned income and levies on ground rents – but he was denounced as 'the advocate of blackmail, confiscation, plunder and communism'.[5]

Joseph Chamberlain is not the easiest of men to understand. He was a powerful but not a charismatic figure. Lord Salisbury once truly said: 'No one ever loved Joe'. He was not a revolutionary in the sense of wishing to overthrow the social order in which he had been born and in which as an individual he had prospered, but his time as Lord Mayor of Birmingham had proved that he had the driving force of the genuine reformer who hated injustice and human suffering. He also hated inefficiency and it is sometimes difficult to tell which he hated most, injustice or inefficiency. But, above all, he was an achiever, a man who if he saw a problem, wanted to do something about setting it right. He did not change his mind about the nature of the social problem or about its urgency but, ten years after his Birmingham speech, he made another speech, on this occasion at Walsall, in which it was clear that he was now looking for very different solutions. This time he told his audience,

> ... to my mind the cause of bad trade, of want of employment, is clear. It is the continual growth of our population at the same time that our trade and industry does not grow in proportion, and if we want our trade and industry to grow we must find new markets for it. Old markets are getting exhausted, some of them are being closed

to us by hostile tariffs, and unless we can find new countries which will be free to take our goods you may be quite satisfied that lack of employment will continue to be one of the greatest of social evils.[6]

It was to try to remedy this situation that he had chosen to take the Colonial Office, in preference even to the Chancellorship of the Exchequer, which had been offered to him. He went on to advocate both the extension of the empire and the treatment of the existing empire as an 'undeveloped estate', which required both investment and planning.

During the seven years he spent at the Colonial Office, Joseph Chamberlain did everything he could to modernise the British empire. It was not simply a matter of replacing candles by electric light and seeing that there were up-to-date maps in the office. He secured legislation to make it easier for colonial governments to raise loans and put in the infrastructure of communications and other facilities which would make poss-ible the development of their economies. Like many men of his time he believed that the future lay with the big states. Only as the centre of a great empire could Britain compete with Germany and the United States. He wanted to see the British empire working as one unit politically, in defence matters and, above all, economically. It was his attempt to bring about an imperial *Zollverein*, or customs union, or at least to reinstate some measure of imperial preference, which broke his party and ended his own political career.

Chamberlain, like Disraeli, had begun his career as a radical but in 1886 he had left the Liberal Party over the Irish question and it was as a member of a Conservative government that he was able to put his imperial policies into operation. But the political right had no kind of monopoly of imperial enthusiasm. Bernard Semmel in his excellent *Imperialism and Social Reform* shows how deeply it permeated into the consciousness of the left. It won the support of the whole Liberal-Imperialist group in men such as Lord Rosebery, H. H. Asquith, R. B. Haldane and Sir Edward Grey. Rosebery expressed his support for the extension of the British empire in language not unlike that of Joseph Chamberlain. If Chamberlain had spoken of 'unde-veloped estates', Rosebery spoke of, in mining language, 'pegging out claims for posterity'. The objective of each man was the same, to secure Britain's economic future. Semmel has gone so far as to say, 'The Liberal programme of 1906–14 . . . was a combination of Radical social reform and imperialist foreign and military policy'.[7]

It was not only one wing of the Liberal party who were converts to imperialism. Many leading Fabians, although they had reservations about the way in which empire had been procured, became enthusiasts for the efficient development of the empire once acquired. Elie Halévy describes Sidney and Beatrice Webb as 'convinced imperialists' and later in his career, in 1929, Sidney Webb willingly took office as Colonial Secretary. George Bernard Shaw was responsible for the publication of the tract, *Fabianism and the Empire* (1900), which supported the British government's attitude to the Boer War. They saw no conflict between their desire for the betterment of the working classes and the support of imperial objectives. Some socialists, such as Karl Pearson, went further and saw a kind of grand design of a Social-Darwinian type in the simultaneous advance of the working classes and of the empire. A similar philosophy, although more mildly expressed, pervades *Fabianism and the Empire*.

The rather scanty evidence available suggests that the working classes themselves favoured the defence and extension of the empire. Friedrich Engels had written despairingly to Kautsky as early as 1882: 'You ask me what the English workers think about colonial policy. . . . There is no workers' party here, there are only Conservatives and Liberal-Radicals, and the workers gaily share the feast of England's monopoly of the world markets and the colonies.'[8] Lenin saw the winning of the working class for the imperial cause as a gigantic confidence trick. In the short run, he believed, the capitalists could use the 'superprofits' they derived from the colonies to bribe the 'aristocracy of labour', that is, the skilled artisans and the small traders, to support them. J. A. Hobson too believed in something not far removed from a conspiracy theory. 'A completely socialist State,' he wrote

which kept good books and presented regular balance-sheets of expenditure and assets would soon discard Imperialism;

an intelligent *laissez-faire* democracy which gave duly pro-
portionate weight in its policy to all economic interests alike
would do the same. But a state in which certain well-
organised business interests are able to outweigh the weak,
diffused interest of the community is bound to pursue a
policy which accords with the pressure of the former
interests.[9]

Many contemporary writers, as well as later historians, have
seen the imperialist expansion of the late nineteenth century
not, as it might appear at first sight, as the overflowing of
confident nationalism but as an essentially defensive reaction
to a threatening situation. Cecil Rhodes saw it as the alternative to civil war. Even in countries like Germany, which
appeared to be on the threshold of great expansion, similar
fears were expressed. Friedrich Fabri who, although he exaggerated when he said that his pamphlet *Does Germany need
Colonies?* (1879) sparked off the whole German colonial movement, was an important catalyst, concluded a grim analysis of a
population explosion, unemployment and 'a rapid growth in
pauperism and in social poverty' with the prophecy that,
without a safety valve, they would have an explosion which
would make 1789 look like child's play. A later historian, H.-U.
Wehler, has taken up a similar point to suggest that Bismarck's
imperialism was an early example of a modern interventionist
state, trying 'to correct the disfunction of the economy . . . in
order to ensure the stability of the economic system'. It was 'an
attempt on the part of her ruling elites to create improved
conditions favourable to the stability of the social and economic
system as it stood'.[10] The acquisition of colonial territory was
merely one of a whole range of measures, some purely fiscal,
including subsidies on steamship lines, the establishment of
banks overseas and special transport rates for export goods
which were deliberately 'anti-cyclical', that is to say, intended
to counteract the downward turn in the economy; a conscious
economic strategy, which had as its ultimate goal the preservation of social stability.

No comparable analysis has been offered for British actions
in this period. A less interventionist government, still firmly
committed to free trade and *laissez-faire*, is unlikely to provide

comparable evidence. But, on the face of it, Britain's situation was a great deal more perilous than Germany's. She was an old industrial society, whose industry was beginning to stagnate; although in absolute terms her iron and steel industries, for example, were still increasing their production, relative to her new competitors, like Germany and the United States, they were declining. In new industries, such as chemicals and electrical goods, Britain was being rapidly left behind. Interest rates were low and opportunities for investments poor by the 1880s. J. A. Hobson, and Lenin, made the defence of investments overseas central to their analysis of the imperial annexations of this period. Strictly contemporary writers – and both Hobson and Lenin wrote some years later – did not. They emphasised rather the defence of markets. In the petitions which poured into the Foreign Office in the 1880s when France, or Portugal, or Germany was recognised as the sovereign of yet another part of the African coast, the complaints were about the erection of customs houses, the imposition of tariffs, the discrimination against British traders who, at least in their own eyes, had been the ones who opened the area to trade in the first place. The Germans were slightly less unpopular than the others because, in their colonies, they still had a liberal tariff policy.

The English working-man did not necessarily mistake his own interest in this. If goods could not be sold, men could not be employed. As Dunraven pointed out, it was not too difficult for the capitalist to switch his investment from unprofitable to profitable stock at home or abroad and not necessarily within the empire – in fact most British investment abroad in this period was still in the United States. But it was virtually impossible for the Lancashire cotton operative, all of whose 'capital' was invested in his skill in his trade, to switch his labour if the textile market collapsed. He was tied to the trade he knew and the place he knew. The working classes were enthusiastic for the Fair Trade League. Their support for imperialism, which Engels noted, may well not have been, as Lenin supposed, simply the result of clever deception by the bourgeoisie.

Whether the newly annexed areas, particularly in Africa, did in fact provide any kind of effective outlet for British industry is a difficult question to answer. Professors Robinson and Gallagher expressed considerable scepticism in *Africa and the Victorians* (1961) as to whether the tribes of tropical Africa would exhibit any interest in the kind of consumer goods of which British industry now had an embarrassing surplus. Contemporary critics, including J. A. Hobson, had little difficulty in demonstrating from the Board of Trade's own figures that by the beginning of the twentieth century the 'new' empire seemed to have contributed little to British trade. In the quinquennium 1855–9 Britain received 23.5 per cent of her imports and sent 31.5 per cent of her exports to her own overseas possessions; in the quinquennium 1895–9 the comparable figures were 21.6 per cent and 37 per cent. Hobson concluded: 'We perceive that the proportions of our external trade had changed very little during the half century; colonial imports slightly fell, colonial exports slightly rose, during the last decade, as compared with the beginning of the period'. An analysis of the proportion of their trade which Britain's colonies did with the mother country was even more devastating. Between 1856–9 and 1896–9 the percentage of their imports which the colonies took from Britain fell from 46.5 to 32.5 and the percentage of their exports to Britain fell from 57.1 to 34.9. Was it worth the expense and international aggravation of acquiring and defending colonies for such small returns? 'The distinctive feature of modern Imperialism', commented Hobson severely, 'from the commercial standpoint, is that it adds to our empire tropical and sub-tropical regions with which our trade is small, precarious and unprogressive.'[11]

The question is not, however, quite so simply answered as Hobson supposed. Even though Africa had been represented as the new El Dorado and even though fabulous riches did come from a few places like Kimberley and the Witwatersrand, contemporary business men seem to have been more concerned with markets than with supplies of raw materials – although a few raw materials such as the vegetable oils of the Niger region were important. The Lancashire – and what is less often appreciated, the Scottish – textile industry did export large quantities of goods to West Africa. Birmingham and Sheffield exported metal goods of all kinds all over Africa. It is significant that a very high proportion of the parliamentary lobbying on colonial questions in the late nineteenth century came from just those areas. When businesses were operating very close to the edge of bankruptcy, as many were during the Great Depression, one fairly large market could be of vital importance for their survival.

It is also possible that Hobson and some of his followers used too short a time scale in assessing the effects of the new colonies on the British economy. When Hobson published the third edition of *Imperialism, a Study*, in 1938 he very honestly published an elaborate appendix bringing his statistics up to date, although he must presumably have been aware that they were capable of leading to very different conclusions from those he had published in 1902. Between 1904 and 1934 the value of British exports to British possessions, other than India and the Dominions, that is to say mainly to the recently acquired empire, rose from £16,687,997 to £61,271,842. The value of imports rose in the same period from £12,916,861 to £76,533,367. The 1934 figures had, in fact, been significantly affected by the worldwide slump and the comparable export and import figures in the late 1920s (with a small exception in 1926) had been consistently well over £100,000,000. The figures published by S. H. Frankel in his *Capital Investment in Africa* (1938) also tend to show that Britain's African colonies did help to cushion the British economy against the worst effects of the depression of the 1930s, rather in the way in which German writers such as H. von Treitschke believed that the British and Dutch economies had been cushioned in the 1870s and 1880s.

Some Marxist writers, including Rosa Luxemburg, believed that so long as the developed capitalist economies could extend into the periphery they could find solutions for the periodic slumps with which capitalism was inevitably afflicted and that this process could go on for a very long time, although not indefinitely. Kautsky, whom Lenin no longer regarded as a Marxist, even thought that eventually some state of equilibrium might be reached. In 1917 Lenin believed that the apocalypse was already very near. Capitalism contained within it the seeds of its own decay and imperialism was simply one of the symptoms of its approaching end. Capitalism had run out of solutions. Perhaps in theory the capitalists could change their policy to one less suicidal but, in reality, this was not possible. It would be, as Professor Kiernan puts it, like asking a tiger to turn vegetarian.

J. A. Hobson, to whom Lenin frankly acknowledged that he owed some of his ideas on imperialism, although he developed them very differently, reached a quite different conclusion. Hobson was an interesting man. The son of a newspaper proprietor, he became best known as a freelance writer and journalist. Like Joseph Chamberlain and Friedrich Fabri he was interested in the social question, long before he became interested in imperialism. In 1891, he published *Problems of Poverty* and, in 1896, *The Problem of Unemployment*. His attention turned to colonial problems when he went out to South Africa as a correspondent for the *Manchester Guardian*, just before the Boer War. Several books resulted from his experiences: *The War in South Africa* (1900), *The Psychology of Jingoism* (1901) and, in a sense, *Imperialism, a Study* (1902). He went on to write a number of books about taxation.

Unlike Lenin, Hobson did not believe that either imperialism or the collapse of capitalism were in any way inevitable. He believed that, faced by undoubtedly grave and distressing problems at home, his countrymen had turned to false solutions, namely overseas expansion. He argued at length in *Imperialism, a Study*, which became an immensely influential book, that the annexation of overseas territories solved nothing. On the contrary, it aggravated the situation. The problem, as Hobson saw it, was that there was a surplus of capital in the system because of the stagnation of industry, which meant that capital could not find profitable employment at home. Investors therefore looked overseas and then called on their governments to protect their investments, which were often in unstable countries. The only reason why that capital could not be used at home to build up British industry was because of the evil of under-consumption, the unnatural constriction of the domestic market, resulting from the maldistribution of wealth in society. 'It is not', he wrote, 'industrial progress that demands the opening up of new markets and areas of investment, but the mal-distribution of consuming power which prevents the absorption of commodities and capital within the country.' This over-saving was the economic tap-root of imperialism. 'If the consuming public in this country', he wrote in another passage, 'raised its standard of consumption to keep pace with every rise of productive powers, there could be no excess of goods or capital clamorous to use Imperialism to find markets.'[12] Hobson did not go into any detail in *Imperialism, a Study* as to how this redistribution of wealth could be brought about but his other writings make it clear that he considered differential taxation an important weapon. Hobson was perhaps unrealistic in supposing the home market to be capable of almost indefinite expansion and he certainly departed from the economic orthodoxy of his mentor, Richard Cobden, in regarding foreign trade as a minor factor in the British economy, as P. J. Cain demonstrates in an interesting article, 'J. A. Hobson, Cobdenism, and the Radical Theory of Economic Imperialism, 1898–1914', in *The Economic History Review* of 1978. In his later writings Hobson returned to a more traditional position. Nevertheless Hobson believed that he had set before his countrymen an alternative model for the solution of their economic problems. Unlike Lenin, he believed that, if they were once intellectually convinced of this, they could use their free will to abandon imperialism and adopt another system.

In the years immediately after 1902, however, the British public showed very little inclination to do any such thing. Although the Boer War had led to a new questioning of some of the assumptions of imperialism, there was still a general acceptance of the propositions that both Britain's role as a great power and her economic prosperity depended upon her position as the centre of a great empire. This had now become associated with a new enthusiasm for what is sometimes called 'National Efficiency'. Joseph Chamberlain had been one of the harbingers of this although it became associated with Rosebery's name. It has been analysed in two fairly recent books, G. R. Searle's *The Quest for National Efficiency* (1971) and R. J. Scally's *The Origin of the Lloyd George Coalition: the Politics of Social-Imperialism, 1900–1918* (1975). It crossed party boundaries but it particularly found its home among the Liberal Imperialists and the Fabians. A very important pressure group was the Co-efficients, founded by the Webbs in November 1902. The original twelve members included, besides the

Webbs, L. S. Amery, Sir Edward Grey, R. B. Haldane, Bertrand Russell and H. G. Wells. The Co-efficients were concerned with national security. The growing challenge from Germany, certainly economic and possibly military, was now becoming generally recognised. It must be met by Britain's becoming an 'efficient' nation. The empire was seen as playing a major role for both security and prosperity. There was a large social element in the Co-efficients' programme. They wanted a 'National Minimum' in living standards. This included the elimination of the 'sweated trades' to give a minimum wage, sanitary reforms and housing reforms which would sweep away the terrible slums which still flourished in many British towns, poor law reforms and education reforms.

Ironically some of the earlier arguments in favour of empire had now been turned on their head. Previously, it had been argued that you needed an empire to improve social conditions. Now it was argued that you must improve social conditions to produce a race capable of defending and governing an empire. The *Observer* had revealed how many young men had had to be rejected for service in the Boer War because they could not meet the required medical standards. Sidney Webb pressed his sanitary reforms on the grounds that they must achieve 'the minimum necessary for breeding an even moderately Imperial race' and asked: 'How . . . can we get an efficient army – out of the stunted, anaemic, demoralised denizens of the slum tenements of our great cities?'[13]

Independently minded men in the now largely self-governing dominions did not always agree but enthusiasts in England increasingly saw Britain and her empire as one indivisible unit. Twenty years earlier it had been hoped that the possession of an empire would safeguard and stimulate British trade so that the economy would revive and the conditions necessary for social improvement would be spontaneously generated. In the eighteenth century the great economist Adam Smith had noted that Britain, unlike Spain or Portugal or Holland, had never levied 'tribute' from her empire, had never expected direct contributions from taxation or other levies. Even that principle was now in danger of being broken. The idea was canvassed of using the profits of the Suez Canal Company, 45 per cent of whose shares were owned by the

British government, to pay for the introduction of old age pensions in Britain.

The Co-efficients never achieved their ambition of turning the Liberal party – and thus the Liberal government which won a landslide victory in the general election of 1906 – into the party of Social-Imperialism but the Liberal administration of 1905–14 incorporated many of their tenets into their political philosophy. By the standards of the times they put through a massive programme of social reform, not just old age pensions but a national insurance scheme, the Trades Boards Act of 1909 designed to put an end to 'sweated' labour, a new Housing Act, other Acts to regulate conditions in shops and mines and, spectacularly in Lloyd George's 1909 Budget, differential taxation. Many would regard the legislation of the Liberal government of 1905–14 as marking the beginning of the welfare state. But a government in which H. H. Asquith was first Chancellor of the Exchequer and then Prime Minister, Sir Edward Grey was Foreign Secretary and R. B. Haldane was Secretary of State for War was not likely to be unmindful of the claims of the empire. The defence and preservation of the empire took a high priority.

The British Liberal government differed significantly from that of Bismarckian Germany. It was certainly not intent on preserving the political and social *status quo* in its entirety. On particular issues, including the abolition of the House of Lords or the curbing of the privileged position of landlords, many of its members held very radical views. But it did wish to ensure national stability at a time when working-class discontent was becoming more vocal. The years 1910–12 saw a series of major strikes, involving railwaymen, miners and dockers among others. The Conservative and Unionist party, even more than the Liberals, saw full-blooded socialism as a menace for the first time. J. L. Garvin, planning the campaign literature for the 1910 election, noted of the working-class voters he wished to win over:

Their dream is Socialism and the earthly paradise and their bogey landlords. Our dream – Imperial Strength and Industrial Security based upon Tariff Reform. . . . We have to concentrate upon the ten per cent or so of undecided voters in town and country, and we have to get them at any cost. For this purpose we must work on their *real* feelings.[14]

Both sides suspected that the 'real feelings' of the electors were based on a realisation that Britain was now completely on the defensive, that her industry was in decline compared with that of her new competitors and that even her days as a world power were limited. The possession of a great empire, an empire which included a quarter of the world's population and on which the sun, quite literally, never set, was a wonderful disguise for such a decline and perhaps even, as has been discussed earlier in this chapter, to some extent a genuine insurance against it. After the First World War the British empire actually appeared to increase in size and strength when Britain received many of the former German colonies as mandated territories. Only with the Second World War did the truth become apparent. Britain no longer had either the will or the material strength to continue to govern a great empire. Attitudes had changed profoundly. Some came close to seeing it as a belated vindication of Hobson's strictures. The possession of an empire had not merely failed to solve the social question. It had been a false solution which had actually aggravated the problem. This is nowhere more clearly expressed than in A. J. P. Taylor's *English History, 1914–45* (1965) in which he says: 'In the Second World War the British people came of age. . . . Traditional values lost much of their force. Other values took their place. Imperial greatness was on the way out; the welfare state was on the way in. The British empire declined; the condition of the people improved.'[15]

It is possible to dispute whether the possession of an empire postponed or hastened Britain's decline but it will readily be perceived that this is an entirely amoral question. It does not ask whether it was morally justifiable for the British public to solve their 'social problem' at the expense of others, even assuming that it could be done. Such a question seems obvious and central to people in the late twentieth century. It occurred to few even of the most idealistic writers of the early twentieth century – indeed, the more idealistic they were, the less likely it was to occur to them. It did not occur to them because to them it was a non-question. Men as diverse as Cecil Rhodes and Karl

Pearson were imbued with a sense of the inevitability of progress and the evolution of mankind, the whole complex framework of thought which is conveniently described as Social Darwinism. Advanced nations would forge ahead. Backward nations would catch up or drop out of history. The working classes would share in the generally advancing prosperity. Colonial peoples would have reason to be grateful to the more advanced, more 'civilised', peoples who, even at the expense of conquest, had rescued them from barbarism and helped them to join the onward march of mankind. Some, like the great pro-consular figure Lord Lugard, believed that the roles of Europeans and Africans were complementary. Europe would have access to the unused riches of Africa to stimulate her industry. Africans would be enabled to cast aside their poverty, heathenism and subjection to harsh and arbitrary regimes and enjoy the benefits of civilisation. The circle had been squared. Imperialism would solve not only the 'social question' of Europe but that of the colonial peoples as well.

8. Sinews of Empire: Changing Perspectives

C. C. ELDRIDGE

I

Was there a British empire? The question is not entirely frivolous. Even the most superficial of surveys quickly reveals that far from being a monolithic structure the British empire never amounted to much more than a series of separate, bilateral relationships between a strong European power and a host of weaker territories. It was a loose and sometimes accidental association of units with few shared characteristics apart from their mutual origins stemming from British economic, political and cultural predominance in the world. Comparatively rarely did the British make any conscious effort to submerge the individuality of their colonies and when they did bestir themselves success was rarer still. No single code of laws, language or religion covered the empire. Above all, there was no single form of government and the authority of the imperial government varied tremendously at the local level.

At the beginning of the nineteenth century, there were huge disparities in the government of the British North American colonies, the West Indian islands, the footholds on the west coast of Africa, the penal settlements in the antipodes and the motley array of islands, naval bases and coaling stations strung across the oceans of the world. By the end of the century, when it might be thought that the cement of empire would have hardened, there were even greater variations in the methods of government and in the effectiveness of British control: British India ruled by a Queen-Empress but with a host of princely states in the interior; self-governing colonies apparently independent except where external defence and foreign policy were concerned; Crown colonies ruled autocratically from Whitehall; protectorates and spheres of influence, some where a British administrator had never been seen and where British writ did not run. Governors, consul-generals, high commissioners, residents and even a hereditary English raja (in Sarawak) abounded; chartered companies had been created to carry out expansion on the cheap and many extensions of authority had taken place under the curious pretence that no additions were being made to the empire at all. And so by the closing years of Queen Victoria's reign, when the empire had expanded to embrace a quarter of the earth's surface and a quarter of mankind, there was still no coherence in the government of the empire. Despite the spread of the telegraph around the world, British politicians and government officials had no more success in imposing their wishes on the prancing pro-consuls than they had had with their predecessors. To this extent the British empire was an illusion. Even in its allegedly finest hour, towards the very end of the 1890s, so vividly portrayed in James Morris' *Pax Britannica: The Climax of an Empire* (1968), when imperial pageantry surrounded Queen Victoria's Diamond Jubilee, and when the British press, the majority of British politicians and most of the nation, including the working classes, appeared to be united in their adulation of the empire, that empire was more fragile than it had been for many a year. British power was on the wane and British weakness was shortly to be exposed when the Boer War severely dented not only Victorian self-esteem but Britain's image throughout the world.

What did this amorphous collection of colonies and protectorates amount to? What purpose in the eyes of contemporaries did the empire serve? What held it together? These questions have exercised historians as much as they preoccupied contemporaries. The whole army of forces at work have been referred to throughout this volume. Economic factors of various kinds have been highlighted; political, diplomatic and strategic motives have also been stressed – along with social imperialism and the impact of chauvinism, jingoism and the yellow press. Missionary zeal, humanitarianism and plans for social reform, ideas of trusteeship, the white man's burden and the civilising mission, clearly played their part at critical stages in the development of the imperial idea. The role of Social Darwinism and racial superiority has also been examined in some depth. The impact of the revolutions in Western technology, especially in the conquest of West Africa, has been outlined and the growing disparity in power between the European centre and the overseas 'periphery' demonstrated. In fact, developments on the periphery – caused by rapidly changing local conditions, insubordinate and ambitious men on the spot, scheming local potentates, local power vacuums, the collapse of indigenous societies or collaborating cliques, the clash of cultures as local polities encountered pressure from the capitalist system – frequently led to events that were so obviously beyond metropolitan control that one may be permitted to wonder whether there ever was any underlying rational purpose behind the façade of empire. Perhaps, like Topsy, the empire just grew, sometimes by accident (as when the Bay Islands off the Republic of Honduras were annexed in 1852 in contravention of the Clayton–Bulwer Treaty of 1850) or by simple error (as when the Cocos–Keeling islands in the Indian Ocean were annexed in 1857 instead of the Great and Little Cocos in the Bay of Bengal). On the other hand, the acquisition of Singapore (1819), Aden (1839), Hong Kong (1842), Labuan (1846), Kowloon (1860) and Lagos (1861), once their geographical position and place in world or local trade is noted, suggests that some larger design and interest *was* at work. On occasion, the empire did advance with a very definite purpose in mind. After all, most empires are concerned with power, profit and prestige. Was the British empire any different?

The idea that the empire constituted a coherent unit, comprehensible in itself, was challenged in 1953 by Gallagher and Robinson in that seminal article 'The Imperialism of Free Trade'. Defining imperialism as the political function of the process of integrating new regions into the expanding economy, they argued that only within the *total* framework of expansion was the nineteenth-century empire intelligible. To confine one's attention to the formal empire alone was 'like judging the size and character of icebergs solely from the parts above the water-line',[1] for other countries could, by one means or another, fall under Britain's sway. Since the British were willing to limit the use of paramount power to establishing security for trade, the phasing of British expansion depended on local conditions and the world situation. Just because the late Victorians were obliged to annex territory more frequently than their predecessors, this did not mean they were more imperialistic in their outlook. Their aims remained the same but external conditions had altered, thus requiring formal intervention.

Yet Gallagher and Robinson shied away from a simple economic interpretation of the role of empire. In *Africa and the Victorians* (1961), they suggested that far from the flag occasionally following trade, the late Victorians, in scraping the bottom of the barrel, planted the British flag in much of Africa for entirely different purposes and then attempted to justify their actions by talking of economic advantages and encouraging traders and investors to make something of the government's newly acquired burdens. In their later work, Robinson and Gallagher give clear priority to strategy, 'local crises' and the break-down of collaborating mechanisms as the most important determinants of British advance.

Many historians have followed their lead. Dissatisfaction with the 'Theory of Capitalist Imperialism', despite recent attempts to correct misunderstandings concerning the theses of Hobson and Lenin, has led many writers not only to ignore different Marxist interpretations, such as those of Luxemburg and Kautsky as well as far more recent refinements of the Marxist case, but to downgrade *all* economic interpretations, even those which do not relate to surplus capital and overseas investment but concentrate instead on the needs of trade, the search for markets and new sources of raw material. However, current diplomatic, strategic and peripheral explanations for such events as the British occupation of Egypt and the Anglo-Boer War at the end of the century have recently come in for some criticism and the pendulum has begun to swing gently back, once again, in favour of economic interpretations. While the requirements of British foreign policy, domestic politics and conditions in the metropolis, as well as developments overseas (the peripheral factor), are of great significance in our understanding of Britain's imperial history, it is equally clear that the economic background to these events is of crucial importance.

The connection between British intervention and expansionist activities in the formal and informal empires with phases in the economic growth of the metropolitan economy is not easy to establish. But in the *Economic History Review* for 1980, P. J. Cain and A. G. Hopkins attempted precisely this in an article entitled 'The Political Economy of British Expansion Overseas, 1750–1914'. Adopting the standpoint of political economy, they proceeded to analyse the management of the national economy and the strategies devised to secure state revenues, domestic employment, and public order in an attempt to show that 'the various phases of the expansion of Britain's presence and power abroad were closely connected with the development of the domestic economy, the shifting balance of social and political forces which this development entailed, and the varying intensity of Britain's economic and political rivalry with other powers'.[2]

Rejecting the common assumption that the industrial revolution provided Britain with an easy route to economic domination and world influence, Cain and Hopkins argued that the rise of modern manufacturing was a much more prolonged and painful process than current theories of imperialism allow. 'Industrialisation, when it came, was accompanied by pronounced regional differences, marked sectoral variations and irregular rates of growth. It also greatly increased the problems of unemployment, distress and the threat of disorder.' Thus British policies and attitudes towards expansion overseas in the late eighteenth and early nineteenth centuries reflected the 'prolonged economic and political importance of agriculture and then the slow, uncertain and incomplete transition to industry'. Further, expansion overseas bore the marks of the shifting alliances among interest groups, each with distinctive sectoral and regional bases, each seeking to identify sectional with national interests. Finally,

The motive, timing and extent of Britain's expansion into the non-European world were determined very largely by her varying ability either to penetrate the markets of other major European powers or to command imports independently of them.[3]

Britain extended her presence overseas in direct relation to her failure to dominate her chief competitors.

Cain and Hopkins concluded that Britain's path to wealth and worldwide influence was an extraordinarily chequered one: the growth of an export economy (based on cotton manufacture from 1780) was finally accomplished only with the reluctant admission by the landed interest of the need to dismantle the old colonial system in the 1840s. Thus the 'stereotyped contrast' between a triumphant Britain before 1870 and a troubled and defensive nation thereafter cannot be sustained; and the complex shifts in overseas markets, resource pools and power bases were, in a sense, reflections of the uneven and highly regionalised development of the first industrial nation:

> This is well illustrated by the partition of Africa, where a changing balance of internal power between industrial and financial sectors was set against a background of Britain's relative decline as an industrial nation. The net result was a 'new imperialism' originating in financial power in Egypt and South Africa coexisting with an older imperialism represented by Britain's traditional and ailing export industries, which were trying to consolidate their hold on markets in parts of tropical Africa.[4]

More than one type of imperialism, therefore, was at work in the late nineteenth century.

In restoring the metropolitan economy to the centre of the analysis, Cain and Hopkins have opened up another way for interpreting Britain's role as a world power. They have also increased our understanding of the changing pattern of British activities in both the formal and informal empires. Moreover, for present purposes, their thesis adds yet another dimension, an essential backcloth, to our understanding of contemporary attitudes towards the empire.

II

It ought to be a commonplace that the function of empire is

never static: once in existence empires usually serve a host of purposes. New justifications frequently arise as original purposes cease to be relevant. In the long run, the continuation of their existence, if only for reasons of prestige, usually becomes an end in itself. In the past, however, historians of the British empire too readily assumed that once the mercantilist system had begun to be dismantled the empire lost its role. Not until after 1870 did the need for empire once again become readily apparent. Armchair historians, seeking corroborating evidence for this preconceived thesis, placed heavy reliance upon secondhand opinion, the 'received version' of events. Conflicting material was ignored, in the interests of coherent analysis, in order to establish one consistent, enduring outlook for the early and mid-Victorian years. Clearly, not until the realities of the situation were taken into account and opinion tied in with the events that actually occurred, would it be possible to come to a more accurate understanding of British policies and opinions. Even today, a great deal more spade-work needs to be done: examining what contemporaries actually wrote rather than what they are said to have written; investigating the context, the occasion, the audience and the intended purpose of their statements; charting the changes and contradictions in the opinions of individuals over a period of time; examining the variety of attitudes towards specific events and themes; and accepting that beneath the rhetoric objective analysis of the unfamiliar problems of distant lands is unlikely to have occurred (contemporaries usually found what they wanted to find in any given situation and then acted according to their previously settled convictions). When this is done, it may be possible to reach tentative conclusions about the real state of British attitudes towards the empire. But, even then, it will almost certainly be impossible to generalise: opinions will be varied and class differences, regional differences and sectoral differences (to name but a few) will still remain.

Nevertheless while much research remains to be done, sufficient work has been carried out, especially in the last twenty years, to challenge previously accepted notions about the changing nature of British responses to empire. And while it will obviously be many years before any new synthesis reaches the textbooks, the demolition of previous misconceptions is worth recording, along with the opening of new areas of debate, and the emergence of at least some areas of general agreement.

The 'received version' of British imperial history outlined at the beginning of this volume – the division of the nineteenth century into phases of imperialism and anti-imperialism with 'turning-points' occurring in the decades after 1815 and around 1870 – was based on a much less sophisticated analysis than that of Cain and Hopkins. But it did appear to have the support of a whole range of corroborating evidence concerning contemporary opinions about empire. Embodied within the writings of the late Victorians, notably Seeley's lectures on *The Expansion of England* (1883), and enshrined in H. E. Egerton's pioneering textbook *A Short History of British Colonial Policy* (1897), was the argument that a period of despair and disillusionment with the idea of empire set in after 1783 which lasted until about 1830. The reason for the despondency was the apparent lesson of the American War of Independence – that colonies were like children who would inevitably separate from the mother country as they reached maturity – and the accompanying belief, following the attacks of Adam Smith, Josiah Tucker, Jeremy Bentham and James Mill on mercantilism and the colonial connection, that colonies were no longer the economic assets they were once deemed to be. After 1830 there was some renewed interest in the empire, mainly attributable to the writings and propaganda of the Colonial Reformers, but indifference soon returned and then, as free-trade ideas triumphed and responsible government was established in most of the British North American and Australasian colonies, colonies came to be viewed solely as burdens on the British exchequer. During the 1860s, when the ideas of the 'Manchester School' were at their most influential, separatism and calls for dismemberment of the empire reached their zenith. However, the British soon became concerned about the changing balance of power in Europe and, as the British economy ran into difficulties, the value of empire was reassessed. By the 1890s, the empire had once again become the panacea for all Great Britain's ills, including declining trade, over-population and growing unemployment.

This interpretation received massive endorsement in C. A. Bodelsen's influential *Studies in Mid-Victorian Imperialism* (1924), the first real attempt to investigate contemporary opinion. Based on a survey of contemporary literature, the book contained an impressive array of public and private statements by politicians and writers as well as coverage of views expressed in parliamentary debates, newspapers and journals. The intention was to analyse the origin and character of mid-Victorian separatism, then to chronicle the rise of the imperialist spirit which arose in reaction to it. Bodelsen endorsed the view that the value of empire had fallen into question after 1815. Quoting Hume, Brougham and Roebuck one moment, the *Edinburgh* and *Westminster Reviews* the next, he agreed that the rising tide of separatism was only temporarily held in check by the activities of a small group of Colonial Reformers whose ideas, though unrepresentative of their generation, had tremendous impact on such influential people as John Stuart Mill, Lord John Russell and the third Earl Grey. However, once the old colonial system had been reduced to rags and tatters, most of the settlement colonies given internal self-government, and Canada had further fallen from grace when she rejected the new economic orthodoxy, the anti-empire views of Cobden, Bright and Goldwin Smith reigned supreme. Although 'pessimists' about the future of the empire may have been more numerous than 'separatists', the 'optimists' who hoped for the continuation of empire had been eclipsed. It was not until attempts to remove the final burdens of the colonial connection, the colonial garrisons, led to a series of crises in relations with New Zealand and Canada that a reaction set in. In the changed conditions of the 1870s, the tide turned in favour of a revival of the imperial spirit and the pro-empire faction eventually won the day.

This interpretation coincided with the view of another influential scholar, the American historian R. L. Schuyler, whose articles written during the years 1917–22 were later reproduced with new material in *The Fall of the Old Colonial System: A Study in British Free Trade, 1770–1870* (1945). Schuyler's work confirmed Bodelsen's central thesis about the rise and triumph of an anti-empire spirit in the first half of the nineteenth century and added a couple of important embellishments. First, he traced back the beginnings of this anti-empire spirit (which Seeley had detected few signs of in the decades before 1860) to the period of the American War of Independence. Viewing Adam Smith as the original Little Englander, he traced a continuous and increasingly influential brand of anti-imperialism from Adam Smith and his contemporaries, through the classical economists, philosophic radicals and Benthamites to the Manchester School of the 1860s. He then claimed the movement reached its climax in the first two years of Gladstone's first administration (1868–70), dubbed the 'climax of anti-imperialism', when the disintegration of the empire seemed to be at hand. Whereupon Disraeli, sensing the changed mood of the day, took up the imperial cause and in the 1874 election promptly routed the Little Englanders.

It was a tidy and appealing thesis apparently backed up by extensive evidence. Repetition ensured sanctification and the framework was embodied in almost all textbooks published up to and soon after the Second World War: the decades before 1870 were a peaceful and prosperous anti-empire interlude between the mercantilist imperialism of the war-torn eighteenth century and the violent neo-mercantilist 'new imperialism' of the late-Victorian age. This view can even be found in Richard Koebner and H. D. Schmidt's *Imperialism: The Story and Significance of a Political Word, 1840–1960* published in 1964, a book which otherwise broke much new ground. The year 1865 is described as perhaps the 'nadir' in political thought about the empire: 'most thinking men in those days had little doubt about the impending dissolution of the British Empire' (p. 83). It was the gospel according to Bodelsen and Schuyler.

By 1964, however, the construction of a 'revised version' was already well under way. If the earlier writings of Paul Knaplund, Donald Wagner, K. L. Knorr and Helen Taft Manning (all of whom had reached conclusions which did not square with the old orthodoxy)[5] had made little impact, after Gallagher and Robinson's atheistic onslaught on the traditional framework in 1953 many of their criticisms were revived as well as new lines of investigation opened up. Generally, the re-examination of attitudes as opposed to policy proceeded at a slower pace (initially some writers drew an awkward distinction between general attitudes towards empire and the actual policies the British government pursued[6]), but by 1961 the revisionists had got into their stride and several important articles had appeared in print.

Once the traditional framework was tested, it was found to rest on very flimsy foundations. Most of the alleged criticisms of empire, for example, were criticisms of the colonial *system* not of colonies *per se*. Many of the quotations used to bolster the framework were also found to be unsatisfactory: words had been taken out of context, outbursts in moments of irritation had been treated as being representative of an individual's general views, biased assertions and the verdicts of political opponents had been accepted without discussion, and derogatory comments about specific problems, such as defence difficulties, the position of Canada or colonial wars, had first been turned into broad generalisations and then into a grand imperial philosophy. As investigation continued a different and far more complex situation was revealed. Many former labels and descriptions were found to be totally unsatisfactory. The classical economists and philosophic radicals, for example, were not so anti-empire in sentiment as was previously thought.[7] Nor were the Colonial Reformers, led by Edward Gibbon Wakefield, swimming against so strong a current of opinion as this rather self-important group would have us believe. They did, however, advocate positive programmes of empire and 'grounding their arguments upon the new economic science', Bernard Semmel has argued, 'constructed and maintained a set of doctrines of which the keystone was the necessity of empire to an industrial England'.[8] Their arguments secured a large number of converts so that by mid-century emigration and colonial investment had become twin pillars in a new economic theory supporting empire.

Clearly, after 1830 not all economists opposed the continued existence of the empire, as has so frequently been asserted. Many actually favoured it. Even the Manchester School has been largely misrepresented. Far from being a coherent body, it consisted of a group of economists with divergent views who did not possess any agreed philosophy concerning empire. Very few of the members were informed about colonies and it was the pacifist wing led by Richard Cobden, opposing the use of power in foreign policy, which gave the group its anti-colonial reputation.[9] Many more members of the group supported the 'imperialism of free trade' by ceaselessly urging the Foreign Office to take strong action in China than backed Cobden and Bright in opposing it. Furthermore, even Cobden and Bright could not agree over British policy towards India. Professor R. J. Moore has pointed out that, in the hope of obtaining cotton, many leading members of the Manchester group, including Bright, condoned the promotion of communications and public works by private capital upon which the returns were secured against the public revenue of India: 'That is to say, in anti-imperialist terms, the Manchester School were associated with the "exploitation" of India as a source of raw material, and as a field for the guaranteed investment of "finance capital" '.[10] And this from the alleged centre of Little England-ism!

In fact, the term 'Little Englander' is of doubtful value as a description of a significant British attitude at mid-century as J. S. Galbraith has shown in his 'Myths of the "Little England" Era' (*American Historical Review*, LXVII [1961] 34–48). It was always a term of derision levelled at political opponents, especially by the rather ruthless group of Colonial Reformers who unfairly caricatured the views of others in order to destroy them more effectively. Separatism certainly existed but it had few public exponents. Cobden bemoaned the fact that there was 'as much clinging to colonies at the present moment amongst the middle class as amongst the aristocracy; and the working people are not wiser than the rest',[11] and he always carefully tempered the tone of his own public speeches. No mid-Victorian electorate, it has been said, spoke its will more clearly than that of 1857 which, after the *Arrow* episode and the Canton bombardment, endorsed Palmerston and drove Bright, Cobden and the Manchester radicals, bag and baggage, from the Commons. This was the age of Palmerston not of Manchester.

The crux of the mid-Victorian debate was not whether there should continue to be an empire but the form a reorganised empire should take in terms of government and defence. Few may have denied that eventual independence was the goal of the colonies of British settlement, but equally few wished to implement immediate separation. The time was always far from ripe. This difference between resigned acceptance of eventual independence and an active desire to promote it, must be clearly drawn. Most so-called separatists looked for the gradual relaxation of ties – usually by mutual consent over an unspecified period of time – as a prelude to the grant of independence which, although regarded as inevitable, would not preclude some form of continuing association. They adopted a permissive attitude towards separation *should the colonies wish for it*. As Bright protested: 'Give up the colonies & dependencies of the Empire? Can any Statesman do this, or any country do this? I doubt it'.[12] This attitude was accompanied by a correspondingly negative assumption that if the colonies were destined for eventual independence, imperial expenditure should be cut to a minimum and further expansion avoided. The end of expensive paternalism satisfied most of the empire's critics. Even those who regarded the colonies as nothing but a burden could still subscribe to the belief that the empire was a trust, however costly and undesirable, handed down by their forefathers. To Gladstone, India was 'a capital demand' upon the national honour. Sir George Cornewall Lewis, Goldwin Smith and John Bright were equally appalled at the thought of abandoning India: 'the whole country, in all probability would lapse into chaos and anarchy and into sanguinary and interminable warfare'.[13] 'While we are opposed to imperialism', declared Gladstone, 'we are devoted to empire.'[14]

While this revision of the tone and temper of British responses to the empire prior to 1870 has been in progress, the 'rise of the imperialist spirit' post-1870 has similarly been the object of attention. A great deal of work has been done on the 'popular imperialism' of the late-Victorian age from A. P. Thornton's imaginative study *The Imperial Idea and its Enemies* (1959) to H. J. Field's *Toward a Programme of Imperial Life: The British Empire at the Turn of the Century* (1982) which attempts to link the imperialist impulse to some of the basic patterns of late-Victorian culture, emphasising the idea of 'character' and the notion of 'duty' and showing how elite and then mass persuasion was achieved by the 'new journalism'. Equally interesting work has been done on the contribution of the popular literature of the day – in particular the writings of Kipling, Henty, Rider Haggard and John Buchan.

But if the anti-empire spirit in the earlier age is now thought to have been over-emphasised, some historians have suggested that the aggressive, expansionist spirit of the late-Victorian era has also been exaggerated. S. R. Stembridge in his recent book *Parliament, the Press and the Colonies, 1846–1880* (1982) doubts whether there was any noticeable change in general attitudes towards the empire around 1870. Considerable doubt has been cast on the hold of imperialism over the working classes. Even during the so-called 'climax of imperialism' in the late 1890s, when Beatrice Webb recorded in her diary 'Imperialism in the air – all classes drunk with sightseeing and hysterical loyalty', and during the near-hysterical patriotism of a crude jingoistic type which characterised the Boer War, it would seem that imperial sentiment may have been less widespread than was once assumed.[15] By no means all observers concurred that the British empire fulfilled the purposes that its more extravagant admirers claimed.

On the political level the British dislike of costly expansion continued well into the 1880s. Most 'imperialists' in that decade were federalists intent on strengthening the unity and security of the British parts of the empire. While a penny off the income tax remained the symbol of sound financial policy, extensions of British rule were avoided whenever possible. Only at the end of the decade did the struggle between expansionists and anti-expansionists really begin. Even so the late Victorians normally extended the area of formal control only when all other diplomatic expedients had failed. Annexation, as ever, remained a last resort. By the end of the century, many believed that Great Britain had finally overreached herself and her worldwide commitments exceeded the limits of her power. Far from adding to Britain's strength, the empire made her more vulnerable in the world. After the conclusion of the Anglo-Boer War, a more sober frame of mind and a sense of guilt came into being. And imperialism, with the publication of J. A. Hobson's book *Imperialism: A Study* (1902), permanently acquired the unpleasant connotations which have surrounded its meaning ever since.

Thus the critics of empire, about whom so much has been written in the early and mid-nineteenth century, surfaced again in the late 1890s.[16] Clearly, 'anti-imperialism' always existed below the surface in nineteenth-century Britain and its fortunes

waxed and waned according to the conditions of the day. But as
J. A. Roebuck accurately observed in 1849:

> The people of this country have never acquiesced in the
> opinion that our colonies are useless; and they look with
> disfavour upon any scheme of policy which contemplates the
> separation of the mother country from the colonies. For this
> opinion, the people have been seldom able to render an
> adequate reason; nor have they been accustomed to describe
> with accuracy the way in which the colonies prove useful to
> us; still they believe them beneficial, and so believing, they
> regard with suspicion those who roundly propose 'to cut the
> connexion'.[17]

The empire thus managed to survive even its darkest moments.

III

There can be little doubt, despite past assertions to the
contrary, that throughout the nineteenth century there existed
an ingrained pride in empire. As Gladstone, who viewed the
colonial connection as one of duty rather than advantage,
declared: 'the sentiment of empire may be called innate in every
Briton. If there are exceptions, they are like those of men born
blind or lame among us.'[18] Even in the late eighteenth century,
when despair and disillusionment were supposed to be the
order of the day, Pitt's government, in passing an India Act in
1784, a Navigation Act in 1786, a Canada Act in 1791, and the
Act of Union with Ireland in 1800, strongly reasserted the
principle of imperial control. Over seventy years separated the
surrender at Saratoga from the introduction of responsible
government into Nova Scotia and Canada. During that period
no self-governing constitution was granted to any British
dependency. It must also be remembered that while contemporaries may have argued about the value and the future of the
colonies of British settlement, few suggested that the empire of
trade and strategy – the long chain of naval bases, dockyards,
entrepôts and coaling stations across the world – should be
dismantled. There was also general agreement that India

should be retained. Thus Gladstone, who accepted the burden of empire as a trust that one day should be shed, willingly continued 'the work which Providence has assigned to this country in laying the foundation of mighty states in different parts of the world'.[19]

It was quite possible, therefore, even for those who did not accept that the empire added either politically or economically to Britain's power, influence and prestige, to endorse the moral view of empire that Britain had an obligation to bring the benefits of civilisation to the backward parts of the world. In the late-Victorian period the sense of mission was strong. But mission was an imperial idea long before the politicians took it up – to spread the laws of Alfred, the language of Shakespeare and the Christian religion was always a noble work. As the *North British Review* stated in November 1860 (pp. 86–7):

> to those who regard a vast empire as founded for some higher purpose than the creation and development of wealth, the wilful dismemberment of such an empire seems nothing less than the breaking up of some vast and complex machinery for the progressive civilisation of the human race, and an impious rejection of an instrument put into our hands by Providence for working out some great purpose of His government.

It was this mystical belief in the role of the British empire that the small group of genuine separatists, with their profit and loss ledgers, found so difficult to combat. It was the one sinew of the connection that rational argument had least chance of severing. Goldwin Smith could only challenge those who claimed that 'Providence' had given Britain colonies to prove their claim. But the truth of the claim was apparently so self-evident, and the challenge itself so seditious, that it could be ignored with impunity.

In fact, an examination of the public statements made in defence of empire by those who took the decisions, and debated them, in the field of politics and administration, reveals not only a marked similarity of approach but a remarkable continuity of ideas throughout the nineteenth century (although, of course, the imperial idea picked up several notable, and not necessarily desirable, adjuncts in the closing decades). Empire was usually justified in political, economic and social terms but the sense of mission, of obligations and responsibilities, as well as pride in British achievements, was always there. For example, William Huskisson, in a speech moving for a select committee on the civil government of Canada on 2 May 1828, declared:

> In every quarter of the globe we have planted the seeds of freedom, civilisation and Christianity. To every quarter of the globe we have carried the language, the free institutions, the system of laws, which prevail in this country; – in every quarter they are fructifying and making progress; and if it be said by some selfish calculator, that we have done all this at the expense of sacrifices which we ought not to have made, my answer is, – in spite of these sacrifices, we are still the first and happiest people in the old world; and, whilst this is our lot, let us rejoice rather in that rich harvest of glory, which must belong to a nation that has laid the foundation of similar happiness and prosperity to other nations, kindred in blood, in habits, and in feelings to ourselves.[20]

Lord John Russell, in a major government declaration on colonial policy on 8 February 1850, spoke in similar terms.[21] And Earl Grey stated, when defending his colonial secretaryship in *The Colonial Policy of Lord John Russell's Administration* (1853, I, 14),

> I conceive that, by the acquisition of its Colonial dominions, the Nation has incurred a responsibility of the highest kind, which it is not at liberty to throw off. The authority of the British Crown is at this moment the most powerful instrument, under Providence, of maintaining peace and order in many extensive regions of the earth, and thereby assists in diffusing amongst millions of the human race, the blessings of Christianity and civilisation.

The same sentiments are repeated and emphasised in the second half of the century. In 1878 the Earl of Carnarvon, addressing the Philosophical Institution in Edinburgh, commented:

> If we turn to that far larger empire over our native fellow-subjects of which I have spoken, the limits expand and the proportions rise till there forms itself a picture so vast and noble that the mind loses itself in the contemplation of what might be under the benificent rule of Great Britain. . . . There we have races struggling to emerge into civilisation, to whom emancipation from servitude is but the foretaste of the far higher law of liberty and progress to which they may yet attain; and vast populations like those of India sitting like children in the shadow of doubt and poverty and sorrow, yet looking up to us for guidance and for help. To them it is our part to give wise laws, good government, and a well ordered finance, which is the foundation of good things in human communities; it is ours to supply them with a system where the humblest may enjoy freedom from oppression and wrong equally with the greatest; where the light of religion and morality can penetrate into the darkest dwelling places. This is the real fulfilment of our duties; this, again, I say, is the true strength and meaning of imperialism.[22]

In a more frequently quoted speech, Joseph Chamberlain explained to the Royal Colonial Institute on 31 March 1897:

> We feel now that our rule over these territories can only be justified if we can show that it adds to the happiness and prosperity of the people, and I maintain that our rule does, and has, brought security and peace and comparative prosperity to countries that never knew their blessings before. In carrying out this work of civilisation we are fulfilling what I believe to be our national mission.[23]

Full of pride these utterances may have been but the dour emphasis on responsibilities and obligations was far removed from the crude jingoism and racial trumpetings of the yellow press. The sense of duty, responsibility and self-sacrifice, so clearly present in Kipling's verse ('The White Man's Burden' is an obvious example), had been there throughout the nineteenth century.

Nevertheless, the habit of authority which had impressed on contemporaries the duty of empire in 1800 – the duty of defending kith and kin and protecting, educating and converting the half-savage and half-child – had gradually assumed in the late-Victorian era all the mysticism of a religious faith. In part this was a deliberate process. In delivering his lectures on *The Expansion of England*, Professor Seeley was aiming to effect a change in attitudes among his young student elite, presumably the coming generation's leaders, by creating an increased imperial consciousness. It was all part of the task of character regeneration. The object was to link the valued character traits of the individual to the spirit of empire at the national level. Two other influential books, C. H. Pearson's *National Life and Character: A Forecast* (1893) and Benjamin Kidd's *Social Evolution* (1894), had similar purposes in mind. The public schools were also geared to inculcating courage, self-discipline, honesty, a sense of service and loyalty to the group. The same qualities were instilled into cadet units, through organised games and, later, the scouting movement. Learning to 'play the game' and being a member of a team was an important experience of life. The same virtues were preached in the popular literature of the day, especially for younger readers in G. A. Henty's many volumes. The works of Rider Haggard, John Buchan, Conan Doyle, Robert Louis Stevenson and Joseph Conrad held esteemed places on the bookshelves of three generations – the generations which produced the schoolboy masters of the empire.

This growing imperial consciousness – hammered home by the 'new journalism', the cheap half-penny newspapers – was closely linked with ideas about Anglo-Saxon destiny in the world. As early as 1868 Charles Dilke in his *Greater Britain* had pointed to the civilising mission of the 'Anglo-Saxon race' linking it with trusteeship of the backward peoples of the world. The new, popular racial theories were used more crudely to justify conquest and dominion over subject populations. However, as Dr Bolt has pointed out, race was more an invaluable adjunct to imperialism than the moving force behind it. So too was jingoism. The outburst of popular xenophobia in the 1890s was not necessarily an integral part of the imperial credo, it just so happened that the heroes and wars upon which it fed were linked with empire at the time. The two parted company after the Boer War. More important was the revived sense of trusteeship as philanthropists, anti-slavers and missionary societies called for British intervention. Thus empire acquired an enlarged moral purpose in the late-Victorian decades and the civilising mission became as popular as it had ever been in the Evangelical era or the early-Victorian age. It may be suggested that this sense of mission, the task Providence had assigned the British nation, provided one of the strongest links in the imperial chain.

Of course it cannot be denied that the political and economic advantages of empire loomed large in the thoughts of contemporaries. The possession of ports and strategic bases around the world and the existence of faithful 'allies' of British stock in several quarters of the globe were frequently paraded as adding to the reputation, moral influence and power of Great Britain. India was an eastern barrack in oriental seas and her army was, on many occasions, used outside the subcontinent for British ends. Disraeli was the statesman *par excellence* who promoted the concept of an armed empire assisting Britain in her role on the world's stage. Gladstone fought a running battle with Disraeli over the future character of the British empire in 1877–80. His was the initial victory but, as the century wore on, he found himself increasingly out of step with the new spirit of the age.

Similarly, economic arguments were always at the forefront of contemporary minds. As the mercantilist system was dismantled a new theory of empire grew up based on the benefits of colonisation and investment. Colonisation was seen as providing a safety valve for tensions within British society by transferring Britain's 'redundant' population overseas, thus opening up new lands and markets, and providing cheap foodstuffs and raw materials, for Britain's benefit. India was the supreme example of the advantages of empire. Her tariffs were frequently manipulated in favour of Lancashire's cotton manufacturers and the Indian cotton industry was put under pressure. By 1870, nearly one-fifth of Britain's exported cotton goods went to India. Overall India was Britain's third largest customer after the United States and Germany. By 1890 she ranked second. India also provided Britain with raw cotton, wheat, oil seeds, indigo, jute and tea. She was also the estate on which opium was grown for the China trade which ensured Britain's favourable balance of trade with the East. During the years 1854–69 alone, some £150,000,000 was invested in India, mainly in railways and other public works, frequently with a guaranteed rate of return. By 1913, India accounted for about one-tenth of Britain's overseas investment. In the late-Victorian age the economic argument became the major *justification* for British expansion everywhere. New international rivalry, economic depression, rising foreign competition and tariff discrimination only increased the need to protect and expand existing markets. Much of private enterprise, many financial interests in the City, and an increasing number of chambers of commerce and manufacturers' associations clamoured for the extension of imperial dominion. Empire had become a general panacea for Britain's ills. Joseph Chamberlain dreamed of developing the 'undeveloped estates', of imperial federation and an imperial *zollverein*. He was to be disappointed. Nevertheless it was still hoped at the end of the century that the newly acquired tropical colonies might yet prove to be the source of future economic salvation.

But political and economic arguments alone would never have secured the almost universal support of the Victorian governing classes. What is missing is the emotional context, for belief in empire was never entirely rational. The 'popular imperialism' of the late 1890s, it must be admitted, was an unusual phenomenon, the product of peculiar circumstances based partly on arrogance and more so on fear. It had many unsavoury aspects which many long-standing supporters of the imperial idea found distasteful. For them empire had always been an ennobling task, a duty, involving self-sacrifice as well as rich rewards. The art of government had a morally bracing effect on the character of the British people as well as incalculable benefits for the governed. Thus in the reassessments of the function of empire currently being undertaken, beside the more tangible *benefits* of the imperial connection must be placed the *duties* and *obligations* of the connection. Providence, so frequently invoked by Victorians, must be given its due. For it was often the sense of mission (and all that it subsumed) which convinced the doubtful and placed the empire above rational argument. It also provided, along with the marked loyalty of the colonies of British settlement, one of the toughest sinews of the relationship.

Notes and References

1. CONTINUITY AND DISCONTINUITY IN BRITISH IMPERIALISM *Paul Kennedy*

* Since the composition of this chapter, the second edition of *Africa and the Victorians* has appeared, with an additional 'Explanation' and 'Afterthoughts' written by Ronald Robinson. Those pieces offer a clarification of the author's original intentions and concede that in some minor areas (e.g. the motives behind the imperialism of foreign powers) their earlier presentation may not have been correct; but in general the second edition defends and reasserts the cluster of 'Robinson and Gallagher theories' and in consequence no major redrafting of this particular chapter seemed necessary.

1. J. A. Gallagher and R. E. Robinson, 'The Imperialism of Free Trade', *EconHR*, 2nd. ser., VI (1953) 1–15.

2. See, for example, A. P. Newton and J. Ewing, *The British Empire since 1783* (London, 1929); A. B. Keith, *Selected Speeches and Documents on British Colonial Policy 1763–1917*, 2 vols (London, 1918) and *The Governments of the British Empire* (London, 1936).

3. J. A. Hobson, *Imperialism: A Study* (London, 1902) pp. 19, 118.

4. V. I. Lenin, *Imperialism, the Highest Stage of Capitalism* (Moscow, 1975 edn.) p. 73.

5. Ibid., *passim*, but espec. pp. 22, 58, 115. See also the analysis in E. Stokes, 'Late Nineteenth-Century Colonial Expansion and the Attack on the Theory of Economic Imperialism: A Case of Mistaken Identity?', *HJ*, XII, (1969) 285–301.

6. Gallagher and Robinson, 'The Imperialism of Free Trade', p. 3.

7. R. E. Robinson and J. A. Gallagher, with A. Denny, *Africa and the Victorians: the Official Mind of Imperialism*, 2nd ed. (London, 1981). See also W. R. Louis (ed.), *Imperialism: The Robinson and Gallagher Controversy* (New York, 1976).

8. Robinson and Gallagher, *Africa and the Victorians*, p. 466ff.; and especially R. E. Robinson, 'Non-European Foundations of European Imperialism: Sketch for a Theory of Collaboration', in E. R. J. Owen and R. B. Sutcliffe (eds), *Studies in the Theory of Imperialism* (London, 1972) Chapter 5.

9. O. MacDonagh, 'The Anti-Imperialism of Free Trade', *EconHR*, XIV (1962) 489–501.

10. Platt's objections are best followed in his articles: 'The Imperialism of Free Trade: Some Reservations', *EconHR*, XXI (1968) 296–306; 'Further Objections to an "Imperialism of Free Trade" 1830–60', *EconHR*, XXVI

(1973) 77–91; and 'The National Economy and British Imperial Expansion before 1914', *JICH*, ii (1973) 3–14.

11. B. Semmel, *The Rise of Free Trade Imperialism: Classical Political Economy, the Empire of Free Trade and Imperialism 1750–1850* (Cambridge, 1970) *passim*.

12. C. C. Eldridge, *England's Mission: The Imperial Idea in the Age of Gladstone and Disraeli 1868–80* (London, 1973) Chapters 3–6 and *Victorian Imperialism* (London, 1978) pp. 92–101.

13. Robinson and Gallagher, *Africa and the Victorians*, p. 466.

14. Robinson and Gallagher, 'The Partition of Africa', in *New Cambridge Modern History*, vol. xi, *Material Progress and World-Wide Problems 1870–1898*, ed. F. H. Hinsley (Cambridge, 1962) pp. 593–640.

15. A. G. Hopkins, 'Economic Imperialism in West Africa: Lagos, 1880–1892', *EconHR*, xxi (1968) 580–606; C. W. Newbury, 'The Tariff Factor in Anglo-French West African Partition', in P. Gifford and W. R. Louis (eds), *France and Britain in Africa* (New Haven, Conn., 1971) pp. 221–59; H. A. Turner, 'Bismarck's Imperialist Venture: Anti-British in Origin?', in P. Gifford and W. R. Louis (eds), *Britain and Germany in Africa* (New Haven, Conn., 1967) pp. 47–82.

16. See especially, D. C. M. Platt, 'Economic Factors in British Policy during the "New Imperialism" ', *P&P*, 39 (1968) 120–38; W. G. Hynes, *The Economics of Empire: Britain, Africa and the New Imperialism 1870–1895* (London, 1979); G. N. Uzoigwe, *Britain and the Conquest of Africa* (Ann Arbor, Mich., 1974).

17. See the array of references on p. 487, fns 2 and 3, of P. J. Cain and A. G. Hopkins, 'The Political Economy of British Expansion Overseas 1750–1914', *EconHR*, xxxiii (1980) 463–90.

18. R. Shannon, *The Crisis of Imperialism 1865–1915* (London, 1974); B. Porter, *The Lion's Share: A Short History of British Imperialism 1850–1970* (London, 1975) Chapter iv; R. Hyam, *Britain's Imperial Century 1815–1914: A Study of Empire and Expansion* (London, 1976) Chapters 3 and 4; P. Kennedy, *The Realities behind Diplomacy: Background Influences on British External Policy 1865–1980* (London/Boston, 1981) Chapters 1 and 2.

19. See, for example, C. W. Newbury and A. S. Kanya-Forstner, 'French Policy and the Origins of the Scramble for West Africa', *JAH*, x (1969) 253–76.

20. Apart from Turner's article (note 15 above), see the references in P. Kennedy, *The Rise of the Anglo-German Antagonism 1860–1914* (London/Boston, 1980) Chapter 10.

21. Robinson and Gallagher, *Africa and the Victorians*, p. 19.

22. Kennedy, *The Rise of the Anglo-German Antagonism*, parts Three and Four.

2. COLONIAL SELF-GOVERNMENT   *Peter Burroughs*

1. William Cobbett (ed.), *Cobbett's Parliamentary History of England* (London, 1810) vol. xvii, pp. 1236–7.

2. W. L. Morton, 'The Local Executive in the British Empire, 1763–1828', *EHR*, LXXVIII (1963) 436–57.

3. Francis Masères, Attorney General of Quebec, 1769, quoted in V. T. Harlow, *The Founding of the Second British Empire 1763–1793* (London, 1964) vol. II, p. 668.

4. *Hansard*, New Series, XIX, 2 May 1828, 300–44.

5. Report of the Select Committee on the Civil Government of Canada, *Parliamentary Papers* 1828 (569) VII.

6. G. M. Craig (ed.), *Lord Durham's Report* (Toronto, 1963) pp. 22–3.

7. G. Martin, *The Durham Report and British Policy* (Cambridge, 1972), and 'The Influence of the Durham Report', R. Hyam and G. Martin (eds), *Reappraisals in British Imperial History* (London, 1975) pp. 75–87.

8. For example, H. E. Egerton, *A Short History of British Colonial Policy* (London, 1897); C. P. Lucas (ed.), *Lord Durham's Report on the Affairs of British North America*, 3 vols (Oxford, 1912); J. L. Morison, 'The Mission of the Earl of Durham', in *CHBE* (Cambridge, 1930) vol. VI, pp. 289–307; C. W. New, *Lord Durham* (Oxford, 1929).

9. J. M. Ward, *Colonial Self-Government: The British Experience 1759–1856* (London, 1976).

10. For example, C. A. Bodelsen, *Studies in Mid-Victorian Imperialism* (Copenhagen, 1924); R. L. Schuyler, *The Fall of the Old Colonial System: A Study in British Free Trade 1770–1870* (New York, 1945).

11. J. A. Gallagher and R. E. Robinson, 'The Imperialism of Free Trade', *EconHR*, VI (1953) 1–15. For a collection of key articles bearing on this historical controversy, A. G. L. Shaw (ed.), *Great Britain and the Colonies 1815–1865* (London, 1970).

12. Some parallels are drawn in J. W. Cell, *British Colonial Administration in the Mid-Nineteenth Century: The Policy-Making Process* (New Haven, 1970) pp. 154–5.

13. Gairdner to Grey, 28 November 1857, *Grey Papers*, University of Durham, GP/Gairdner.

3.   INDIA AND THE BRITISH EMPIRE   *R. J. Moore*

1. Percival Spear (ed.), *The Oxford History of India*, 3rd ed. (Oxford, 1958) p. 572.

2. Cited in C. H. Philips, *The East India Company, 1784–1834*, 2nd ed. (Manchester, 1961) p. 240.

3. Ibid., p. 241.

4. P. J. Marshall, 'British Expansion in India in the Eighteenth Century: An Historical Revision', *History*, LX (1975) 28–43.

5. Ibid., p. 30.

6. For the recourse to force in the interests of trade in the seventeenth and early eighteenth centuries, see I. Bruce Watson, 'Fortifications, Force and English Trade in India', *P&P*, 88 (1980) 70–87. See also K. N. Chaudhuri, *The Trading World of Asia and the English East India Company, 1660–1760* (Cambridge, 1978).

7. Marshall, 'British Expansion', p. 37.

8. Ibid., p. 41.

9. P. J. Marshall, 'Economic and Political Expansion: The Case of Oudh', *Modern Asian Studies*, IX (1974) 465–82.

10. Ibid., p. 482.

11. Ibid., pp. 481–2.

12. J. C. Heesterman's phrase in his 'Was there an Indian Reaction? Western Expansion in Indian Perspective', H. L. Wesseling (ed.), *Expansion and Reaction* (Leiden, 1978) pp. 39–40, n. 25.

13. G. J. Alder, 'Britain and the Defence of India – The Origins of the Problem, 1798–1815', *Journal of Asian History*, VI (1972) 14–44; Edward Ingram, 'The Rules of the Game: A Commentary on the Defence of British India, 1798–1829', *JICH*, III (1975) 257–79.

14. E. Ingram, *The Beginning of the Great Game in Asia, 1828–1834* (Oxford, 1979).

15. M. Yapp, *Strategies of British India: Britain, Iran and Afghanistan, 1798–1850* (Oxford, 1980).

16. For the careful policies that segregated the external and internal threats in the 1850s (during the Crimean and Persian wars and the Indian Mutiny) see G. J. Alder, 'India and the Crimean War', *JICH*, II (1973) 15–37.

17. A. G. Stone, *Indian Campaigns, 1778–1914* (London, 1974).

18. 'The first century of British colonial rule in India: social revolution or social stagnation?', in E. Stokes, *The Peasant and the Raj: Studies in agrarian society and peasant rebellion in colonial India* (Cambridge, 1978) p. 26.

19. Ibid., p. 27.

20. Ibid., p. 28.

21. P. J. Cain and A. G. Hopkins, 'The Political Economy of British Expansion Overseas, 1750–1914', *EconHR*, XXXIII (1980) 463–90, p. 479.

22. Stokes, *Peasant and the Raj*, p. 28.

23. Gallagher and Robinson, 'The Imperialism of Free Trade', reprinted in W. R. Louis (ed.), *Imperialism, The Robinson and Gallagher Controversy* (New York, 1976) p. 58.

24. For an analysis of Manchester's 'anti-imperialism' see Oliver Mac-Donagh, 'The Anti-Imperialism of Free Trade', *EconHR*, XIV (1962) 489–501.

25. See R. J. Moore, *Sir Charles Wood's Indian Policy, 1853–66* (Manchester, 1966).

26. Introduction to R. Jeffrey (ed.), *People, Princes and Paramount Power: Society and Politics in the Indian Princely States* (Delhi, 1978) p. 7.

27. Ibid., pp. 7–8.

28. Ibid., p. 10.

29. Stokes, *Peasant and the Raj*, p. 91. Cf. the Utilitarians' attempt to encourage development by adjusting the revenue to the yield from the land: Stokes, *The English Utilitarians and India* (Oxford, 1959) Chapter II.

30. Even Professor Robinson, who joined with J. A. Gallagher to assert the continuity of nineteenth-century imperialism, has recently recognised the Mutiny as prompting a fresh cost-benefit analysis of expansion (in Wesseling, *Expansion and Reaction*, p. 142).

31. Moore, *Wood, passim* (e.g. p. 134).

32. Cain and Hopkins, 'Political Economy', pp. 483, 489.

33. B. R. Tomlinson, 'India and the British Empire, 1880–1935', *Indian Economic and Social History Review*, 12 (1975) 340.

34. See P. Harnetty, *Imperialism and Free Trade: Lancashire and India in the Mid-Nineteenth Century* (Manchester, 1972).

35. L. H. Jenks, *The Migration of British Capital to 1875* (London, 1938) pp. 206–7.

36. Daniel Thorner, *Investment in Empire: British Railway and Steam Shipping Enterprise in India, 1825–1849* (Philadelphia, 1950) Chapter 7.

37. See A. P. Kaminsky, ' "Lombard Street" and India: Currency Problems in the Late Nineteenth Century', *Indian Economic and Social History Review*, XVII (1980) 307–27.

38. See H. L. Hoskins, *British Routes to India* (London, 1928); R. E. Robinson and J. A. Gallagher, with A. Denny, *Africa and the Victorians: The Official Mind of Imperialism*, 2nd ed. (London, 1981).

39. Tomlinson, 'India and the British Empire', p. 349.

40. A. Seal, *The Emergence of Indian Nationalism: Competition and Collaboration in the Later Nineteenth Century* (Cambridge, 1968).

41. *Report on Constitutional Reforms* (Montagu-Chelmsford), Cd. 9109 (1918) 69.

42. M. D. Morris, 'Towards a Reinterpretation of Nineteenth Century Indian Economic History', *JEH*, 33 (1963) 606–18, reprinted with critical papers by Bipan Chandra, T. Raychaudhuri and T. Matsui, and Morris's rejoinder, *Indian Economic and Social History Review*, 5 (1968) 1–100, 319–88.

4. BRITAIN AND THE NEW IMPERIALISM *James Sturgis*

1. W. D. McIntyre, *The Imperial Frontier in the Tropics 1865–75* (London, 1967) pp. 378–9.

2. P. J. Durrans, 'A Two-Edged Sword: The Liberal Attack on Disraelian Imperialism', *JICH*, x (1982) 262–84.

3. For the conflicting interpretations regarding Egypt see: E. R. J. Owen, 'Egypt and Europe: from French expedition to British occupation', in *Studies in the Theory of Imperialism*, E. R. J. Owen and R. B. Sutcliffe (eds) (London, 1972) Chapter VIII; A. Schölch, 'The "Men on the Spot" and the English Occupation of Egypt in 1882', *HJ*, XIX (1976) 773–85; D. C. M. Platt, *Finance, Trade and Politics in British Foreign Policy 1815–1914* (Oxford, 1968) pp. 154–80; R. E. Robinson and J. A. Gallagher with Alice Denny, *Africa and the Victorians*, 2nd ed. (London, 1981) Chapter V; A. P. Thornton, *For the File on Empire* (London, 1968) pp. 220–51.

4. Peter Marshall, 'The Imperial Factor in the Liberal Decline, 1880–1885' in *Perspectives of Empire*, J. E. Flint and G. Williams (eds) (London, 1973) pp. 143–7.

5. J. E. Flint, *Sir George Goldie and the making of Nigeria* (London, 1960) p. 270.

6. S. Koss, *The Rise and Fall of the Political Press in Britain* (London, 1981) pp. 215, 356–408.

7. T. Boyle, 'The Liberal Imperialists, 1892–1906', *Bulletin of the Institute of Historical Research*, LII (1979) 48–67.

8. A. N. Porter, *The Origins of the South African War. Joseph Chamberlain and the Diplomacy of Imperialism 1895–9* (Manchester, 1980) pp. 258–64.

9. P. J. Cain and A. G. Hopkins, 'The Political Economy of British Expansion Overseas, 1750–1914', *EconHR*, XXXIII (1980) 463–90. See also P. J. Cain, *Economic Foundations of British Overseas Expansion 1815–1914* (London, 1980).

10. D. C. M. Platt, *Finance, Trade and Politics*, pp. 363–4.

11. W. G. Hynes, 'British Mercantile Attitudes towards Imperial Expansion', *HJ*, XIX (1976) 969–79. See also W. G. Hynes, *The Economics of Empire. Britain, Africa and the New Imperialism 1870–1895* (London, 1979).

12. C. C. Wrigley, 'Neo-Mercantile Policies and the New Imperialism', in *The Imperial Impact: Studies in the Economic History of Africa and India*, C. Dewey and A. G. Hopkins (eds) (London, 1978) Chapter 2.

13. A. G. Hopkins, 'Economic Imperialism in West Africa: Lagos, 1880–92', *EconHR*, XXI (1968) 580–606. See also A. G. Hopkins, *An Economic History of West Africa* (London, 1973).

14. F. Harcourt, 'Disraeli's Imperialism, 1866–1868: A Question of Timing', *HJ*, XXIII (1980) 87–109.

15. H. Cunningham, 'Jingoism in 1877–78', *Victorian Studies*, XIV (1971) 429–53.

16. W. Baumgart, *Imperialism. The Idea and Reality of British and French Colonial Expansion, 1880–1914* (Oxford, 1982) pp. 32–46.

17. Tony Smith, *The Pattern of Imperialism* (Cambridge, 1981) pp. 42–9.

18. Robinson and Gallagher, *Africa and the Victorians*; D. K. Fieldhouse, *Economics and Empire* (London, 1973); R. E. Robinson, 'Non-European foundations of European imperialism: sketch for a theory of collaboration', in Owen and Sutcliffe, *Theory of Imperialism*, Chapter V.

19. R. Foster, *Lord Randolph Churchill* (Oxford, 1981) pp. 206–13.

20. J. D. Hargreaves, *West Africa Partitioned*, vol. I, *The Loaded Pause 1885–9* (London, 1974) p. 22.

5. THE EXTRA-EUROPEAN FOUNDATIONS OF BRITISH IMPERIALISM: TOWARDS A REASSESSMENT   A. E. Atmore

1. Ronald Robinson, 'Non-European foundations of European imperialism: sketch for a theory of collaboration', in E. R. J. Owen and R. B. Sutcliffe, *Studies in the Theory of Imperialism* (London, 1972) pp. 138–9.

2. Ibid., p. 139.

3. Ibid., p. 129.

4. The basic information in this section has been culled from the standard works on the Ottoman empire: Bernard Lewis, *The Emergence of Modern Turkey* (London, 1961); P. M. Holt, *Egypt and the Fertile Crescent* (London, 1966); R. H. Davison, *Reform in the Ottoman Empire, 1839–1876* (Princeton, 1963); W. R. Polk and R. L. Chambers; *Beginnings of Modernisation in the Middle East; the nineteenth century* (Chicago, 1968); Stanford Shaw, *History of the Ottoman Empire*

and Modern Turkey (Cambridge, 1976); M. A. Cook (ed.) *Studies in the Economic History of the Middle East* (Oxford, 1970).

5. Robinson, 'Non-European Foundations', p. 129.

6. Immanuel Wallerstein, 'Ottoman Empire and Capitalist World Economy: some questions for research', *Review*, II (1979) 389–98.

7. Huri Islamoglu and Suraiya Faroqhi, 'Crop Patterns and Agricultural Production Trends in Sixteenth Century Anatolia', *Review*, II (1979) 436.

8. Robinson, 'Non-European Foundations', pp. 132–3.

9. See Freda Harcourt, 'Disraeli's Imperialism, 1866–1868: a question of timing', *HJ*, XXIII (1980) 87–109. This perceptive article demonstrates (indirectly) how Africa was almost partitioned in the 1860s.

10. John D. Hargreaves, *Prelude to the Partition of West Africa* (London, 1966) p. 169.

11. For details of these British wars in West Africa see Michael Crowder (ed.), *West African Resistance: the military response to colonial occupation* (London, 1971).

12. A. S. Kanya-Forstner, *The Conquest of the Western Sudan: a study in French military imperialism* (Cambridge, 1969).

13. For the Dahomey war, see David Ross in Crowder, *West African Resistance*, pp. 144–69.

14. For somewhat different views, see Agneta Pallinder-Law, 'Aborted Modernisation in West Africa? The Case of Abeokuta', *JAH*, XI (1974) 65–82.

15. Edward I. Steinhart, *Conflict and Collaboration: the Kingdoms of Western Uganda, 1890–1907* (Princeton, 1977) pp. vii–viii.

16. Ronald Robinson and John Gallagher with Alice Denny, *Africa and the Victorians: the official mind of imperialism*, 2nd ed. (London, 1981).

17. Owen and Sutcliffe, *Theory of Imperialism*, p. 141.

18. Ibid.

19. John Lonsdale and Bruce Berman, 'Coping with the Contradictions: the development of the colonial state in Kenya, 1895–1914', *JAH*, XX (1979) 487–505. In the sentence, 'peasant expansion might also, from initially strengthening the patronage relations by which chiefs and others made these contributions to the politics of collaboration, go on to transform these props of colonial authority into exploitative employers or landlords through the discontinuities of class formation', pp. 491–2.

20. Gwyn Prins, *The Hidden Hippopotamus: reappraisal in African history – the early colonial experience in Western Zambia* (Cambridge, 1980) pp. 2–3.

21. See A. N. Porter, *The origins of the South African War: Joseph Chamberlain and the diplomacy of imperialism, 1895–99* (Manchester, 1980) on this point. Probably the most resolute supporters of British imperialism in South Africa at that time were Africans. But that is another matter.

22. S. Marks and A. E. Atmore, 'The Imperial Factor in South Africa in the Nineteenth Century: towards a reassessment', in E. F. Penrose (ed.), *European Imperialism and the Partition of Africa* (London, 1975) p. 132.

23. Robert G. Gregory. 'Cooperation and Collaboration in Colonial East Africa: the Asians' political role, 1890–1964, *African Affairs*, 80 (1981) 259.

6.   RACE AND THE VICTORIANS   *Christine Bolt*

I should like to thank Dr Brian Harrison for his detailed and valuable criticisms of an earlier version of this chapter, and especially for suggestions relating to notes 10, 20 and 25.

1. G. M. Frederickson, *The Black Image in the White Mind* (New York, 1971) pp. 97–130, quotation from p. 97.

2. H. Temperley, *British Antislavery, 1833–1870* (London, 1972) pp. 115–16, 221 – though later on in the century, unity and a greater degree of financial security would be restored: see ibid., pp. 265–6.

3. Ibid., p. 266; C. C. Eldridge, *England's Mission* (London, 1973) pp. 242, 253 and Chapter 6; W. D. McIntyre, *The Imperial Frontier in the Tropics, 1865–1875* (London, 1967) pp. 39–41; L. H. Gann and P. Duignan, *The Rulers of British Africa, 1870–1914* (London, 1978) pp. 23–5.

4. The next five paragraphs have drawn on: C. Bolt, *Victorian Attitudes to Race* (London, 1971) Chapter 1; D. A. Lorimer, *Colour, Class and the Victorians* (Leicester, 1978) Chapter 7; M. Banton *Race Relations* (New York, 1967); J. W. Burrow, *Evolution and Society* (Cambridge, 1966) especially pp. 263–77; G. Jones, *Social Darwinism in English Thought* (Brighton, 1980); and L. Poliakov, *The Aryan Myth* (London, 1974) pp. 175–82, 223–4, 292–4, and Chapters 7–11.

5. M. Nadis, 'G. A. Henty's Idea of India', *Victorian Studies*, VIII (1964) 49–58; A. J. Greenberger, *The British Image of India* (London, 1969) pp. 2, 4–7.

6. Lorimer, *Colour, Class and the Victorians*, Chapter 3, especially pp. 60, 68.

7. J. Walvin, *Black and White* (London, 1973) pp. 189–99.

8. L. P. Curtis, *Apes and Angels* (London, 1971) pp. 13–14, and *Anglo-Saxons and Celts* (Bridgeport, 1968) pp. 19, 53–4, 61–2; S. Gilley, 'English Attitudes to the Irish in England, 1780–1900', in C. Holmes (ed.), *Immigrants and Minorities in British Society* (London, 1978) pp. 81–110; J. A. Garrard, *The English and Immigration, 1880–1910* (London, 1971) pp. 13, 76, 206; L. P. Gartner, *The Jewish Immigrants in England, 1880–1914* (London, 1960) pp. 107–8; B. Gainer, *The Alien Invasion* (London, 1972) pp. 114, 118, 212, 214.

9. Gilley, 'English Attitudes', pp. 93, 98, 103–5; Gainer, *Alien Invasion*, 212–13; N. Kirk, 'Ethnicity, Class and Popular Toryism, 1815–1870', pp. 64–5, 68, 73f., 82–3, 92–4, in K. Lunn (ed.), *Hosts, Immigrants and Minorities* (Folkestone, 1980).

10. J. Amery, *The Life of Joseph Chamberlain* (London, 1951) Vol. IV, pp. 14–15.

11. E. Stokes, *The Political Ideas of English Imperialism* (London, 1960) pp. 171, 181; R. Wilkinson, *The Prefects* (London, 1964); G. Best, *Mid-Victorian Britain, 1851–1875*, revised ed. (St Albans, 1973) pp. 171, 183, 276–7.

12. Greenberger, *British Image*, pp. 11, 25, 28, 42, 44, 48–52, 56, 64; G. Arnold, *Held Fast for Empire* (London, 1980) pp. 68, 93, 126; Gann and Duignan, *The Rulers*, p. 263.

13. V. G. Kiernan, *The Lords of Human Kind*, revised ed. (Harmondsworth, 1972) pp. 167–70, 179; T. G. Fraser, 'Imperial Policy and Indian Minorities

Overseas, 1905–23', in A. C. Hepburn (ed.), *Minorities in History* (London, 1978) pp. 154–5.

14. M. Green, *Dreams of Adventure, Deeds of Empire* (London, 1980) pp. xi, 23–4, 65; J. Meyers, *Fiction and the Colonial Experience* (Ipswich, 1973) pp. vii–viii; Gann and Duignan, *The Rulers*, pp. 20–1.

15. T. W. Clark (ed.), *The Novel in India* (London, 1970) pp. 16–18, 149, 158; S. P. Cohen, *The Indian Army* (Berkeley, 1971) pp. 50–1; Arnold, *Held Fast*, pp. 43–5.

16. P. Narain, *Press and Politics in India, 1885–1905* (Bombay, 1970) pp. 166–73.

17. Lorimer, *Colour, Class and the Victorians*, Chapters 5–6; W. L. Burn, *The Age of Equipoise* (London, 1968) p. 82; H. Perkin, *The Origins of Modern English Society, 1780–1880* (London, 1969) pp. 273–90, 428–30.

18. N. Canny, 'Dominant Minorities: English Settlers in Ireland and Virginia, 1550–1650', pp. 51–69, in Hepburn, *Minorities in History*.

19. Burn, *Age of Equipoise*, p. 33; R. Price, *An Imperial War and the British Working Class* (London, 1972) pp. 237–9.

20. Narain, *Press and Politics*, p. 167.

21. G. Shepperson, 'The World of Rudyard Kipling', pp. 130–1, in A. Rutherford (ed.), *Kipling's Mind and Art* (Edinburgh and London, 1964).

22. E. Stokes, *The English Utilitarians and India* (London, 1959); S. N. Mukherjee, *Sir William Jones* (London, 1968) pp. 3, 16, 42, 83, 111–12, 119–20, 125–7, 131, 133–6.

23. S. D. Singh, *Novels of the Indian Mutiny* (New Dehli, 1973) p. 227; M. Edwardes, *Bound to Exile* (London, 1969) Chapters 10–12; G. D. Bearce, *British Attitudes to India, 1784–1858* (London, 1961) pp. 233–41; F. Hutchins, *The Illusion of Permanence* (Princeton, 1967) pp. 153–4, 156–8, 171–4, 194–5; Greenberger, *British Image*, p. 33; Meyers, *Fiction*, pp. 19–20, 35–6.

24. Gann and Duignan, *The Rulers*, pp. 257–8, 264–5, 337.

25. H. Arendt, *Imperialism* (New York, 1968, formerly published as *Origins of Totalitarianism*, Pt. 2) pp. 47, 61; R. Koebner and H. D. Schmidt, *Imperialism* (Cambridge, 1964) pp. 89, 186, 194–5, 207, 215–17; C. A. Bodelsen, *Studies in Mid-Victorian Imperialism* (London, 1968 ed.) p. 69; J. L. Garvin, *The Life of Joseph Chamberlain* (London, 1934) Vol. III, p. 27.

26. B. Porter, *Critics of Empire* (London, 1968) pp. 313–29, 337.

27. Quotation from Stokes, *English Utilitarians*, p. 10; A. P. Thornton, *Doctrines of Imperialism* (New York, 1965) pp. 2, 25; P. Mason, *Patterns of Dominance* (London, 1970) especially Part II, Chapters IV and VI.

7. IMPERIALISM AND SOCIAL REFORM *M. E. Chamberlain*

1. V. I. Lenin, *Imperialism, the Highest Stage of Capitalism* (Foreign Languages Press, Peking 1975), pp. 93–4.

2. The evidence taken by the Royal Commission on the Depression of Trade and Industry is in *Parliamentary Papers* (1886) XXX, 1, 231; XXII. 1; XXIII, 1. The final reports are in *Parliamentary Papers* (1886) XXIII, 507. For the role

of Dunraven and the Fair Trade League see M. E. Chamberlain, 'Lord Dunraven and the British Empire', *Morgannwg*, xv (1971) 50–72.

3. J. A. Hobson, *Imperialism: A Study*, 3rd ed. (London, 1938) p. 101.

4. F. Harcourt, 'Disraeli's Imperialism, 1866–1868: a question of timing', *HJ*, xxiii (1980) 87–109.

5. J. L. Garvin, *Life of Joseph Chamberlain* (London, 1932) i 548–58.

6. *The Times*, 16 July 1895, quoted in G. Bennett, *The Concept of Empire*, 2nd ed. (London, 1962) pp. 313–14.

7. B. Semmel, *Imperialism and Social Reform* (London, 1960) p. 27.

8. V. I. Lenin, *Imperialism*, p. 129.

9. J. A. Hobson, *Imperialism: A Study*, pp. 47–8.

10. H.-U. Wehler, 'Bismarck's Imperialism, 1862–1890', *P&P*, xlviii (1970) 123, 124.

11. J. A. Hobson, *Imperialism: A Study*, p. 38.

12. Ibid., p. 81.

13. Sidney Webb, 'Twentieth Century Politics: a Policy of National Efficiency', *Fabian Tract*, no. 108 (1901) p. 9.

14. Quoted in R. J. Scally, *The Origins of the Lloyd George Coalition; the Politics of Social-Imperialism, 1900–1918* (Princeton, 1975) p. 373.

15. A. J. P. Taylor, *English History, 1914–1945* (Oxford, 1965) p. 600.

8.   SINEWS OF EMPIRE: CHANGING PERSPECTIVES
C. C. Eldridge

1. J. A. Gallagher and R. E. Robinson, 'The Imperialism of Free Trade', *EconHR*, 2nd ser., vi (1953) 1–15.

2. P. J. Cain and A. G. Hopkins, 'The Political Economy of British Expansion Overseas, 1750–1914', *EconHR* xxxiii (1980) 489.

3. Ibid., p. 466.

4. Ibid., pp. 489–90.

5. See, principally, P. Knaplund, *Gladstone and Britain's Imperial Policy* (London, 1927); D. O. Wagner, 'British Economists and the Empire', *Political Science Quarterly*, xlvi (1931) 248–76; K. L. Knorr, *British Colonial Theories, 1570–1850* (Toronto, 1944); H. T. Manning, 'The Colonial Policy of the Whig Ministers, 1830–37', *CHR*, xxxiii (1952) 203–36, 341–68.

6. For example, J. R. M. Butler, 'Imperial Questions in British Politics, 1868–80', *CHBE*, iii, 18–26.

7. See B. Semmel, 'The Philosophic Radicals and Colonialism', *JEH*, xxi (1961) 513–25.

8. Ibid., p. 513.

9. See W. D. Grampp, *The Manchester School of Economics* (Stanford, 1960).

10. R. J. Moore, 'Imperialism and "Free Trade" Policy in India, 1853–4', *EconHR*, xvii (1964) 135–6.

11. Cobden to Bright, 23 December 1848, quoted in J. Morley, *The Life of Richard Cobden* (London, 1903) pp. 502–3.

12. Bright to E. Sturge, 24 September 1857, quoted in J. L. Sturgis, *John Bright and the Empire* (London, 1969) p. 92.

13. Bright to E. Ellice, 16 December 1859, *Ellice Papers*, National Library of Scotland, MSS. Acc. 1993.

14. Speech at Leeds, 7 October 1881, quoted in Sir P. Magnus, *Gladstone, A Biography* (London, 1954) p. 287.

15. See H. Pelling, *Popular Politics and Society in Late Victorian Britain* (London, 1968) and R. Price, *An Imperial War and the British Working Class* (London, 1972). Also H. Cunningham, 'Jingoism and the Working Classes, 1877–8', *Bulletin for the Study of Labour History*, 19 (1969) 6–9.

16. See B. Porter, *Critics of Empire: British Radical Attitudes to Colonialism in Africa, 1895–1914* (London, 1969); S. Koss (ed.), *The Pro-Boers: The Anatomy of a Anti-War Movement* (Chicago, 1973); and A. Davey, *The British Pro-Boers, 1877–1902* (Cape Town, 1978).

17. J. A. Roebuck, *The Colonies of England* (London, 1849) pp. 8–9.

18. W. E. Gladstone, 'England's Mission', *The Nineteenth Century*, IV (September 1878) 569.

19. W. E. Gladstone, 16 April 1849, *Hansard*, 3rd ser., CIV 352.

20. Quoted in G. Bennett (ed.), *The Concept of Empire: Burke to Attlee, 1774–1947*, 2nd ed. (London, 1962) pp. 90–1.

21. Ibid., pp. 181–4.

22. Carnarvon, 'Imperial Administration', *Fortnightly Review*, XXIV (December 1878) pp. 763–4.

23. Quoted in Bennett, *Concept of Empire*, p. 318.

Suggestions for Further Reading

1. CONTINUITY AND DISCONTINUITY IN BRITISH IMPERIALISM   *Paul Kennedy*

The most comprehensive survey of British imperialism in the nineteenth century is R. Hyam's *Britain's Imperial Century 1815–1914: A Study of Empire and Expansion* (London, 1976); there is also a good coverage in C. C. Eldridge, *Victorian Imperialism* (London, 1978). B. Porter's excellent and spirited account, *The Lion's Share: A Short History of British Imperialism 1850–1970* (London, 1975), only begins in mid-century, but compensates in many other ways.

To get the 'flavour' of Robinson and Gallagher's writings, students should read the now classic work, *Africa and the Victorians: The Official Mind of Imperialism*, 2nd ed. (London, 1981). The shorter pieces – including their seminal essay on 'The Imperialism of Free Trade' which provoked the whole continuity debate – are now conveniently collected in W. R. Louis (ed.), *Imperialism: The Robinson and Gallagher Controversy* (New York, 1976), which also contains a wide-ranging analysis of the debate by the editor. Another very useful survey of the historiography is P. J. Cain's *Economic Foundations of British Overseas Expansion 1815–1914* (London, 1980). British imperial policy and attitudes in the early-to-mid-nineteenth century are examined in the essays collected in A. G. L. Shaw (ed.), *Great Britain and the Colonies 1815–1865* (London, 1970).

There is no space here to list the numerous *regional* studies of British imperialism, although the most important of them have much to say about the larger debate. But the following works, which cover general themes, should be noted: D. C. M. Platt, *Finance, Trade and Politics in British Foreign Policy 1815–1914* (Oxford, 1968); A. P. Thornton, *The Imperial Idea and its Enemies: A Study in British Power* (London, 1959); and D. K. Fieldhouse, *Economics and Empire 1830–1914* (London, 1973).

Finally, one should note an important general article: P. J. Cain and A. G. Hopkins, 'The Political Economy of British Expansion Overseas, 1750–1914', *EconHR*, xxxiii (1980) 463–90, with a wealth of references and an intimation of a larger work to come.

2. COLONIAL SELF-GOVERNMENT   *Peter Burroughs*

The only comprehensive, scholarly study of colonial self-government is John M. Ward, *Colonial Self-Government: The British Experience 1759–1856* (London, 1976). Other accounts deal with particular aspects of the subject. The imperial dimension of the American Revolution is surveyed by Ian R. Christie, *Crisis of Empire: Great Britain and the American Colonies 1754–1783* (London, 1966). British policy towards Quebec is fully analysed in Vincent T. Harlow, *The Founding of the Second British Empire 1763–1793*, vol. II (London, 1964), and viewed from a Canadian angle in A. L. Burt, *The Old Province of Quebec* (Minneapolis, 1933; Toronto, 1967). The problems of Canadian government and the character of British policy between 1791 and the rebellions are examined in P. Burroughs, *The Canadian Crisis and British Colonial Policy 1828–1841* (London, 1972), and in Helen T. Manning, *The Revolt of French Canada 1800–1835* (London, 1962) and her article 'The Colonial Policy of the Whig Ministers 1830–37', *CHR*, XXXIII (1952) 203–36 and 341–68.

A lively, readable introduction to the history of Lower Canada and the rebellions is presented by Joseph Schull, *Rebellion: The Rising in French Canada 1837* (Toronto, 1971). A celebrated but controversial economic interpretation is offered by Donald G. Creighton, *The Commercial Empire of the St. Lawrence 1760–1850* (New Haven, 1937), reissued as *The Empire of the St. Lawrence* (Toronto, 1956), with the thesis summarised in 'The Economic Background of the Rebellions of Eighteen Thirty-Seven', *Canadian Journal of Economics and Political Science*, III (1937) 322–34. The causes of agrarian discontent are traced in Fernand Ouellet, *The Economic and Social History of Quebec 1760–1850* (English translation, Toronto, 1979). The reform movement and rebellion in Upper Canada are discussed in Gerald M. Craig, *Upper Canada, The Formative Years 1784–1841* (Toronto, 1963), and in Aileen Dunham, *Political Unrest in Upper Canada 1815–1836* (London, 1927; Toronto, 1963). Mackenzie's career is graphically portrayed in William Kilbourn, *The Firebrand, William Lyon Mackenzie and the Rebellion in Upper Canada* (Toronto, 1958). W. S. MacNutt, *The Atlantic Provinces, The Emergence of Colonial Society 1712–1857* (Toronto, 1965) covers developments in the Maritime provinces.

Britain's handling of colonial self-government in the 1840s and 1850s is examined in John W. Cell, *British Colonial Administration in the Mid-Nineteenth Century: The Policy-Making Process* (New Haven, 1970), and in two books by W. P. Morrell, *British Colonial Policy in the Age of Peel and Russell* (Oxford, 1930) and *British Colonial Policy in the Mid-Victorian Age* (Oxford, 1969).

3. INDIA AND THE BRITISH EMPIRE   *R. J. Moore*

Many of the most pertinent studies are mentioned in the notes. In addition, for the pre-Mutiny period of expansion the following works may be consulted: P. J. Marshall, *Problems of Empire: Britain and India, 1757–1813* (London, 1968), and *East Indian Fortunes: The British in Bengal in the Eighteenth Century* (Oxford, 1976); M. Greenberg, *British Trade and the Opening of China, 1800–42*

(Cambridge, 1969 ed.); K. N. Chaudhuri (ed.), *The Economic Development of India under the East India Company, 1814–1858* (Cambridge, 1971); G. D. Bearce, *British Attitudes Towards India, 1784–1858* (Oxford, 1961); K. A. Ballhatchet (ed.), *East India Company Studies, Essays in Honour of Sir Cyril Philips* (London, 1984); C. H. Philips (ed.), *Indian Society and the Beginnings of Modernization, c. 1830–1850* (London, 1976).

For the post-Mutiny period the following items are suggested: T. R. Metcalf, *The Aftermath of Revolt: India, 1857–1870* (Princeton, 1964); R. J. Moore, *Liberalism and Indian Politics, 1872–1922* (London, 1966); F. G. Hutchins, *The Illusion of Permanence: British Imperialism in India* (Princeton, 1967); S. Gopal, *British Policy in India, 1858–1905* (Cambridge, 1965); I. Copland, *The British Raj and the Indian Princes: Paramountcy in Western India, 1857–1930* (London, 1982); R. I. Crane and N. G. Barrier (eds), *British Imperial Policy in India and Sri Lanka, 1858–1912* (Columbia, Missouri, 1981); B. Martin, *New India, 1885: British Official Policy and the Emergence of the Indian National Congress* (Berkeley, 1969); S. R. Mehrotra, *The Commonwealth and the Nation* (New Delhi, 1978); C. H. Philips (ed.), *The Evolution of India and Pakistan, 1858–1947: Select Documents* (Oxford, 1962); D. Dilks, *Curzon in India*, 2 vols (London, 1969–70).

For the economic aspects of the imperial connection, see V. Anstey, *The Economic Development of India* (London, 1957 ed.); S. Ambirajan, *Classical Political Economy and British Policy in India* (Cambridge, 1978); Bipan Chandra, *The Rise and Growth of Economic Nationalism in India, 1880–1905* (New Delhi, 1966); the journal *Indian Economic and Social History Review*; and P. G. Robb, 'British Rule and Indian "Improvement" ', *EconHR*, xxxiv (1981) 507–23.

For a collection and brief synthesis of J. A. Gallagher's writings, see John Gallagher, *The Decline, Revival and Fall of the British Empire*, ed. A. Seal (Cambridge, 1982).

4. BRITAIN AND THE NEW IMPERIALISM   *James Sturgis*

Of books not mentioned in the text or notes the most helpful guides to an understanding of the different conceptual approaches to the scramble for Africa are an analytical essay by Professor G. N. Sanderson which is contained in F. E. Penrose (ed.), *European Imperialism and the Partition of Africa* (London, 1975) and C. C. Eldridge's *Victorian Imperialism* (London, 1978) which examines the theories of the motivation for imperialism and the immediate events prior to Partition.

5. THE EXTRA-EUROPEAN FOUNDATIONS OF BRITISH IMPERIALISM: TOWARDS A REASSESSMENT   *A. E. Atmore*

Many of the studies by Robinson and Gallagher, and by Robinson alone, which appeared in the 1960s and 1970s, have been reprinted in the 1980s. The seminal work, *Africa and the Victorians*, was published in a second edition in 1981 (London, paperback). Robinson contributed a new introduction and

'Afterthoughts', which attempted to relate the original 1961 book both to earlier and later writings on imperialism and the partition of Africa. The 1961 text of *Africa and the Victorians* was reprinted unaltered: the great corpus of historical studies on this vast topic remained largely unassimilated. Robinson's article, 'Non-European foundations of European imperialism' was reprinted in John Gallagher (ed. Anil Seal), *The Decline, Revival and Fall of the British Empire: the Ford lectures and other essays* (Cambridge, 1982). A further paper by Robinson, 'European Imperialism and Indigenous Reactions in British West Africa, 1880–1914' appeared in H. L. Wesseling (ed.), *Expansion and Reaction: essays in European expansion and reactions in Asia and Africa* (Comparative Studies in Overseas History, Vol. 1, Leiden, 1978).

The 'peripheral crises' theory of Robinson and Gallagher has received a great deal of critical attention from historians, both in the global context of European imperialism, and in the causes and consequences of this imperialism in key regions of the world. A brilliant neo-Marxist (and anti-Leninist) assessment is Bill Warren (ed. J. Sender), *Imperialism: Pioneer of Capitalism* (London, 1980). P. J. Cain and A. G. Hopkins, 'The political economy of British expansion overseas, 1750–1914', *EconHR*, xxxiii (1980) 463–90, is a cogently argued examination, and on a smaller scale, also of great interest is Freda Harcourt, 'Disraeli's imperialism, 1866–1868: a question of timing', *HJ*, xxiii (1980) 87–109. Excellent articles, reviewing much of the recent literature, are Shula Marks, 'Scrambling for South Africa', *JAH*, xxiii (1982) 97–113 and Robin Law, 'Imperialism and Partition', *JAH*, xxiv (1983) 101–4. Michael Brett, 'Modernisation in 19th Century North Africa', *The Maghreb Review*, 7 (1982) 16–22, is most instructive and thought-provoking.

For European imperialism and the Ottoman empire, there are: S. J. Shaw, *A History of the Ottoman Empire and Modern Turkey* (Cambridge, 1978); Charles Issawi, *The Economic History of Turkey, 1800–1914* (Chicago, 1981); Carter V. Findley, *Bureaucratic reform in the Ottoman Empire: the Sublime Porte, 1789–1922* (Princeton, 1980); Elie Kedourie, *England and the Middle East: the destruction of the Ottoman Empire, 1914–1921*, 2nd ed. (Hassocks, 1978); and J. L. Wallach (ed.), *Germany and the Middle East, 1835–1939* (Tel Aviv, 1975). Marian Kent (ed.), *The Great Powers and the end of the Ottoman Empire* (London, forthcoming), will be of considerable interest.

6.   RACE AND THE VICTORIANS   *Christine Bolt*

In addition to the books mentioned in the notes, readers will find the following works helpful: J. Rex, *Race Relations in Sociological Theory* (London, 1970); J. Barzun, *Race: a Study in Superstition* (New York, 1965 ed.); P. D. Curtin, *Image of Africa* (London, 1965); H. A. Cairns, *Prelude to Imperialism: British Reactions to Central African Society, 1840–1890* (London, 1965); M. Crowder, *West Africa Under Colonial Rule* (London, 1970 ed.); B. Semmel, *The Governor Eyre Controversy* (London, 1962); T. R. Metcalf, *Aftermath of Revolt: India, 1857–1870* (Princeton, 1964); J. K. Stanford, *Ladies in the Sun: The Memsahib's India, 1790–1860* (London, 1962); C. C. Eldridge,

Victorian Imperialism (London, 1978); K. Ballhatchet, *Race, Sex and Class Under the Raj: Imperial Attitudes and Policies and Their Critics, 1793–1905* (London, 1980).

7. IMPERIALISM AND SOCIAL REFORM   *M. E. Chamberlain*

Two contemporary, or near contemporary, sources are fundamental; J. A. Hobson's *Imperialism, a Study* (first published 1902) and Lenin's *Imperialism, the Highest Stage of Capitalism* (first published 1917). Both have been reprinted many times. Bernard Semmel's *Imperialism and Social Reform* (London, 1960) is a sometimes difficult but always important study. Two other important studies, sometimes raising controversial points, are G. R. Searle, *The Quest for National Efficiency: A Study in British Politics and Political Thought, 1899–1914* (London, 1971) and R. J. Scally, *The Origins of the Lloyd George Coalition; the Politics of Social-Imperialism, 1900–1918* (Princeton, 1975). P. S. Gupta, *Imperialism and the British Labour Movement, 1914–1964* (London, 1975) carries the discussion rather beyond the limits of the present paper.

Robert Blake's *Disraeli* (London, 1966) is by far the best biography of the statesman. There are now many biographies of Joseph Chamberlain but the works most relevant to the present discussion are: J. L. Garvin and J. Amery, *Life of Joseph Chamberlain*, vols III and IV (London, 1934, 1951); P. Fraser, *Joseph Chamberlain: Radicalism and Empire, 1868–1914* (London, 1966); Enoch Powell, *Joseph Chamberlain* (London, 1977); and R. V. Kubicek, *The Administration of Imperialism: Joseph Chamberlain at the Colonial Office* (Durham, NC, 1969). E. Halévy's *Imperialism and the Rise of Labour* (first published in French in 1926, 2nd revised ed. in English reprinted 1961) is still useful. Also, for the earlier background, K. E. Knorr, *British Colonial Theories, 1570–1850* (Toronto, 1944, reprinted 1964). Lord Lugard's views are to be found in his *The Dual Mandate in British Tropical Africa* (Edinburgh & London, 1922, reprinted 1965).

Relevant articles include H.-U. Wehler, 'Bismarck's Imperialism, 1862–1890', *P&P*, 48 (1970) 119–55 for a thought-provoking analysis of the German situation which invites comparison with Britain and P. J. Cain, 'J. A. Hobson, Cobdenism, and the Radical Theory of Economic Imperialism, 1898–1914', *EconHR*, XXXI (1978) 565–84. W. Baumgart's *Imperialism: the Idea and Reality of British and French Colonial Expansion, 1880–1914* (Oxford, 1982) contains an interesting chapter on 'British Social Imperialism' and a critique of H.-U. Wehler's approach.

8. SINEWS OF EMPIRE: CHANGING PERSPECTIVES
C. C. Eldridge

Of the older works mentioned in the text, C. A. Bodelsen's *Studies in Mid-Victorian Imperialism* (Copenhagen, 1924) remains useful even though the central thesis of the book has been heavily undermined. R. Koebner and H. D. Schmidt's *Imperialism: The Story and Significance of a Political Word, 1840–1960* (Cambridge, 1964) also provides a number of useful insights into British responses to empire during the nineteenth century. Many of the more important revisionist articles are collected together in A. G. L. Shaw, *Great Britain and the Colonies, 1815–65* (London, 1970) and contemporary extracts and a valuable commentary are to be found in P. Burroughs, *British Attitudes towards Canada, 1822–1849* (Scarborough, Ontario, 1971). A wealth of illustratory material is included in G. Bennett, (ed.) *The Concept of Empire: Burke to Attlee, 1774–1947*, 2nd ed. (London, 1962). Ged Martin's article 'Anti-imperialism in the mid-nineteenth century and the nature of the British empire, 1820–70' in R. Hyam and G. W. Martin, *Reappraisals in British Imperial History* (London, 1975) argues the case for continuity in imperial thinking, an interpretation supported by S. R. Stembridge in his detailed study, *Parliament, the Press and the Colonies, 1846–1880* (New York, 1982). Unfortunately, the vast amount of secondary material published since the mid-1960s is not discussed in the latter volume. The alleged 'climax of anti-imperialism' during Gladstone's first administration and Disraeli's subsequent ministry is covered in C. C. Eldridge, *England's Mission: the Imperial Idea in the Age of Gladstone and Disraeli, 1868–80* (London, 1973) and the ethos in which the governing elite made its decisions in the late nineteenth century is evoked in A. P. Thornton, *The Imperial Idea and its Enemies* (London, 1959). Bernard Porter sets out the critical position of the radical opponents of empire in *Critics of Empire: British radical attitudes to colonialism in Africa, 1895–1914* (London, 1969). H. J. Field's *Toward a Programme of Imperial Life. The British Empire at the Turn of the Century* (Oxford, 1982) is a fascinating contribution to the intellectual history of imperialism. The best short introduction to the role of empire within the wider context of British expansion overseas remains P. J. Cain, *Economic Foundations of British Overseas Expansion, 1815–1914* (London, 1980).

Notes on Contributors

A. E. ATMORE, Research Fellow at the School of Oriental and African Studies, University of London, is the author, with Roland Oliver, of *The African Middle Ages, 1400–1800* (1981) and *Africa Since 1800*, 3rd ed. (1981).

CHRISTINE BOLT is a Reader in American History, University of Kent. Her publications include the *Antislavery Movement and Reconstruction* (1969); *Victorian Attitudes to Race* (1971) and *A History of the U.S.A.* (1974).

PETER BURROUGHS is Professor of History, Dalhousie University. His publications include *Britain and Australia, 1831–55: A Study of Imperial Relations and Crown Lands Administration* (1967); *British Attitudes Towards Canada, 1822–49* (1971) and *The Canadian Crisis and British Colonial Policy, 1828–41* (1972).

M. E. CHAMBERLAIN is Senior Lecturer in History, University College of Swansea. Her publications include *The New Imperialism* (Historical Association pamphlet, 1970); *The Scramble for Africa* (1974) and *Lord Aberdeen* (1983).

C. C. ELDRIDGE, Senior Lecturer in History, Saint David's University College, Lampeter, is author of *England's Mission: The Imperial Idea in the Age of Gladstone and Disraeli, 1868–80* (1973) and *Victorian Imperialism* (1978).

PAUL KENNEDY is J. Richardson Dilworth Professor of History at Yale University. His publications include *Samoan Tangle: A Study in Anglo-German-American Relations, 1878–1900* (1974); *The Rise and Fall of British Naval Mastery* (1976) and *The Realities Behind Diplomacy: Background Influences on British External Policy, 1865–1980* (1981).

R. J. MOORE is Professor of History, The Flinders University of South Australia. Among his publications are *Sir Charles Wood's Indian Policy, 1853–66* (1966); *Liberalism and Indian Politics, 1872–1922* (1966) and, most recently, *Escape from Empire: the Attlee Government and the Indian Problem* (1983).

JAMES STURGIS, Lecturer in History at Birkbeck College, University of London, is the author of *John Bright and the Empire* (1969).

Index